# 23

## A Memoir of 1939

### By

# Antoni 'Joe' Podolski

Second Edition

Yellow Wheel Publishing Ltd., UK
2014

©2014 Jeremy Podolski. All rights reserved.
First paper back edition printed 2014 in the United Kingdom

All rights reserved. No part of this publication may be reproduced, distributed, or transmitted in any form or by any means, including photocopying, recording, or other electronic or mechanical methods, without the prior written permission of the publisher, except in the case of brief quotations embodied in critical reviews and certain other non commercial uses permitted by copyright law.

Published by Yellow Wheel Publishing Ltd.
For more copies of this book contact www.23days.eu

First Edition printed: March 2014
Second Edition printed: May 2014

Acknowledgements and thanks are due to:

Keith Flatman for his encouragement
and the services of his ever-willing secretary
for transcribing Joe's spoken word into type

Tim Russell for his careful editing of the original text

Charlotte May for her cover design

BookPrintingUK.com for their printing expertise

Other members of the Podolski family
for their help and support

Although every precaution has been taken in the preparation of this book, the publisher and author assume no responsibility for errors or omissions. Neither is any liability assumed for damages resulting from the use of the information contained herein.

ISBN : 978-0-9929331-0-4

# Contents

|  | Foreword | 1 |
|---|---|---|
|  | Introduction | 4 |
| 1 | A Magical Childhood | 8 |
| 2 | Invaded from both West and East | 23 |
| 3 | Captured by the Reds | 45 |
| 4 | Judgement Day at Orsha Prison | 72 |
| 5 | 23 Days Awaiting Death | 91 |
| 6 | 9 days in Lubyanka Prison | 112 |
| 7 | Escape from an Arctic Gulag | 131 |
| 8 | Two On Our Own | 150 |
| 9 | Freedom in England | 174 |
| 10 | Mission to Lithuania | 187 |
| 11 | To join the Polish Army | 207 |
| 12 | Scoring a Double | 229 |
| 13 | The Thought of Freedom | 245 |
|  | Epilogue | 251 |

## Photographs  253 -

Baby Joe at 6 months of Age

Inscription on reverse of photograph.
to my dearest Grandma and Grandpa, from loving Józio

My mother Maria 1931

My Dad Jozef 1945

At School 1935

Russian Justice 1939

Squadron Photo (2nd Left back Row)

309 Squadron 1945 (front row, last)

Family Group 1956
**Joe with Dad Jozef, wife Mil, sons Andrew and Nigel**

# Foreword

Having been born just six years after the end of World War 2, a frequent topic of conversation amongst my friends was "What did your Dad do during the War?". In that way I learned of Dads who had flown on the Dam-buster Raid, been at Dunkirk, sailed in submarines or in ships, commanded a tank, been on commando raids, or been captive in German or Japanese POW camps. Further details were rarely available mainly because the Dads, almost to a man, were reluctant to talk about what they had gone through and survived to those who had not lived through similar experiences. In many cases they found it painful to recall experiences of a war that they really needed to forget.

In that way I grew up knowing that my Dad had been born and brought up in Poland before the start of the War. I knew that he was just 16 in 1939 enjoying an idyllic childhood when Hitler invaded Poland. I also knew that at the end of the War he was in the Polish Air Force, as part of the Royal Air Force, flying one of the fastest and most advanced single-seater fighters of the War, the American P-51 Mustang. So as far as I was aware Dad had been a pilot for most of the War. In my young mind that conjured up thoughts of the Battle of Britain, dogfighting, chivalry and glamour. A fun way for a teenager to fight a war.

Dad rarely talked about his war to me even when asked directly. Questions about flying during the War were ignored or brushed aside and apart from a few random incidents he said little about those days. As I grew up Dad continued his flying either in a Tiger Moth biplane or later in gliders, something that I followed him into gratefully. How many people did I know who could fly aerobatics with their Dad before they became a teenager? Dad went on to become Chief Flying Instructor for over 25 years at our local Norfolk Gliding Club based at Tibenham. In the course of that, on a number of occasions, he met Hollywood movie star and ex-Colonel Jimmy Stewart who had flown from Tibenham during the War. But that's another story and I digress.

Dad fitted a stereotype of what many thought was a typical Polish pilot: skilled, brave, slightly mad, hard drinking and hard living and he did his best to live up to that. In his private life he married my mother soon after the War then left the Air Force before starting a family, my brother Andrew and myself. Having put aside thoughts of his pre-War ambition of studying medicine he trained as a cabinet maker. He worked first as a coach-maker before becoming self-employed in a succession of roles: as a door to door Washing Machine renter, as a freelance cabinet maker, a pallet repairer, a garden fencing manufacturer and a boat-builder. He subsequently became an Inspector and repairer of gliders and a builder of glider trailers. In parallel with those activities he learnt silversmithing and jewellery repairing and established a jeweller's shop in Norwich. But he still had time to enjoy himself. Oh, and he also was a founder member of the first Judo Club in Norwich after the War and often mentioned that he had taught many dozens of Norwich police officers using the unarmed combat skills he had acquired during WW2.

But in all that time he rarely said anything about his wartime past. I have just one memory of seeing a school exercise book in which he had scribbled a couple of pages of writing entitled "23 days". At the time it seemed to be some fragmentary notes about his experiences in Poland at the outbreak of war. It meant nothing to me at the time. I realised that I had no idea how Dad had escaped the war in Poland and ended up in England but I never bothered to ask.

At the age of 61 life suddenly changed for Dad when he suffered a stroke that nearly killed him. At the time only a pioneering operation involving bypass surgery of an artery in his brain saved his life. However it instantly put an end to much of Dad's exploits. He slowed down, was forced to retire and gave up flying. Fortunately it was at a time when he could become a very welcome and doting Grandad to four lively grandsons.

At this point he resolved to put into words an account of the life changing events he had experienced at the start of World War 2. The following is the account of those times in his own words. His handwriting was not sufficiently legible and he was not much of a typist so he acquired a tape recorder and dictated his memoirs, passage by passage. His solicitor at the time, Keith Flatman, lent Dad the services of his secretary and she painstakingly transcribed it to printed pages, well over 600 of them.

For many years afterwards Dad attempted to find a publisher who could take his manuscript and expertly, but sympathetically, edit his thoughts and put them into a published form. Despite many efforts he never managed to get it published in his lifetime. Sadly he passed away in 1999 at the age of 76. He willed the manuscript to my two sons, Jeffrey and Jeremy, with the hope that one day they would get it published.

Since then it has taken many hours of further work to turn it into what you have today. It involved scanning the many hundreds of pages of sometimes very poor quality type, then converting into a form that could be read by a word-processor, This had to be checked, edited, revised and laid-out in a form to provide to a publisher.

The results are here to see. It is a personal memoir written by a Pole who was forced to flee his home as a boy never to return. After the War that home had become part of the Soviet Union as although the German occupation ceased in 1945, the Russians remained in residence until 1991. At the time of writing his memoirs the Soviets were still there as can be deduced by some of his comments. He experienced many horrific events but survived and made a new life in England, a country that offered him asylum. He learnt a new language, married and made a happy and successful life for himself and his family. In writing this he has created an everlasting link from the most traumatic times of 1939 to you, dear reader, today.

Nigel Podolski 2014

# Introduction

At long last I have decided to put something on paper. As I begin to write this the year is 1984, nearly half a century after the start of the Second World War and the times I wish to recall. It is also a significant year for anybody who has read George Orwell's novel describing what he predicted would happen to our society. Fortunately it has not turned out that way but if events had been different during that War maybe Orwell's predictions would have been a lot closer to the truth.

In many ways I feel I have been bullied by others into this crazy idea of writing my life story. I have given it very deep thought. The majority of people who tried to persuade me to write are expecting me to include something about my flying career, as most people know me from my flying circles. Maybe one day I will venture into that field as I have done some exciting flying in my life. But frankly, so many books have covered this subject so thoroughly that I feel I have very little to add. All my experiences as a flyer in a Polish Air Force Fighter Squadron have already been written down over and over again. The magic of the shout, "squadron scramble!", has been experienced and explained by so many people to so many readers, that I feel it has been worn out, just like a pair of old socks. I was fortunate enough to be the Chief Flying Instructor in a local gliding club for many years, but so many excellent books have been written on this subject for me to be able to add to. I am nowhere near a good enough writer to compete with the literary geniuses who already written about those subjects.

However there is one part of my life that very few people can say they experienced, and that I can record, and that is the horror of some five months at the beginning of the Second World War in 1939 trapped between two armies in the middle of Poland. It was my own private nightmare and I have relived it so many times over and over again during the past forty years.

At times I feel that these experiences made it more difficult for people to deal with me than it would have been otherwise, but that is all water under the bridge. Having eventually resolved to write this book I recently asked my long-standing friend, my solicitor, "Where do I begin?" "At the beginning", he simply replied. OK then, but where is the beginning?

I suppose I had better say something about my family, as they were all involved in this tale, and our background. Many readers might not realise that, in the past, Poland had been a very powerful Central European state, with territories that stretched from the Baltic Sea in the north to the Black Sea in the south-east. Due to unfortunate quarrels between some very rich, influential and powerful families the Polish state was brought down to a point where its ancient enemies, Russia, Germany, Austria and Hungary, were able to carve up the Polish territories for the first time in 1772. The population in Poland was divided into two kinds - noblemen and yeomanry. The rest were traders, commercial people and peasants. Only the top tier of society had family crests, which you could be either born with, or awarded through exceptional service to the King.

Chronicles state that my family was awarded a coat-of-arms on the battlefields around 1450 or 1460. Ever since, there was no generation that did not take part in numerous wars or bloody uprisings. There were many actions of Polish forces against our eastern neighbour, Russia, and vice-versa. We especially had problems on our south-east border with the Cossacks, Tartars and Turks. For a long time, Poland was accepted by Western Europe as a bastion defending Christianity from the Turkish Empire. While it was under occupation by Austria, Germany and Russia, just before the First World War, there was a very strong nationalistic underground movement, and members of this formed the nucleus of the Polish Army in 1914. Every occupying state had their own ways of dealing with rebellious Poles. As well as open executions of fighting men, the Russians had used deportation and resettlement of the population as a particular punishment. They had very vast territories, some very inhospitable, and found it was a lot better to send rebels to the Siberian salt mines than keep them in prisons. The scourge of Communism, which came to power in 1917, extended this punishment system to their own people. So rebellious individuals and their whole family would be sent two or three thousand miles to live in completely new surroundings. This is still happening at the moment in the twentieth century, in 1984.

Throughout the occupation of Poland, many thousands of Poles were sent to Siberia following any insurrection or armed uprising. All dissidents and national activists and their families shared the same fate. In the 18th and 19th centuries, chained prisoners were sent in horse-drawn Black Marias all the way to Siberia. In the 20th century railway cattle trucks were used to send thousands more unfortunates into the depths of Russia. My Mother's parents, as young children, had been sent to Siberia in 1865, where my Mother was born. After 40 years in Siberia, they trekked back west. They progressed in many short hops by horse and cart. On the way they had to make frequent stops in order to earn some food before moving on. When they got to a place called Orsha, more or less in a straight line between Moscow and Minsk, my Mother worked for several months as a machinist in a factory making army uniforms. By some twist of fate, this was the place where I was to spend 23 days in a condemned cell in 1940.

My Father had been born at Mielec, near Krakow, in the southern part of Poland in 1897. When he was 14, he ran away from home in order to join a secret Polish force that eventually formed the nucleus of the Polish Army. At the end of the First World War this force liberated Poland under the command of the future First Marshall Pilsudski. History records a big advance by the Russian Bolshevik army that was stopped at the gates of Warsaw. That particular campaign was written into the Polish history books as The Miracle of the Vistula. My Father took part in it, when the Polish forces pushed the Bolsheviks from the outside of Warsaw all the way to Minsk through Orsha and beyond. During subsequent armistice negotiations the pre-1939 Russian Polish border was established, and that is when and where my parents met and married in 1921.

The far-eastern part of Poland was like the American Wild West with a lot of banditry going on by renegades from the Red and Polish Armies. A brave few could grab large parcels of land for very little money or very cheap loans. But, due to the unrest and banditry, you had to be brave in order to settle in that part of the country, and indeed there were very few takers. Nevertheless that is where my Father settled down on some 1000 hectares of land, most of it forested. In order to survive the lawlessness one really had to have a gun in one hand and a plough in the other.

## Chapter 1 : A Magical Childhood

On the whole I had a very happy childhood. Only my Mother was difficult at times. She liked to travel to Warsaw and loved to attend concerts there. Frequently when she returned, after having seen one virtuoso or another, as an only child, I was the target of her attention. Once, having heard an international violinist, she got my Father to buy me a violin and arranged lessons for me. At that particular time I was conducting a private war with a pair of twin brothers two years older than me. Due to their attentions, I frequently felt as though I had more ice packs on my face than could be found in all the champagne buckets in the whole of Warsaw. At that time my sole aim in life was to catch the twins one at a time. On finally meeting one of them after a music lesson, I tried to wrap the violin strings around his neck without taking them off the instrument. Needless to say, that was the end of my fiddle and also my future career as an international violinist. Some time later I remember that my Mother became most keen on me learning to play a brass instrument but my Father refused, with the excuse that brass instruments were a lot harder to be hit with than stringed ones, and the twins were still about! Looking back, I realise I was a bit of a hard nut in reality which was probably the reason I was later kicked out of three schools, mainly for fighting or playing practical jokes, For some reason the school authorities did not seem to share my sense of humour.

Our home was a very large rambling house with extensive cellars and an enormous wooden roof. Behind the house was a massive courtyard of some 150 by 200 metres surrounded by stables, barns and all kinds of farm buildings and cottages which were occupied by tenant families and farm workers. The whole complex was surrounded by heavy wire stretched on poles whilst guard dogs on chains patrolled all the property. And what dogs they were! They were offspring of Alsatian bitches who, when in season, had been taken to the forest and left there for the night, in order to be sired by wild wolves. They were completely unapproachable and only tolerated the man who fed them. My Father regularly bought or was given all kinds of peculiar animals, one of the most memorable being a sickly baby ram who subsequently turned into a real terror of the yard. One of our men spent many hours with the young ram and a scarecrow. We found out too late that he had been teaching the dumb animal to charge anything resembling a backside, especially if it was dressed in trousers. Later on I had a lot of laughs with the animal. In the middle of the yard was a very old-fashioned well with a large U-shaped deep trough. Many a time I threw a silver Polish coin into the trough and encourage some unsuspecting visitor to fish it out. Then of course, the ram, seeing a backside stuck near the trough, would attack it without hesitation. I introduced all my school pals to this ram or should I say that he really needed no introduction from me?

Inside the house we had two highly trained Alsatians which we kept as guard dogs. Immediately outside the house was a gander with four wives, who would raise the alarm if even a mouse ran into the hazelnut bushes where his harem took permanent residence. On many occasions my Mother would end up chasing me with a kitchen towel for causing a fight between the gander and the ram.

Every year my Father had two or three glass fifty-litre carboys filled with black stoned cherries and topped up with sugar. By Christmas all the sugar had dissolved in the cherry juice leaving quite a large empty gap on top. This he would fill with almost neat alcohol he bought from the local distillery. After a long period the alcohol would produce a liqueur which was as smooth as silk but very powerful to drink. The cherries were used for pies, etc. I got into trouble quite a few times whilst at a residential grammar school for feeding the cherries to my pals who in turn got quite drunk. When at home I would go to the cellar and pinch a one litre aluminium mug full of them and have fun with my gander. He loved them but was rather greedy. After some fifteen or twenty cherries he would become totally intoxicated. The result was always disastrous. At the first sign of trouble I had to make myself scarce in order to avoid my mother.

The drunken gander would get very aggressive and in the first place, would attack the poor ram. The ram had no stomach to fight the gander, ever since the time that the latter had managed to attach its powerful beak to the ram's personal male pride. This had made the poor old ram bolt across the muddy path around a horses' trough. As the gander was holding tightly onto the ram's under anatomy, he was sliding in the mud for some considerable distance just like a water-skier. Ever after, the ram had great respect for the drunken gander and preferred to run than to stand and fight, although fight he could, possessing a beautiful flat head surrounded on each side by double twisted horns. Seeing the ram in retreat, and his wives hiding in the dense hazel bushes surrounding the house, the gander would then pick on one of the huge red hens that always scratched around near the troughs.

Full of amorous feelings, he would take a little jump onto one of the hens. Under the gander's great weight, it would fall beak first into the mud and shriek blue murder. At this distress signal, a huge cockerel would run from wherever he was in the yard to help and that was when the real fun would begin. The cockerel was a type of fighting bird with huge spurs on his legs. Black and white feathers and blood would fly everywhere. My Mother would often join in the commotion looking for me. I made sure I was nowhere to be found and always knew places to hide. Normally one of our men had to separate them with the aid of a birch twig broom to prevent them killing each other.

I was born on the 17th January 1923 in Baranowicze, in the Eastern part of Poland. My mother's grandma, who at that time was reputed to be 105, took complete charge of my upbringing. My earliest recollection of her, at the tender age of 5, was that she was very strict and that I was expected to obey her without question. She was definitely the boss and didn't care who knew it. Even our guard dogs, which were on the vicious side, had great respect for her. She was continually pestered by newspaper men asking about her age. She had no official birth certificate but was very proud to show them letters received by her father about 100 years before. Her prized possession was a receipt dated from that time for her handmade knee length boots, which her father had bought from the local Jewish shoemaker. The only doubt was whether she was 8 or 10 years old when she got her them. According to the receipt the length of the boots was only 8cm.

I started my rather robust career at the tender age of 4 when a neighbour's gander attacked me. In the resulting fight I apparently lost most of my hair, but also managed to strangle my adversary. I personally cannot remember the incident but had heard it repeated many times. I do remember being told that, as a result of my escapade, my father very nearly shot the neighbour, the manager of the local railway station.

I began getting into serious trouble when I started at prep school. Glass in particular had some kind of strange attraction to me. It would shatter at my slightest contact. My father was constantly having to pay for windows, mirrors large and small, panes of glass, etc.

In line with very old Polish tradition, I had no haircut, at least nothing to speak of, until I was around 7 years of age. At that time, during a great family ceremony, I had my first haircut and was fully recognised as a male member of the family. I then started attending school full-time.

I honestly cannot remember a time when I was free of knocks from fighting. I was always on the side of the underdog. I hated bullies and was very often beaten up by them. Unlike most kids I did not lose my first set of teeth naturally, they were mostly knocked out by other boys. Mind you, I gave a good account of myself in fights and always had sore and swollen knuckles. Altogether I was kicked out of three different schools, mostly for fighting or for pranks that the other lads had dared me to do. My dislike of pampered mummies' boys was well known to all my mates, and looking back I guess that at times I was rather over-boisterous with them. Their parents, who were often serving, high-ranking Army Officers, always made representations to my father about my fighting. He was very strict and insisted I should never start a fight. But he always said I had the right to defend myself when attacked. Looking back it makes me smile how often I would engineer situations so that somebody would take a swipe at me and I could fairly retaliate. Despite my boisterous disposition, I never missed school unlike many other youngsters of my age. Many would not attend school for a week or more at a time, but instead would sunbathe near the river or hang around the travelling circus, both favourite pastimes for youngsters of my age.

The schools I attended were very strictly segregated and, having no sister at home, girls were a bit of a mystery to me. I do remember being kicked out of one school for being caught in the dressing-room of the girls' grammar school gym across the road. That was when, on my mother's insistence, I was packed off to a so-called "closed" school run by the teaching order of the Selenizian monks. The school buildings, together with several hectares of orchards and gardens, were surrounded by a 2-metre high wall, and it was strictly against the rules to go to the local town or surrounding villages. Unfortunately, to me, this represented a challenge that I could not resist. I soon found a safe way over the wall, with the aid of a rope ladder and a huge lime tree.

I had been told by some of the older boys that there were a number of young ladies in the nearby villages, who were eager to meet our lads. I saw the possibility of making some pocket-money by guiding lads over the wall for a fee. Twice I was caught going over it by a prefect monk and got walloped by him. When I first joined the school I wondered why all the lads had a short back and sides haircut instead of sideburns that many others wore. I was soon to find out why. One of the prefects, a lad with ginger hair, had a nasty habit of twisting long sideburns and practically lifting their wearer by them. While doing so, he gave a lecture on the advantages of good behaviour. Any time one of us was in his office the other boys would listen to find out how long his victim could stick his torture without screaming.

Within two hours of my arrival in that school, I got involved in a fight with a much bigger lad and received a fair hiding, but not before I had managed to make a spectacular fountain out of his nose. As a result, I was soon introduced to our ginger prefect. There and then I made a solemn promise to get rid of my sideburns. With the new intake and plenty of "freshers" I soon realised that a pecking order had to be established amongst the lads. It was quite a job not to shout out when punished by the prefect, but I could usually manage it. There were some big strong lads about and it took me around three weeks to establish myself as a handy fellow with my fists. Many duels were fought behind the small chapel next to a huge pile of coke. A few times bigger lads managed to use my face as a sledge and the heap of coke as a snowy-hill to slide down on, but in the end I could normally manage to dislodge their ears or noses. I had one big advantage over my opponents as I never had a nosebleed. My opponents were not so lucky. Their noses were my first target and they would quickly panic when a punched nose started bleeding.

Our home was next to a very marshy river with thousands of wild ducks on it. In the spring, shortly after my seventh birthday I continually badgered my father to let me go duck shooting on my own. Eventually he relented and gave me a loaded shotgun and told me to go into the marsh up to my knees and wait for the ducks. The gun was a beautiful three-barrelled model, two barrels containing shot-filled cartridges and the third on the top for a bullet. I remember standing there gradually sinking into mud praying for at least one duck to pass by. At long last a large flight of the creatures came and after taking careful aim, I pulled the trigger. There was a very large bang; I felt as if I'd been kicked by a mule and was promptly knocked on my back into the marsh. The kick was so bad because, in my excitement, I had fired both barrels of the shotgun together. I would probably have drowned if my father had not heard my screams and come to my rescue. That was my introduction to a real weapon. It took a good week and a few hot baths to get rid of the stiffness in my neck and back, but I was delighted to have fired it.

I cannot remember when I actually started riding horses bareback, but I do remember climbing onto one from a water trough in our backyard but then slipping into the cold water. For my shame and wet bum I got whacks from my mother with a tea towel, which was one of her favourite weapons. I remember that I always tried to keep out of her way as she was quick tempered and rather generous with her tea towel, which could hurt badly especially when slightly wet.

Whilst at home I can never remember going to the doctor's as my great-grandma treated all my ills with her herbal recipes. She was so good at it that she even held an unofficial surgery for the locals. As I grew up, I helped her collect herbs all year round. There was always something to gather and pick for her store, from young nettles growing on the cinders to lime tree flowers to be picked only on certain days of the year. In later life I regretted the fact that none of her recipes had been written down and that all her vast knowledge died with her in 1935, by our calculations, somewhere around the ripe age of 117! My childhood was a time of great joy. All around me I had everything that a young lad could wish. I was surrounded by different animals that sometimes got me into trouble, like a pet squirrel which once decided to have forty winks in my father's hunting boots. He nearly had a heart attack when he tried to put them on. I remember him running around with one boot on and a gun in his hand, trying to shoot the squirrel. Unfortunately he stood in a bowl of lukewarm fat dripping while pursuing the squirrel. I'm sure they could hear him shouting a mile away!

In the nearby river there was an abundance of fish of all sorts, and the forest was full of game. On my seventh birthday I was given a beautiful short-barrelled .22 rifle and 10,000 rounds of ammunition. In a short time I won a gold medal for my proficiency at target shooting. Father had a lot of firearms in the house and often took me for practice shooting with different weapons. When I was eleven, I stalked and shot a young wild pig with my .22 rifle and my father was very proud of the fact. Around that time on the Estate we were over-run with rats and I sat for hours in a pigsty shooting them off the rafters.

Generally speaking I was not badly behaved, being an only child used to having my own way. My only bad spells of behaviour were during visits of friends of my father from Warsaw who brought children of my age. They were ignorant snobbish city dwellers and I could not get on with most of them. They had no respect at all for life in the country. Most of them belonged to all kinds of clubs, boxing being one of the more popular. Quite a few times I had to defend myself from so-called boxing experts and collected black eyes, split lips and all kinds of abrasions, but I had a favourite punch which never let me down. I found that one mediocre thump on an opponent's nose would frequently do the trick; after the ensuing red nose fountain I had to hide from my mother as, according to her, the fight was always my fault.

Some of my despised visitors even had medals for horse riding proficiency but, unlike me, they could not ride bareback. In my early school days, I rode to school on a favourite mare of mine. On arrival I'd smack her hindquarters and say, "Go home", and she would retrace her steps some three kilometres, before returning to pick me up after school. She was a rather bad timekeeper and often galloped back to school early. She would wait for me outside on the grass full of clover, which she adored. On the way from school I had to be careful of my tame squirrel, which would jump onto my back from the trees looking for nuts in my pocket. Once, one of our visitors, an especially obnoxious boy, but supposedly expert horseman, was riding my horse in our driveway when the squirrel missed his back and landed on the horse's hindquarters. The sharp claws of the squirrel made the horse bolt and the lad was taken for the ride of his life. After a good 100 metres he fell off with a thump and broke two ribs on the large stones. All hell ensued as he was an Army Colonel's son, his father being in charge of troops guarding a Government residence in Warsaw. An Army ambulance arrived from some 10 kilometres away to take him away. The incident was a blessing in disguise for me, as from then on visitors were not allowed to ride my horses.

I was never taught the facts of life by my parents or discussed them with pals as they were as ignorant as I. I think I was 12 or 13 when a neighbour's daughter on school holidays from a very posh school tried hard to demonstrate to me the intricate facts of life. Unfortunately she chose the pigeon coop in their loft. It took me a few hours to pick the feathers from my smart wool suit and, there and then, I decided it was not worth the bother, at least for the time being. Some years after the local kindergarten teacher explained to me what it was all about during one of my holidays from grammar school.

In my whole life I experienced many incredible coincidences, which at the time were baffling to say the least. Here is one worth mentioning. Many years after the War, in 1981, while in Warsaw, I was invited with friends to dinner at the house of a man I did not know. During the course of the evening he kept staring at me. I began feeling very uncomfortable and began to suspect that he might be a KGB agent or some undercover militia man, especially when he told me that he felt that he had met me somewhere before. As he seemed to be a complete stranger, I started losing my temper and was on the point of leaving the dinner when he suddenly produced an enormous album and showed me a group photograph of my school at the monastery. There was a cross on my chest. He was apparently an amateur historian who had been at the same school as me and had been collecting information about our school's ex-pupils for years. According to his information I had died somewhere in Russia in 1940. I was most surprised to find that he had recognised me after more than 40 years. He told me that I had apparently prevented a bully in a dormitory we stayed in together from taking a cake from him.

Unfortunately my ginger prefect died in a labour camp in Russia, but the young monk in charge of our dormitory was still alive in when we met in 1981. We had a rather tearful reunion and exchanged our stories. Apparently, when the Russians invaded they bulldozed the chapel and main church with tanks. The main church tower fell on a tank and killed four of its occupants.

Academically, I was perhaps average or slightly above, but looking back my behaviour at times was quite outrageous. My pet hates were maths and German language, as both subjects were taken by the same teacher, or professor, as we called them in grammar schools. My favourite subject, funnily enough, was Latin, which was despised by most kids. Chemistry and anything involving the bodies of animals fascinated me, and I was very useful at mending the broken wings of birds and limbs of all kinds of animals. When I was about ten I was knocked off the high bar in the gym by one of the other pupils. It resulted in a rupture that was eventually repaired in hospital in Krakow. During the post operation period in casualty, I spent two weeks watching all kinds of surgical treatments. The staff tolerated me as I wore a silk dressing gown supplied by the hospital and resided in a select part of the hospital. It really gave me my first interest and leaning towards medical school. In 1936 I had a further operation for a perforated appendix, which gave me rather a bad time. Because of this, I nearly had a change of heart regarding my future; but by then I was fairly committed to medicine, so I decided to stick with my ambition for a career in it.

As mentioned my childhood was very happy and I never minded the lack of brothers or sisters. Indeed, I considered myself lucky to be on my own as most of my friends were forever complaining about their siblings. So my idyllic years went by until the 1939 War, when Europe was raped by the two biggest perverts and maniacs at that time in Europe, namely Stalin and Hitler. On reflection, I preferred the Germans as we knew where we stood with them. For killing a German you knew you were likely to be killed At least they operated in daylight, unlike their friends the Communists who always carried out their evil deeds at night.

The Germans, through their Teutonic efficiency, mostly admitted and documented the killings they carried out during the War. The Russians for their part murdered many thousands in secret, the most infamous example being the massacre of fifteen thousand Polish Army and Police officers at Katyn in 1940. They have never admitted the crime, which was subsequently proved beyond any shadow of a doubt by the International Red Cross, who were called in, funnily enough, by the Germans, when they discovered the mass graves in Katyn forest. When exhumed bodies were examined it was found that all the victims had been murdered in the same manner – a bullet in the base of the skull, a favourite method long-used by the Russians.

My childhood home was a dream for growing up in as a boy. I was the only child and one might think I was rather spoilt. Well, perhaps I was but at school I had to be tough to survive. The boys from the surrounding villages were big and tough, real healthy peasant stock and I had to hold my own with them. I was an active member of the Scout movement and having at our disposal a beautiful forest, there were many summer camps held there. In fact my Father arranged a sort of semi- permanent Scout camp in one of the clearings with two log cabins and water wells. I loved it and, looking back, that gave me a chance to show off. When I was twelve or thirteen it was nothing unusual for me to stalk and kill a young wild pig for the camp's pot. Three years before the War, my Father had bought me a beautiful Arab stallion foal that I adored and we became great friends. I could ride bareback horses since I was four and use skis quite expertly at about the same age.

At least once a year my Father took me to see his Dad, my Grandfather. He was a very tall man and always seemed like an almighty giant. He had been his county's mill stone carrying champion for many years. On the opposite side of the street to where my Grandad lived was a fire station where an annual competition of strong men took place. Round mill stones were laid flat on the ground and all competitors had to lift and carry a stone along an oblong grass courtyard. The distance marker of the winner was set into the turf and left there until the following year. I was very proud of my Grandad and loved him very dearly. He would take me fishing in a nearby river for trout, which he taught me to catch with my hands in the water. When I was there, we would spend every second together. It broke my heart when he died in 1935. I was also very close to my Father who also was a powerful man and had been through a few sticky patches in his life especially during the First World War. He had been gassed with his brother; my Father suffered no great ill effects from it but my uncle went blind a few years after the war and died blind in 1980, some fourteen days before the death of my Father.

Whilst at Grammar school at the monastery. I was introduced and became hooked on another hobby, flying. From most points in the grounds of the college I could see a gliding school operating on a nearby hill. It fascinated me to see the gliders going up and down. I badgered my father to find out more about it and to let me go on a course to learn to fly. He was afraid to tell my mother about my new fancy but through his friends in Warsaw he soon found out about the details and said I could go on the course provided I didn't tell my mother about it. So in 1937 and 1938 I attended the gliding school. The school was situated on a plateau on top of a mountain ridge where hangars, workshops and sleeping accommodation in tents under canvas were situated. There were no two-seater gliders for teaching and the single-seater we had had to be seen to be believed. You sat on a wooden seat with nothing around you at all. In front you had the stick and rudder pedals to control the glider. Somewhere above and behind you was the cloth-covered wing, which you could not see when sitting in the seat. To start with it seemed crazy to me to even try to fly in such a contraption but my ambition would not allow me to give in.

It is essential for any fixed wing flying machine to have and maintain forward speed. This in turn creates lift on the wing, which then overcomes your drag and the structure's weight, and keeps you in the air. To start with, we sat in a glider that was hung just above the ground on a construction that reminded me of a hangman's gibbet.

We had to try to keep it level and in a flying attitude. After a few 15-minute sessions on the 'gibbet' we were ready to go on to the skeet pad. There was a long bungee similar to one with which you fix luggage on a car's roof rack but a lot thicker and some 20 yards in length. The middle of the bungee was secured by a large ring on an open hook under your seat. On each end of the cord some five or so boys were placed and they gently pulled forward. The glider's tail was secured to the ground on a bollard.

When the bungee was suitably extended, the instructor released the tail and the contraption shot forward like a crossbow bolt. While moving forward on the wooden skids underneath, you tried to hop a few inches up to simulate free flying. After a number of successful hops you were ready to go solo. This moment was a great achievement and milestone in my life. After eight days having completed all necessary exercises my instructor said I was ready to fly on my own. He stressed the great importance of keeping the right speed. As we had no instruments to indicate our air speed we had to rely on the bottoms of our trousers. Just before take off you needed to pull your trousers back straight so while flying you could see and feel the behaviour of the airflow. The trousers had to flap in the wind in a steady motion. If flapping too hard you were too fast and had to heave the nose up to prevent the wings from breaking off. If, heaven forbid, your trousers stopped flapping, you were in dead trouble as you were too slow and most likely to go into a spin. There wasn't a day when somebody hadn't spun down. Luckily the structure of the glider was very light and usually would strike the ground with the wing first so that this would break before anything else so that the pilot was reasonably safe, except perhaps maybe for a broken bone or two. But this was an acceptable risk to all concerned.

My instructor took me to the edge of the plateau and pointing with his arm down the hill said, "Can you see that long field some 500 to 600 metres away. That is your landing field. Don't worry, it is quite a soft field and we have had it fairly freshly ploughed and raked, and spread some straw on it" He told me to take my long scouts socks off in order to feel the flapping of my trousers on my bare ankles. This time there were ten beefy boys at each end of the bungee.

My heart was pounding as if it was trying to leave my petrified body. They stretched the bungee to the full and I could hear the glider's timbers and ply starting to creak underneath me. Eventually, out of my bone-dry throat, I managed to croak the word "Go". The instructor released my tail and I was shot out like an arrow down the hill. Momentarily the rush of wind took my breath away. I was glad I had a pair of goggles shielding my eyes as immediately a huge fly hit the left glass and obliterated my vision with blood and the remains of his body. In a blind panic I pushed the goggles up on to my forehead and regained my composure. Luckily I did not encounter any further flies during this flight. To my surprise I found I could control the beast quite easily and concentrated on getting to my landing field. When I crossed the boundary my trousers stopped flapping and I sank very rapidly indeed to mother earth. With a sickening thump I hit the ground and stopped immediately. Jumping off I examined the glider. After such a thump I was convinced something must be broken. To my great relief I could find no damage whatsoever.

Very soon, a local peasant, hired for this purpose, with horse and a small trailer, joined me to take my glider back up the hill. We loaded it onto his trailer and holding one wing walked a very long way up the twisting field road. We were nearly at the top when the ruddy horse decided to have a rest again. On starting it gave a sharp and sudden pull. It caught me unawares and my aching legs could not cope. On falling flat on my face I let go of the wing which in turn fell on top of a few hard stalks of cut down bush protruding from the ground and I heard the sickening tear of the fabric. My instructor did a mad jig and told me to go with the glider into the hanger and repair it, under the supervision of peasant mechanics. So I spent the rest of the day and well into the night repairing the wing. Despite my shame I was delighted when my instructor came into the hangar and congratulated me warmly on not breaking the glider badly and making such a good job of my first "solo".

On looking back, there was usually structural damage on the first solos so I suppose I had something to be proud of. I became the target of admiration by other boys who had not yet gone solo. Some idiot brought a whole litre of vodka the next day. A number of us got helplessly drunk. The windy weather stopped us flying for a few days. Then the summertime returned in full beauty. We were sunbathing and enjoyed life to the full. The 15 day course was nearly over and in order to get my 'A' and 'B' Certificates I had to make at least three independent flights. My instructor was very keen on me getting my licence so one day, first thing in the morning, he dragged me out of my sleeping tent and told me I had go off again.

The first flight was normal and uneventful as was the next. The third flight I shall remember for the rest of my life. In order to get my licence I had to demonstrate a turn to the left and to the right. So on my third flight I decided to make a turn to the right before landing in a different grazing field. That is when my luck ran out. On turning onto my final approach, to my horror I found a horse and a huge cart on my line of approach.

The cart was loaded very high with hay and a peasant sitting at the front operating a primitive brake on the cart as the whole thing was rolling down the hill. Then I experienced an incredible state of mind, which in later years I witnessed many times while training some hundreds of pilots to glide. I felt that bloody cart hypnotise me and I could not turn away from the damn thing. Just 50 metres from it I could see I was going to end up underneath it. In my desperation I pulled the stick to me in order to lift the nose and jump over it. When right on top of it my trousers stopped fluttering and I fell like a stone onto the top of hay. Luckily I did not touch the peasant, but the shake of the hay made him fall forward on top of the horse. That in turn startled the horse, which bolted down the road like a mad thing. So there I was sitting strapped in a glider on top of the galloping horse and cart. I was completely bewildered and did not know what to do. I remember trying to lift the nose up in order to start flying again. We were travelling at speed for a good 200 or 300 metres. Then I saw on the side of the road a huge wooden cross, which had been put up by the locals as is customary in that part of the world.

Moments later the right wing struck the cross with a sickening thump and the glider and I fell off the cart. Luckily by then I had undone my straps and just fell off on my own. I was lucky as it was nearly the end of the course and it saved me from long ribbing and general embarrassment. The incident got into the national papers, one of which very kindly paid for a new glider. My father gave the knocked about peasant a cow for his injuries as the cart ran over him and broke his leg. So in the end everybody was happy. On returning to my school I had quite a few fights and black eyes over the incident. But eventually its memory died a natural death.

So that was my first attempt to simulate the birds in the intricate art of flying. As already mentioned I witnessed similar incidents when young pilots go for the one and only obstruction on the field for no reason at all. Many years later, while Chief Flying Instructor of a gliding Club, I witnessed pilots time and time again hypnotised by an obstruction. Once one very nearly hit my car while landing. Luckily I was sitting inside and managed to rapidly drive out of harms way.

On reflection, there was one sinister side to the gliding courses in Poland – they were run by Polish Air Force personnel. In their misguided wisdom the Polish authorities also accepted hundreds of young German boys, at a price, for training as pilots. I had a pen-pal in Berlin, who I had met at the Berlin Olympics in 1936. After being trained as a pilot by the Poles, he later bombed our country in a Stuka.

## Chapter 2 : Invaded from both West and East

The first few months of 1939 were wonderful for me. We had a very happy family Christmas, which was always a magic time at home; but that particular Christmas was something very special. My Father announced that he had made provisions to leave the family estate exclusively to me. We were all in good health and I was anxiously awaiting the result of my entry exams to medical school, which I felt had gone very well for me.

I eventually got the results in early March with confirmation of a place in medical school at Lwow, one of the better colleges in Poland. I felt that I'd really got the whole world at my feet. There was another reason for great excitement, an impending war with Germany, but our country's very strong pact with Great Britain and France meant we were confident about our future.

All the young people of my generation were awaiting the war with excitement. After several centuries of fighting by our forefathers, we were keen not to miss out on a war. For ages, every generation in Poland had been involved in a war or some kind of bloody uprising. I could never have suspected that, after a five-year nightmare, I would find myself in the Polish Air Force in England, while three so-called friendly powers would carve up central Europe and give my beloved birthplace to Russia. But no recriminations, let's get back to my story.

As mentioned before, my family had an estate of some 1000 hectares in the eastern part of Poland, about 16 kilometres from the Russian border. Some 500 plus hectares of this land was in a forest full of wildlife, including some brown European bears, thousands of wild pigs, foxes, beaver, deer, etc. During the hard winters we had thousands of unwanted illegal immigrants in the form of wolves, which were crossing the border from Russia at will. Even 500 metres of mined no-man's land set up by the Russians could not stop these starving packs of animals. We also had frequent Russian escapees who, by some miracle, managed to cross the border. They were mainly allowed to cross for money by border guards who were escapees themselves and, of course, there were a number of people sent as spies. Polish security services had a mammoth problem to separate spies from genuine refugees.

At times we had so many refugees that my Father set up a sort of field kitchen to warm the unfortunates. Some of their stories we could hardly believe. Many of them insisted that genocide on a massive scale was in progress in Russia, and huge work camps were being set up in the northern part of Russia, where many thousands perished without a trace. Detailed reports of these were sent to the West but ignored as being anti-Communist propaganda. The Communist party in the West was very well-organised and worked very hard to subdue and ridicule these reports. In view of the danger of serious infiltration from Russia, the whole population of Eastern Poland was instructed to report any strangers in their districts. However, all those who had reported strangers regretted it bitterly later. When the Russians invaded they arrested many of those informers and most of them were put to death.

That is how I became a rather unwilling witness to the very first series of executions in that year. Amongst those first arrested were the father and uncle of a very close school friend. We knew that those arrested were being held in the village Council offices cum Police Station. There were three large buildings in a compound surrounded by young trees, which reminded me of old American forts during the period of Indian unrest that I had seen in films at the time. Living near the Russian border, we were well informed as to what was going on in Russia from refugees who were crossing over in ever increasing numbers. But frankly, we could not believe all their stories, as some of them were hard to swallow. It was hard to believe that even very young children in Russia were encouraged to report on their parents to teachers with information about what they had said or done. Many fathers, uncles or brothers were sent to labour camps for bringing a few potatoes from the fields of collective farms they worked on. Many mothers ended up in the same camps by mentioning that the flour they made bread with was not what it used to be. Any criticism regarding the party was punished ruthlessly by the NKVD, the Soviet secret police.

Stories were coming thick and fast that genocide on a large scale was being carried out in Russia. My Father was very uneasy regarding these stories, as he knew the Communists only too well. Some landowners around us had already made plans to move west. We knew that Ribbentrop, the German Foreign Minister, had been seen kissing Molotov, his opposite number, in Moscow. While my Father was presiding at a meeting of local people, he said openly that, in his opinion, a further partition of Poland was a possibility. Government officials in Warsaw, on hearing this, called him hysterical and he was formally reprimanded.

My Father also made provisional plans for us to move to Mielec, his home town in the West. Many of his friends, a number of whom were Generals or in the Government, were trying to persuade him to stay as they assured him what he had heard was only gossip and, after all, Poland had signed a treaty with Great Britain and France, which pledged mutual help in case of a war with Germany. Looking back, nobody in the West or in the Polish Government believed that there might be any danger from the east. After all, Poland had signed a non-aggression pact with Russia as well. Furthermore, they did not believe the Red Army was capable of being aggressive after the purges of high-ranking Officers following the famous trials of 1936-1938. As early as March '39 we had heard reports of Russian Red Army Divisions massing on the Polish borders, but nobody believed there could be any danger from them. In addition Communist undercover units in Poland had spread rumours that the Red Army would join forces with Poland if war with Germany should start. Then came the German ultimatum regarding the so-called Danzig corridor and the war began in earnest on September 1st 1939. On the pretext of having to protect Germans living in the western part of Poland, Hitler ordered an invasion.

At the beginning, we were not affected. There were no bombings and no action. Then we noticed increasing numbers of transports carrying wounded men from the front line. My Scout troop had been co-opted to assist with civil defence and I, together with a number of other Scouts, was given the task of keeping a lookout for enemy aircraft. We sat for many hours in a church steeple searching the skies for aircraft that never came. There was, however, one sinister development that disturbed us all – a great increase in local radio traffic, obviously in code, from some kind of secret station. Germany's fifth column spies had moved into the district, and were reporting on all movements. A Polish Army unit moved into the local vicarage with some radio monitoring equipment. I remember seeing a Polish Warrant Officer sitting at a sort of typewriter wearing headphones.

One day an Army Corporal came up the steeple and said they had detected brief, but repeated, transmissions from very close by. We all looked around the terrain close to the church to search for anything unusual. One of our Scouts pointed out two horses with carts parked next to the cemetery wall. Three occupants of those carts appeared to have bandages on their heads, one had his arm in a sling. Our Corporal decided that his patrol should check them and then left. We saw his patrol of four soldiers plus the NCO walking towards the cart and talking to the occupants. As soon as the NCO put his hand in the cart to remove some straw, we saw flashes of fire and all the soldiers fell to the ground. We had a field telephone in the steeple connected to the vicarage but, despite my frantic attempts to contact the rest of the Army unit, there was no reply.

The day before that incident I had pinched a Mauser pistol out of my Dad's gun room together with a box of ammunition. I remember very well the ammo was pulling my trousers down as it was so heavy. I rushed as quickly as I could down the staircase and ran to the vicarage. A Second Lieutenant treated me with contempt but, to get rid of me, told a few of his soldiers, armed with light machine guns, to go and check the cart. Soon after we heard automatic gunfire from the direction of the cemetery and saw an officer take his pistol out and run madly towards it. At that moment, I remember it struck me as funny that he had spurs on his officers' boots. Apparently he was a cavalryman but there were no horses to be seen and his spurs were making a hell of a din. Suddenly, there was a short burst of fire from behind a barn and he fell, presumably dead. A Warrant Officer nearby

He asked me if I knew how to use a grenade; he quickly showed me how and then gave me two. He told me to approach the barn from the back while he went in a line to where his comrade had fallen. I grabbed the grenades and rushed behind the barn. In my excitement I pulled the pin out of one of them and held it tightly. I went right round the barn but saw nothing. The Warrant Officer waved me towards the cemetery some 100 metres away. We both reached the cart and looked into it. Under the straw there was a huge radio transmitter, our five Polish soldiers lay dead and, nearby were the bodies of two men dressed in Polish uniforms. The third one was nowhere to be seen. We ran back to the vicarage to telephone for help. By the time we got back, the wires from the set had been pulled out and the typewriter was missing. The Warrant Officer said to me, "That bastard was here. I know what he was doing, he took our coding machine."

Then suddenly he stopped in mid-sentence and started screaming at me that I was a little so-and-so. He had just noticed that I was holding a grenade in my hand but the safety pin was missing. This was when I realised that grenades do not explode, even without the safety pin, providing you hold them tight and don't let go of them. Frantically he started searching for a piece of string to secure my grenade but with no luck.

I suggested that I should throw the grenade into a big dip near the river behind a house. We went together to get rid of the damn thing, walking past an outside lavatory, which was just a deep hole in the ground with a wooden hut on top of it. Whilst we were walking past, we heard a sort of muffled splash as if something heavy had been dropped into the pit. As I threw the grenade away, the Warrant Officer shouted at the lavatory door asking who was in there. There was a big bang and his left arm flew backwards. "That son-of-a-bitch has shot me", he shouted. We both ran back into the kitchen through the back door. As the Warrant Officer rushed for a weapon I pulled my Mauser out, put the magazine into it and by the time he came back with the rifle I had emptied the whole magazine into the toilet through the kitchen window. The toilet door flew open and there was a dead man sitting there. The Warrant Officer could still see movement in the corpse and shouted to be careful in case he was still alive. He could not use his rifle because a bullet had shattered his left arm. I assured him that I knew how to use a rifle, so he handed me it and told me to shoot the sitting man. We saw clearly a peaked hat with the Polish insignia, which showed he was a Major. I got such the jitters and could hardly hold the rifle still. I leant it on the windowsill and took a very careful aim. The Warrant Officer said, "You'd better shoot him in the head, just to make sure". As the distance was not more than some four or five metres, I hit him just on the bridge of the nose. His hat flew off, up over his head and disappeared. The Warrant Officer went and dragged the corpse out and looked into the hole in the toilet. It was fairly freshly dug and we could clearly see a typewriting machine at the bottom of it. The Warrant Officer got into a real panic because he was in charge of this machine and said he would most probably be court-martialled and shot for losing it. There was a very old range in the kitchen with some huge hooks hanging in the chimney for holding meats, etc. The poor beggar picked one up and spent some two hours trying to fish the writing machine from the toilet. I refused to take part in it as I had had enough excitement for one day. I often wonder what eventually happened to that machine. Before long, the local police and some Army men arrived and reached the bodies. Apparently the three men were a German fifth column unit transmitting information to the German Army. They were masquerading as wounded Polish Officers. They all had German identity cards and one of them was a Berliner.

It was the first human being I had killed, and it had no effect on me whatsoever. I didn't feel sick or anything, as is often portrayed in films or books. At the time I felt a great satisfaction that we had managed to catch a spy, literally with his trousers down. Excited I definitely was, but it was the same feeling as I had when killing a wild boar in the forest. The date of the above incident was around the 10th September and for us at that time the writing, in very big letters, was on the wall.

The following day we had some ten or so Russian refugees on the farm. They all lived in very close proximity to the border and said there were massive concentrations of Red Army units there. I remember my Father spent a good hour on the 'phone to Warsaw. He was trying to persuade his old Army pal, a General, that an attack by the Russians was imminent. After a lot of explanations and excuses he was told in no uncertain manner to mind his own business. According to Warsaw sources, they were just rumours – there was no basis to any of them or cause for alarm. My Father gathered his family and farm workers together and told us all that he believed an invasion by Russia was imminent and that he would have to evacuate to our neighbouring country, Lithuania, with his family. He said that there would be no immediate danger to the farm workers as the Red Army would reckon they were all oppressed peasants, and made arrangements for us to go to Lithuania on the 19th September, aboard the night train.

My Mother was terrified of these developments. She mainly spoke to the refugees, as she was fluent in Russian. Then on the 17th September, at about 4am, our telephone rang. It was an Internal Security man informing my Father that a massive Red Army force had crossed the border. Father rang his local friends and within half an hour was picked up by one of our neighbours. They went to join a last ditch stand in the marshes of the Pripyat Delta, but, being pressed by Russian units, they had to change their plans and managed to slip into Lithuania.

The River Pripyat was a very marshy river with massive deposits of thick peat whose waters were fed by a number of very boggy rivers. This formed a natural and impenetrable part of Poland to German armour, which, after all, was eventually the downfall of the Polish, French and British forces on the continent of Europe. There was another part of southern Poland that the German soldiers would have to take on foot, and that is the Carpathian mountain range where armour could not enter. The Germans knew that very well, hence a secret pact with Russia to partition Poland. Several divisions of the Polish Army were concentrated in these massive areas. We lived on the edge of the Pripyat Delta and had great hopes of stopping the German armour. All our plans were going well until the 17th September, when the Red Army crossed our eastern border and attacked us from the back. What chance did we have to fight completely surrounded? The massive concentration of Polish forces just laid down their arms and, where possible, went home. The glorious Red Army were picking up every man in uniform, or part uniform, of the Polish Army and pronouncing them prisoners of war. War, but what war? We had a pact of non-aggression with Russia still in force, but what could one expect from Stalin and his bunch of perverted butchers. They slaughtered millions of their own people, so why not a few million of their old enemy, the Poles. That was the point where the tragedy of millions of Poles, and my own, began. The Russians were picking everybody up who had even part of the Polish Army kit on. If some local civilians picked up an army water bottle and were found with it, they were arrested and sent to the POW camp. My Father evacuated to Lithuania. My Mother was soon taken and sent to the far eastern part of Russia and I was left bewildered, angry and frightened on my own.

Just to put the events of 1939 into context, Germany had unexpectedly invaded Poland on September 1st. 16 days later, on September 17th, Russia invaded Poland from the East, meeting the Germans on the so-called Curson Line on the banks of the River Bug. 21 days later they announced the "annexing of the 2nd Polish Republic... acting to protect Ukrainians and Belarussians in the eastern part of Poland."

The Red Army put my Mother under house arrest on the very first day of the invasion, on 17th September, but I managed to get away and lived in an isolated barn with my school pal. We decided to find out more about the arrested men, so one night we managed to crawl up to a fence surrounding their camp. Its buildings were actually part of the fence of the compound and were nothing more than a type of log cabin. We hoped that we could remove moss from between the logs in one of the walls and perhaps talk to some of the men inside. I remember the night was very dark and wet.

We were practically paralysed with cold when we got to the outside wall. We immediately started looking for a wider gap between the logs from which we could pull out the moss that was used to prevent draughts in the buildings. We soon found a weak spot in the form of mortar which was used to render part of the wall. While my friend was attempting to find a crack in the mortar to prise it off, I moved a few metres to the fence that had numerous gaps between the split logs. Nearby were Russian troops. We had to be very careful not to make a noise because by now we knew that they would shoot to kill without any warning and practically on any pretext. My friend was in luck. He managed to chip out a lump of plaster but the sound of it falling made a noise like an exploding 1000-pound bomb, or so it seemed to me at the time. Rapidly he made contact with the prisoners inside, but the news was not good at all. He spoke to his uncle who told him that they were being accused of informing on Russian refugees. Only the previous evening the Red Army had tied some of the prisoners' hands behind their backs with wire. From the men's description and stories the Russians were thinking of executing these men. We could not believe it. How could they possibly contemplate executing them?

By this time it was either very late or very early the next day, and we knew that only the rain was delaying daybreak. To our good fortune, a nearby field of ripe flax had been harvested and the sheaves were stacked very close to the fence where we were so we were able to use those as cover. We had no option but to stay put as we clearly saw troops moving out of the school buildings. My friend joined me near the fence as some guards entered the cell. Through the gap in the fence I could clearly see the entrance to the building and I saw the red flashes on the army overcoats and hats. I immediately recognised them as being the insignia that was feared and despised by all, the so-called NKVD - the secret internal security forces of the Red Army. I also recognised a man walking slowly across the compound, a man that we already knew as the "red butcher". Later on he got an infamous reputation as a specialist in shooting women in the head whilst raping them. But at that particular time we just watched with misgivings and wondered what was going to happen next.

In the next ten or so minutes, we were faced with horror beyond any description. A number of men were brought out from the building, bent forward, and shot with a revolver in the base of the skull. Three or four bodies were left in the mud, mixed with horse and cow dung, as horses and animals had used it as an exercise yard. The next victim, realising what was going on, decided to have a go at his executioners. He kicked out viciously and started shouting. Immediately the red butcher called for help and some three or four more troopers rushed out of the adjoining building. They jumped on the maddened man and jammed hands full of dirt from the courtyard into his mouth, to subdue his shouts. The end came quickly and mercilessly. There was a muffled shot as from an air-gun and the body ended up in the mud, but he was a very powerful man and was still kicking and moaning as he lay there. The red butcher told his troopers to hold him and then fired three more bullets into his head.

At that point my friend could not contain himself any longer. He groaned and exclaimed "Jesus Mary". Immediately we heard the clink of a rifle bolt. I instinctively moved back about a foot towards the sheaves of flax behind me, and instantly felt something soft and wet splash my face. It was followed by the sound of a rifle shot. For a couple of seconds I thought the wetness on my face was mud, but then I realised it was warm and, seeing my friend laying on the ground with the side of his head missing, I realised that it was blood and brain. The taste in my mouth was distinctly salty and I was very nearly physically sick.

Luckily for me, I had previously worked as a volunteer at the local hospital as a general dogsbody and seen some post-mortems and a lot of blood. I lay there paralysed with emotion and tried to keep quiet between two sheaves of flax, hardly daring to breathe. Then the trooper who had fired the shot rushed up and dragged my friend away by one leg, informing the red butcher that he had caught a son-of-a-bitch peeping tom. I am certain that the American expression "son-of-a-bitch" came straight from Russian émigrés as it has been used for centuries in Russia, where it is a favourite expression. Whilst the body of my friend was being dragged away by one leg, the remaining part of his head started falling off in bits. By the time he had travelled four or five metres, the rest of his skull had fallen off. The guard's bullet, which entered around his ear had done the job properly and shattered the skull like a coconut. A few days later, I went back to the spot with some friends and, on the pretext of collecting flax, recovered a few pieces of his skull. His Mother eventually had them buried by an Orthodox Church priest as the Roman Catholic priest had already been arrested.

This was only the beginning of my nightmare; much worse was still in front of me. During my pre-war days of tracking and hunting I had got to know the forest very well. There were a number of small shacks built by foresters and pulpits from which we would shoot wild pigs. A pulpit was a small platform, a sort of tree house, raised from the ground by some ten or twenty metres on a tower. From here a hunter had a perfect view of animals coming into a clearing to eat or perhaps raid a field of potatoes. They were mainly used to hunt wild pigs, but on occasions were used for culling stags and deer. I had sat in a pulpit for many hours in sub-zero temperatures, with a heap of straw to keep myself warm. As a very severe winter was approaching, a handful of straw went a long way. Despite being only 16-years-old, I was intending to form or join some kind of partisan group. I decided to abandon the isolated barn and move into the forest. I was soon joined by some of my young friends and when our group was eventually dispersed by the Russians, there were more than 600 of us. A lot of partisans were ex-members of the Polish army, especially members of the 78th Infantry Division, which was ordered by the Polish command to lay down their arms some 10km away.

We had no problems with arms and ammunition – there were mountains of the stuff available. With the prisoner executions and the death of my friend fresh in my memory, I wanted to kill any men from the NKVD that I could. From Polish army arms dumps we had acquired a number of marvellous sniper rifles with extra long barrels and excellent sights, so we began a campaign of sniping. It was great sport to us, but not so funny for the Russian commissars. The forest was ours in every respect. We had plenty of arms and plenty of food. Only bread was a bit of a problem, but there were many local villagers who were prepared to make it for us. We ate plenty of venison or wild pig with bread. Looking back on it now, it was real madness to start a kind of private war but we didn't think about it too much. We were also encouraged by a number Russian deserters who had joined us.

According to them, the NKVD and commissars were so despised that they felt it was only a matter of time before some kind of revolt against them took place. Our circumstances and conditions at the time were so unreal that we lost a sense of proportion in our thinking. I personally was prepared to die and, frankly, I was certain that this would actually happen. Never in my wildest dreams could I see myself sitting and trying to write this book some 45 years later, in 1984.

The Russians eventually became very methodical in their approach to the problem of our activities they were facing. Most of the pulpits were just chopped down or, if they were defended, blasted with artillery or tanks. I remember one time when three men in our group died when a tank knocked down their pulpit. During this particular operation, a tank commander with red flashes on his uniform had his head blown off by a sniper when he emerged from the top door to examine the remains of the pulpit. The sniper in question was actually a Russian army deserter who celebrated his kill by getting so helplessly drunk that we very nearly had to shoot him to keep the peace. He said he had been waiting some ten years to shoot at least one of these bastards. He was a great character and could out-drink anybody. He eventually got killed while drilling a hole in a railway tank full of vodka, which was being transported to Germany. Rail traffic was moving 24-hours a day without stop, as the Germans and Russians were great friends at that time. Many petrol tanks on their way by train to Germany went up in smoke in December 1939 when our partisans managed to set them alight, creating a massive explosion at a railway junction. I personally missed the firework display as, by then, I was in custody under interrogation.

I had one aim in life at this time, and that was to get the "red butcher". My hatred of this man bordered on the insane. I was stalking him like I would a wild animal. Twice I tried to kill him and twice he got away, but only just. The second time I shot the peak of his hat and he lived. Eventually his perverted habits became his downfall. He got drunk in one of the local villages and took the local blacksmith's 13 or 14-year-old daughter into a storeroom next to the forge and raped her. Before he could shoot her while having sex, the blacksmith found him and smashed his left hand into pulp with a sledgehammer. He would have killed him there and then, but was afraid of killing his daughter.

The news of the incident came to us within two hours and three of us went to pick him up. I persuaded the blacksmith to hand him over to us. He wanted to drop a white-hot horseshoe in his crotch but was persuaded that we would deal with him. With his left hand heavily wrapped in rags from the forge, we took him by horse and cart to a very isolated farmhouse. To start with we intended to blow his head off with a rifle round. A bullet had been prepared in such a way that its tip was flattened by the smithy's rasp. He also melted out some of the lead from the centre of the bullet, which was temporarily removed from the shell, making the bullet into a so-called dumdum, which would be able take his head clean off. The blacksmith told me that he knew what he was talking about, as he had poached many wild boar in our forest before the War with similar illegal bullets.

When we eventually got our prisoner into the farm outbuildings we found that the bullet would not fit our rifles, but we were determined not to let him go. With us we had some practice grenades, which were the size of a large chicken's egg. The son of the farmer in whose barn we were had a square piece of black rubber that he used to propel model aircraft out of, and I made a sort of rubber band out of it. Putting it around his head restricted the opening of his mouth, but not before we had inserted the grenade in it. We pulled the pin and let him go. Unfortunately the band on his head slipped and he managed to spit out the grenade together with some of his teeth. It exploded in some manure but to our disappointment left him alive, so we dragged him back into the buildings. I had noticed a horse cart with flat pneumatic tyres in the yard and asked the farmer for part of an inner tube, which we made a band out of. This was much wider than the previous one and it worked like a dream. After letting him go with another grenade between his teeth, he started running towards the muck heap that had saved him before. This time he didn't quite manage to spit out the grenade. There was a muffled explosion and his head just took off.

Never had I imagined there could be so much blood in a human being. There was literally a fountain of blood followed by the remains of his head. To this day, I have a very vivid memory of him running around without his head, and his two collarbones sticking straight up from his shoulders. Seeing him still running my friend screamed, "For Christ's sake, shoot the bastard because he will get away". At that particular time I had around my neck a captured Russian machine pistol with 64 rounds of ammo in it. I let fly towards him and we saw the dust coming off his army jacket and cutting into his waist belt. He fell front down into a valley in the muck heap. The farmer, who, incidentally, was an army reservist, brought out two large home-made forks and within minutes he was neatly buried in the heap. As far as I know he was never found and during my interrogation his name was never mentioned. Russian Command probably came to the conclusion that he had been murdered by his own men like a number of other officers had been. He was a Colonel and was well-known as a particularly vicious pervert, who even took advantage of young soldiers under his command.

Things started getting very complicated when the Russians decided to get rid of all opposition in our area. They brought in two full divisions of the army, and an armed brigade of some 100 tanks. They combed the forest on foot and adopted a strict policy of shooting first and asking questions later. They also introduced a massive resettlement programme. Whole villages and big parts of towns were packed into railway cattle trucks and taken deep into Russia, well beyond the Ural Mountains. My Mother was sent with others to Kazakhstan, a far-eastern state and left to her fate. The majority of people on the trucks had to beg for food, as no provisions were made at all for food supplies. Some lucky ones were sent to work on collective farms, where the food supply was a lot better. In the main all resettled people were treated as free slave labour. As everybody was only allowed to take 20 kilograms in weight it was impossible for people to take anything substantial. Those who took jewellery, gold coins, etc., soon found they had to sell everything to survive.

Before my Mother was taken away, I went to our old house to take a last look at the place. It had to be seen to be believed. All 600 of our fruit trees had been chopped down with axes. Some people who worked for us said that after chopping down the trees, the Russians continued into the night to destroy with axes some 400 beehives in the orchard. We had three fairly large fish ponds containing carp, which is still a must for Christmas Eve supper, and it gave my Mother pin money, as some ten tons were taken out every December. The invading Russians were so determined to destroy everything belonging to so-called kulaks (a Russian word for an independent farmer or landowner) and intelligentsia that nothing we had was sacred. It was a total repeat of their 1917 revolution, in which they had destroyed all their own intelligentsia, and to this day have never fully recovered from their folly.

Our men told me that the Russians put some anti-tank mines into the ponds. After the mines exploded everything in the lakes was dead, including masses of beautiful green frogs. All our cheese stores were emptied and what they could not eat was thrown into a manure pit. Our guard dogs were shot and thrown into a well in the middle of the yard. The devastation was enormous. Every room in the house was used as a toilet and the stench was overwhelming. This was their perverted way of destroying the bourgeoisie and landowners. Some eleven families still lived in the houses on the estate and, as the well's water supply had been destroyed by the Russians throwing dead animals into it, they had to fetch water in buckets from the river, some two kilometres away. All the workers were questioned and told to sign prepared statements that accused the landlords of being cruel to them. Some refused to sign but most of them, seeing the madness and destruction, duly signed. All of my Mother's clothing, including some fur coats, was looted and, with winter approaching most of the officers, who had only light army coats on their backs, used the fur coats themselves.

Anywhere they went they would simply walk into a house, go to the wardrobe and, without a word, help themselves to whatever they fancied. There was one thing in our house they did not discover, however, and that was the gun-room in the cellar. In here was quite an arsenal of weapons, all sporting guns and rifles, as we did a lot of hunting before the War. There were also several pairs of high hunting boots made of wolf skin and some of the family silver. With the help of one of the men from the estate, I buried the guns and silver in an old machine gun bunker from the First World War and it is probably still there to this day. I was told that during the main shooting and slaughter of animals, my Arab stallion had bolted and had not been seen again. I immediately knew where he might be. I would take him to a spot on the river nearby, where I caught crayfish. I knew he was very fond of the place. True enough, he was there but lame as a bullet had hit him in the hindquarters and most probably shattered a bone. It was the first and last time I cried like a small boy when I had to shoot him, but unfortunately there was no other way out. Two or three divisions of

Red Army troops stationed locally were from the south-east part of Russia and they were Tartars. They preferred horse-meat to any other kind and I was not going to allow my friend to be eaten by those barbarians.

Before they crossed the Polish border on the 17th September, the Russians had been told by their political officers or commissars that they were going into Poland to liberate the peasant masses from the vicious and wicked rule of landowners and capitalists. The very first time we saw them we could not believe our eyes. They were advancing like locusts across our country, on foot with rifles slung across their backs, mostly hanging on a string. Many of them were bare footed or in improvised footwear made from car tyres. Whenever they managed to find a car tyre they would cut it into lengths of 12 inches or so, put their feet wrapped in any rags in the cavity and attach this to their legs just below their knees, with four pieces of string leading to each corner of the segmented tyre. Incidentally at the time, their pockets were stuffed with roubles, paper money worthless in Poland.

They would stop at literally nothing. They had orders to advance and they were blindly doing just that. There was a very marshy river nearby that was practically impassable by human beings. Locals often lost cattle in the treacherous bogs nearby. We could not believe our eyes that, instead of crossing by the bridge some half kilometre away, they actually got across the river on foot with the help of buoyant marsh weeds strapped to their sides like life jackets. When eventually they emerged from the marshes, they marched on to the shouts of "Forward, Forward" from the commissars. They would not even stop to rest. Many of them perished in the bogs but the rest marched on.

In every village the commissars would organise meetings with the local peasants saying, in effect, how proud they were to liberate their comrades. The soldiers immediately bought all the stocks of the village shops, whatever it was, from a small item like a sewing needle to working boots or wellies, and then childishly boasted about everything. I personally witnessed the following conversation.

"What have you got to sell keeper?" asked a soldier.

"Well, I've got a box of oranges. Have you got oranges in Russia?", came the reply.

"Oh yes, plenty but our oranges are the size of footballs. Not like these little ones. What else have you got?"

"I've got some salted herrings," said the shopkeeper. "Have you got herrings in Russia?"

"Oh yes, plenty," said the soldier, "but our herrings are like this," stretching his hands out about a yard to show the shopkeeper the huge size of the fish. "How many boxes of oranges have you got? I'll take the lot. You see, we have got plenty of money in the Communist regime."

The bewildered shopkeeper was forced to accept a few handfuls of money, which the soldier thrust in her apron pocket without counting. When the woman half-heartedly mentioned that she did not understand their money, he explained, "Don't worry, you are liberated and it is Russia now. When we liberate people we never leave again. You will only use our money from now on"

On reflection, how right the bastard was. At that particular time they had already "liberated" all the Baltic States, Lithuania, Latvia, Estonia and very nearly Finland. Since those years, they have gradually liberated, or attempted to liberate, some more oppressed people. For example, the rest of Poland, East Germany, East Prussia, Czechoslovakia, Hungary and Afghanistan.

Now let's go back briefly to the young soldier in the village shop. He took a salted herring out of the wooden barrel by its head and hit the top of his jackboot with it, like a horsewhip, to shake off the loose scales. Then, taking an unpeeled orange from the box, started eating it. He pulled a face a bit and exclaimed, "Ah, son of a bitch. It's nice and strong like good vodka". Onlooking locals dared each other to do the same but nobody could bring themselves to eat unpeeled orange and salted herring. Perhaps local Polish peasants could not read or write, but they had enough intelligence to discover in a very short time that the glorious Red Army was something exceptional. Officers, especially, were making fools of themselves in more ways than one. In one day one of my friends sold the same wristwatch three times in an empty matchbox to different soldiers by switching the box.

For some reason, wristwatches were in particular demand and that led to some bizarre situations. Later, in January 1940 I met our local watch repairer in prison. He had been arrested and accused of counter-revolutionary activities, and told me what had actually happened. A Russian Colonel brought him a highly polished brass carriage clock and demanded that the repairer should make this into four wristwatches. He thought it was a joke. But two days later an officer came to collect the watches and finding them not ready, called a passing NKVD security man and had the repairer arrested on the spot. The watchmaker told me that he had offered four new wristwatches to the Russian, but he had refused them all because they were not highly polished brass like the carriage clock, and he wanted them for his family to mark the occasion of the Polish liberation. When I met the watchmaker in prison he had some broken ribs, a broken wrist, his face and body were black and blue, and he could not hear in one ear. All this for not obeying the order of a glorious Red Army Colonel!

Stories and incidents like this were so sinister and scary that we tried to find out what made the Red Army Officer corps so backward and plainly stupid. They were literally a bunch of screw-balls. Their average I.Q. was so low because, following the infamous political trials in Russia in the 1930's, most of the officers corps had been sent to concentration camps or shot as spies. Some officers even boasted about their rapid advancement through the ranks. An illiterate Private, whose father was a peasant or manual worker, could go from Private to Colonel in one week. They were openly boasting and very proud of the fact that, "only in a Socialist state, could someone get such rapid promotion".

There was one part of the occupation forces that everybody feared and despised. They were the members of the internal security forces, the so-called NKVD, nicknamed "Robins" by us. They had red bands on their hats and red colour flashes on their jackets, hence the name "Robins". They were in a class of their own. A bigger collection of perverted thieves and murderers was never bunched together before.

They were feared and despised by all without exception. Local people soon realised the power of the Robins. During frequent robberies or rapes, or any other criminal activities, all you needed to do was to shout that the NKVD were coming and all activities stopped immediately.

It was nothing unusual to see a Robin shooting a Red Army member. The thin shell of respectability they were ordered to preserve gave the Robins an excuse to perform all kinds of atrocities on all civilians or members of the armed forces. Once they put their finger on somebody that was it. The person knew he was dead. The question was only whether he would be killed quickly by a bullet in the base of the skull, or slowly via a labour camp. Members of the motorised Russian units were terrified of getting their charges, such as guns or lorries, stuck in the mud. This crime would be classified as sabotage and, if proved, the justice would be very swift. Roads and fields were littered with counter-revolutionaries and saboteurs as there was plenty of mud around and field guns often got stuck in the clay on the crop-bare fields.

Seeing the rough justice they dished out to their own kin, we knew not to expect preferential treatment and, sure enough, the locals were not much better treated than their own kind. The reign of terror started immediately after their "invasion of liberation" on September 17th. The Robins entered the villages and towns with prepared pre-War voting lists of inhabitants on which were marked candidates for immediate arrest or so-called resettlement. You had to give them credit for their very detailed information of all Polish nationals. Old or new scores were settled very quickly. They even had a list of all members of the Polish liberation forces from the First World War, which had pushed the Red Army from the outskirts of Warsaw to beyond Minsk, well into pre-1939 Russia in 1919 and wished to settle old scores with them.

The Robins were particularly interested in the whereabouts of my father who had evacuated to Lithuania on the 17th September. As the Russians had also invaded Lithuania on that date, my father ended up as one of their prisoners of war and had missed an infamous massacre by the skin of his teeth. Whilst in captivity, he had developed a high temperature and, by giving a Russian doctor a silver cigarette case, had been withdrawn from being transported from his camp at the very last moment. None of the men who left without him realised they were to be executed. Following their attack on Russia the Germans discovered mass graves in the woods of Katyn, the last resting-place of fifteen thousand missing Polish Officers murdered by the NKVD.

The system of NKVD operations was especially designed to create terror. They never operated in the daylight, always at night. They would sit and observe a village all day but never arrest anybody until dark came. To start with we thought they were just a band of insomniacs in our district, but it was like this everywhere. Like rats, they were always going after their prey at night. This was especially designed to have the maximum terror effect on people. In the dark you could only meet the Robins or looters of the Red Army. Many Russian soldiers had to go and rob as their food supply was very sparse and very poor. Only vodka was in plentiful supply.

There was a lot of heavy drinking done in Poland, but when the Red Army came our pre-war drinking looked like kindergarten parties in comparison. The strongest Polish vodka contains 96% alcohol by volume, the purest alcohol you can bottle. On a number of occasions I witnessed Russians drink a half litre of the stuff without taking a breath. The Robins were particularly heavy drinkers and you could always smell the stale smell of alcohol on their breath. Their most favourite alcoholic tipple was aftershave lotion, the reason being that it smelled better and it sold out rapidly from all the shops. After their invasion, the Russkies, as we called them, started to put real pressure on us. Thousands of troops were engaged in searching for us. A strict curfew was imposed, and more and more often we heard the splatter of bullets hitting a tree or the wall of a building to signify their application of rough justice on anyone they suspected of breaking their rules.

We moved our main operations from the forest to other areas, blowing up a few bridges, viaducts and plenty of railway transport. The operations chopped and changed every few days. Eventually we started taking heavy casualties in men and equipment. We also lost our main explosives dump in a huge explosion that also destroyed five Russian tanks, which had been parked on top of them. The whole dump went up when an idiot Russian fired his tank's gun at a white hare some twenty metres away. This was typical of their mentality – use a sledgehammer to crack a small hazelnut. For example, to catch a few fish for the frying pan they would use a grenade to kill everything in a fish pond.

At the end of October we planned to blow up the Robins' HQ in Baranowicze, which was a large building surrounded by a big courtyard. We packed a massive refuse bin with explosives and were going to push it into the yard, armed with 9mm revolvers and two grenades each. The bomb was prepared in a small yard of a brass instrument maker and repairer some 800 metres from the target building. Halfway to the target there was a Jewish seminary with a main building set well back.

As we pushed the bomb towards our target, out of the darkness a Robin appeared. "Stop. Hands up," he barked. At the same moment there was a loud report and my left arm was pushed violently back as if somebody had pulled it by string. In a split second I lifted the gun in my right hand and fired two rapid rounds. As the distance between us was no more than two or three feet I could not miss. The Robin gave out some kind of wheezing noise and fell backwards. Next I saw a blinding flash and heard a crack of gunfire as a patrol fired towards us, and a bullet hit the waste-bin. Afterwards I have often wondered why the hell the whole thing did not blow up, but at that particular time I was more preoccupied with a soldier lunging at me with his bayonet of needle sharp, tipped steel. Momentarily, I thought he was going to fire but fortunately for me his breech was already empty and he tried to stick me like a wild pig. It happened so quickly I had no time to use my gun, so instinctively I tried to brush aside the bayonet. I felt a sharp prick in the palm of my left hand and my hand became very hot as though scalded. The tip of the bayonet entered my palm at the bottom of the thumb and got stuck somewhere in my wrist. I felt as if my hand was attached to the tip of the bayonet for a moment. I fired a further two rounds into his chest and, as he fell backwards, he pulled my left hand forward which was attached to the bayonet. I had to put my foot forward in order to stop myself falling. While I was busy with my own argument, my colleagues opened fire on the rest of the patrol, killing the three remaining members.

Unfortunately, the Robin's first shot had hit my friend behind me in the hip and it was only the explosion and wind from the muzzle that had knocked my left arm backwards. Our back-up group of four, which followed us several metres behind, took my wounded friend and me to a Jewish doctor's surgery a few doors from the seminary, and that was the end of our escapade. A few days later the bin with its contents was duly delivered to its target and made a very considerable bang and an even bigger hole. After this episode many of us felt there was no future in town, so eleven of us decided to try our luck in the villages and forest again.

## Chapter 3: Captured by the Reds

It was well into November by now and the weather was cold and uncomfortable. One of the boys knew a very isolated farm where he and his friends had hidden some machine pistols, ammunition and grenades and we started walking towards there early one evening. It was some twelve kilometres distant, so it was a fair march, especially at night. But the journey was fairly comfortable as the ploughed and raked fields were quite easy to walk on. The most difficult part was the last 150 or so metres, as it was a potato field and the ground was uneven with the potatoes still in there, and we had to be very careful not to break our ankles. It was just about daybreak when we eventually got to the sty on the farm. The warmth from the animals was very welcome and we settled down to a well-earned rest. The friend who had hid the grenades immediately went to retrieve them and after some half an hour of hard work, we settled down to have a longer rest.

Somebody started humming an old scout's tune and we all joined in a song. This paradise did not last very long, though. There was an explosion and a star shell lit up the grey sky just above the farm buildings. We tried to assess our situation. Our only possible way out was to dash towards the forest some 200 to 250 metres away on one side of the farm. Some of the boys were eager to try it straight away but four of my friends and I decided to wait until it was completely light. The remaining six lads grabbed some grenades and machine pistols and started running towards the forest. Outside the building there was a steaming heap of manure, surrounded by a 'U' shaped wall. I grabbed a few sacks from the building and took two snipers rifles and ammo. All five of us lay on the top of the manure and decided to defend ourselves. The reasoning was quite sensible and simple. If only a Russian patrol was involved, we had a very good chance of winning the argument with the help of two sniper rifles, but within the next few minutes we knew that all was not well.

Continuous flashes from the forest were swiftly followed by machine gun fire and we knew that our comrades were in real trouble. A few grenade explosions and two more star shells lighting up the scene told me that this was probably it. I was rather sorry it had to end, as I felt very comfortable lying on top of the warm muck heap. With the aid of field glasses we could see over a hundred soldiers advancing from the forest. After a quick discussion we decided to set up as many booby traps as possible with grenades and withdraw across the potato fields. As there were deep valleys between the potato crops, I felt this was our best chance. As I knew I could hit a playing card every time from 300 metres with a sniper's rifle, I decided to wait to try and recognise the commissar. Sure enough, within a minute I could see him waving his charges forward with a revolver in his hand. I felt my heart beating against the cow dung while I took a very careful aim and squeezed the trigger.

There was a hefty kick from the rifle butt and two seconds later, the commissar fell as if he'd been pole-axed. At the same moment, a three-ton lorry on the edge of the forest opened up towards us with machine gun fire. I knew the type of lorry very well. Crude steel plates slung on the sides meant they were usually used by NKVD troops. I decided to have a go at them, so I took off among the potatoes dragging the rifle behind me. With a pocket full of ammunition and a machine pistol around my neck, dragging the rifle behind me, it was real hard going. I crawled some 50 metres and felt my position was good enough to have a go at the Robins. One of them was sitting next to the driver of the lorry and moments after firing I saw him falling out of the cab onto the frozen ground. I examined the lorry through my telescopic sights and I saw the red-banded cap of another Robin observing the field through glasses. After firing my last shot I saw his cap leaping into the air. That was my last shot for a very long time....

The gunfire had exposed our position and all hell broke loose. At least four heavy machine guns opened up blindly on the field. Ricocheting bullets were whining and passing like a swarm of mad bees. The tops of the potatoes and bits of earth were flying everywhere. It was almost impossible to crawl or even to move. I dumped my rifle and weapons and managed to crawl very carefully some 50 or so metres away before

I saw scores of running soldiers with a blood-curdling scream of "Hurrah." Suddenly, the hard smack of a rifle butt between my shoulder blades dazed me. The next thing I knew, I was being dragged across the potato fields towards the lorry. There I saw one dead Robin near the cab on the ground and another with his head practically blown off in the truck. I was particularly pleased that my last two shots had been on target. The rest of my group was lying on the ground nearby. One was immediately spiked down with a bayonet. The other one had some terrible abdominal injuries after activating a grenade and killing himself and two nearby Russkies. "Who are you and what are you doing here?" was the first question. I did not answer. I heard my friend say, "We only came to pick some potatoes to eat. The last words I heard on the field were, "Don't kill them all now. We want to interrogate some of them." The journey to prison, lying on the floor of the lorry with my hands tied behind my back, was very painful and uncomfortable.

Lying on the floor of the shaking lorry, presumably on the way to prison, I tried to piece together my scrambled brain. I would probably have passed out but for the intense pain between my shoulder blades, which kept me awake and thinking very intensely. Escape seemed to be out of the question, as I was tightly trussed like a capon with my hands at the back. My legs were also tightly bound together with a piece of wire above my ankles. After a while my feet started to go numb, especially in my left leg, and I thought about a case of gangrene I saw in hospital due to lack of circulation. "What the hell am I going to say to the thousands of questions they are going to throw at me?". There and then my plan of defence was born. I had decided to insist that the reason we were in that potato field was to steal some potatoes for food. I knew if I wanted to survive I must not change my story.

At last we arrived at our destination. I heard a loud squeak and guessed we were about to go through the massive hardwood entrance gate to a pre-war Polish prison. I knew the prison vaguely as I had been there a few times with a doctor from the hospital to dress wounded prisoners. One of the men had to have over 50 stitches all over his face and neck after a fight between prisoners and I had to wash the wound on a warder's arm that had been badly slashed with a glass. The lorry stopped near the entrance to the building with one wall completely covered by a grapevine. I was luckily pulled by the collar on to the huge cobblestoned yard, as one of the other arrested men was pulled by the feet. His head hit the stones and split like a rotten apple. But as he was probably dead on arrival, it made no difference to him. The side of my face also hit the stone and I felt the swelling immediately closing my right eye. I found to my great relief that the guards at the entrance wore Polish uniforms. They were Polish guards who had been ordered to stay on and guard the prisoners. On crossing the border, the NKVD had opened all the prisons and let the prisoners out. They only kept in habitual criminals and had detailed information papers regarding all prisoners and staff. A Sergeant, whom I vaguely remembered from my previous visits, undid my feet and lifted me up under the armpits, but it was to no avail as I could not feel my feet and it took about 20 minutes before I could stand on my own.

The place I was taken to was next to a guardroom with an interconnecting door. There was a long pine oblong table against the wall with a wide heavily barred window behind it. There was a huge tiled stove reaching nearly to the ceiling, which was radiating intense heat. The Polish guard told me to "Strip down completely and wait. That is where my duty ends." I stripped down to my long johns and tried to sit on the bench near the stove. The bench was so hot that if I had been naked I would have blistered. I stood near the hot stove with my back to it. The intense heat seemed to relieve the pain in my back. My eye closed completely and my ear felt like it weighed several pounds in weight. I felt it with my hands and to my horror it was the size of a huge puff mushroom. In the intense heat my head and ears started throbbing painfully.

I heard somebody look into the room a few times through a small spyhole in the door. I was left on my own for a good half hour or so, and kept massaging my feet and hands to restore circulation, all the time thinking of my plan of defence, or rather survival story. Eventually four Robins came into the room, including a woman. A Colonel called the Polish Sergeant from the adjoining room and started screaming and swearing at him as to why I was not undressed. Soon I had lost the last piece of my clothing, my long johns, and all my clothing was searched, then there followed the indignity of a very personal search. I soon realised the purpose of all this. The fairly young female wanted to intimidate me. They cut off all my metal buttons from my trousers, took the belt off and also removed my leather bootlaces.

They asked my surname, first name, father's first name, address. As planned in the lorry, I gave the address of the village blacksmith who had nearly killed a Robin. I knew that he and his family were somewhere in a railway cattle truck on the way to Russia, so I knew it would do no harm. Their questioning stopped for a while as a doctor arrived to examine me. To my delight it was a doctor from the hospital where I had served my apprenticeship just before the war. He told the Robins that my ear needed ice and his assistant went to fetch it from the ambulance. We could not talk but, on the pretext that he was examining my hearing, he whispered to me that he would let people on the outside know where I was.

The Robin insisted that the doctor signed a declaration that I did not suffer from VD or any contagious disease. Then he started asking the same questions over and over again. He asked me what I was doing at the blacksmiths. I told him that I came from Warsaw, my family was very poor and I was hoping to become a smithy in order to shoe the horses at the riding school for the officers' families in Warsaw. I got a brief lecture as to how oppressive our system was, as I had to go 400 kilometres to learn to shoe horses for the capitalists and parasites. After some two hours questioning they all left bar one. He told me to dress and stand with my back against the wall next to the stove. He also left, I was so hot it started to be unbearable to stand there. Frankly I was thankful to be left alone. I went through the story again and again in my mind. The night must have been frosty and still as I could faintly hear as the town clock chimed the hours. After a couple of hours or so I asked a guard if I could sit on the floor, but he told me to "Stand up you son of a bitch and no talking". The stove was protruding into two rooms and, after a while, I could hear my friend talking in the next room, telling his guards that we are innocent and just wanted to pick some potatoes. I started telling the guard my life story hoping that my friend would hear me and would know what to say during interrogation. I was told to be quiet but after a while he gave up on this idea and half listened to my story. I told him why I was apprenticed to the smithy, my life in Warsaw and my fictitious address there.

The address was really that of our dentist in Warsaw. Years later I found that the dentist was questioned about me by the Gestapo but was clever enough to say that he had let some rooms to the family and he didn't know their names exactly. At that time I did not realise that the Russians and the Germans had decided to partition Poland on the so-called Curson line, so the Russians never got as far as Warsaw, but their great friends the Gestapo were doing investigations on their behalf. At around one in the morning, another Robin came in with an armful of wood to make up the fire. I remember it was split hornbeam and I thought they had gone mad as this timber gives as much heat as coal, and this place would be impossible to bear in an hour or so. On top of the wood he brought another pail full of peat and packed the stove to capacity.

By the time the clock struck four, the heat in the room was unbearable. My guard shed his jacket, thick padded body-warmer, boots and an oblong piece of cloth that was wrapped around the foot and calf that served as socks. The nauseating smell of his feet, the stale spirit on his breath and his dirty body smell became worse by the minute. My fast-flowing adrenalin began to settle down and I started feeling really miserable and desperate to escape. My head felt as though it was made of solid lead and I could hardly keep it upright. The very small bag of ice on my ear had long since melted and the throbbing and ringing came back with a vengeance. I asked the guard if could to go to the toilet but his reply was quick and to the point. "Pee in your trousers, you son of a bitch. There is no toilet for you". I felt I just had to get out of this room even if only for one minute. As I could not stand against the wall any longer, I started sliding down onto the floor. He immediately picked up a piece of split hornbeam and hit me on the shins and knees. "Stand up, you bastard. I am not going to Siberia for you," he howled. "You might as well get used to not sleeping because you will not sleep for a long time". "Oh God", I thought, "I have heard about this sort of questioning before. They just will not let me sleep".

As they had taken my belt away my trousers were secured like a sort of wrap with the ends tucked into each other. All night there were different noises coming from around the building. The comings and goings were continuous. At about 5am, the guard asked for a samovar to be lit for tea and when he came back he stood facing me. I distracted him by coughing gently and started relieving myself into his jackboot. For ten seconds or so he didn't notice anything. When he did he howled like a wolf and I thought I was going to kill a Robin without actually shooting him, by giving him a heart attack. He grabbed me by the neck and threw me on the floor. The Polish guard opened the interconnecting door to see what was going on. The stream of cold fresh air hit me and I started shouting and pretending I could not get up. It only lasted half a minute, but it gave me a priceless opportunity to recover from a desperate situation. When my guard went to the toilet, the Polish guard gave me a very large mug of cold water, which I poured over my head and back. By the time it reached my calves and heels, it was warm and steaming.

The Polish guard winked at me as he shouted at me to stand against the wall, so as not to upset the Robin even more. When my guard returned he took his trousers off and draped them over the stove to dry, swearing like mad as the smell of quickly evaporating urine seemed to upset him. He went to the window and pulled out a piece of rag, which was stuffed into the small broken pane of glass. This greatly upset the senior Robin when he came in with his henchmen and, to my great delight, he added some strange and rather colourful words to my vocabulary of White Russian dialect, as he called my guard some strange names. My mind boggled when I heard my guard's ancestors being dragged from the grave and appropriately abused. My guard stood to attention and only kept saying "No, Comrade, yes, Comrade". The chief Robin threw the half dry trousers in his face and screamed at him to get out. He turned his rage at me and screamed the question, "Are you ready now to tell the truth? What were you doing there in the forest and who was with you?" One of his henchmen was the same beautiful Russian girl, who was half sitting on a table with one leg hanging loose. She said in a quiet sophisticated voice, "Come closer, Galubczyk (dearie) and tell me the truth." To get her boss off my back, even temporarily, I moved innocently towards her, holding my trousers up with one hand. When I was about two feet from her, she suddenly kicked out with her leg towards my crotch. Luckily she was slightly off the target but broke the little finger on my left hand, the same hand that was still very tender after being hit with a bayonet in the fairly recent skirmish with the Robins. Whilst kicking, she over balanced and fell backwards onto the table, showing me, and the two guards behind me, that she was not wearing any underwear. This caught me by complete surprise and I pretended I didn't notice anything, but one of the guards behind me started giggling uncontrollably. The chief jumped towards him, hitting him on the face and chest. I started laughing and duly got a backhander on my good ear, so I ended up with ringing in both ears, but it was well worth it to see them fighting amongst themselves.

By now it was getting light outside and, as the Robins never worked in the daylight, he told the Polish guard to take me to cell number 9. The cell was a short walk from the office and while he was unlocking it, he put his thumb and forefinger on the top and bottom of his lips. I presumed he was warning me not to talk in the cell. There were already five men in there and they soon surrounded me, asking me all kind of questions. Remembering the sign the Polish guard made I told them my story about the potatoes and said that I expected to be released soon as I had done nothing wrong. They said I was lucky as the Russians had shot a lot of people here. Then they proceeded to tell me how. The victim was given an army overcoat and his hands tied behind his back. The coat's high collar was then held tightly above his head, and a bullet was fired from a revolver into the base of the skull. This was no news to me as I had seen it with my own eyes in a village police compound. I felt that they were describing it for some effect. I could not think why, but I didn't have to wait long for the answer. Breakfast was 100 grams of clay-textured bread with a half-litre of lukewarm unsweetened so-called tea.

After a sleepless night in a very hot room, with my head badly knocked about and my left hand and head throbbing badly, I was looking forward to a day's rest and so lay on the concrete floor and attempted to sleep. I soon found that there was no respite to my torment, as the other prisoners were talking to me loudly all the time. I was so tired that I went to sleep despite their gibbering but they then started deliberately standing on my feet and hands while were walking across the floor trying to keep me awake.

I just hid my painful left hand in my crotch and went to sleep, but a very painful kick on my bad ear woke me up and I saw a huge bare foot in front of my face. It belonged to a red-faced peasant of about 40 with a very wide smile. Without a thought I lashed out with my right fist and caught him squarely in the crotch. He let out a scream and fell on top of me, his head ending up near mine. In a split second I managed to sink my teeth into his ear. The taste of blood filled my mouth immediately. The rest of the inmates started kicking my body and tried to pull him away. The general commotion and his howling brought in two Polish guards, who thankfully took me outside into the corridor and eventually into the main reception. From their conversation, I realised that cell number 9 was a special cell with Robins as inmates. One of the guards took me to the toilet and told me that they had been ordered to keep me awake all day. He said he would try to help me sleep and I was taken to the hot interview room and left there on my own. Soon after I was told in a whisper to come and stand near the door. Through a spyhole I was told that two sticks would soon be passed to me, which I should use as a kind of crutches to rest. I was not to lie on the floor, however, as the cell would be regularly checked by the Robin on duty through the spyhole, and the Polish guards would get in trouble if I was found on the floor.

The two sticks were quickly passed to me but they were impossible to use and hurt the pits of my arms too much to rest. So I took my boots off and put them on the top of them as a cushion. By moving my feet forward, away from the wall, I found that only they were visible from the spyhole and immediately fell asleep. I must have slept some good five hours. I was disturbed by a Polish guard only once, who was told by the Robin to check on me in case I had hanged myself as my feet were very still.

There were indeed many cases of suicide and the Robins were not prepared to let anybody die without their permission. The sleep refreshed me and I was eventually woken up and my sticks taken away in the late afternoon. Then came the main meal of the day, about three-quarters of a pint of soup in the evening. Well, at least they called it soup. I was told later that prisoners of my category had their soup topped up with cold water if the Robin decided it was too thick. As soon as the night fell, my tormentor turned up with his henchmen and asked me the same questions, over and over again. "We know everything", they said, "you are a saboteur, counter-revolutionary and enemy of the people, so who are your friends and where are they?". I pretended I was very tired and wanted to sleep, which gave me a chance to be very vague and not remember things, and I pretended to see flies and bees flying in the room. Eventually in the early hours of the next morning, the Robin told me that if I did not give them names they were simply going to shoot me. Seeing how agitated the boss was, I felt they would most probably do just that. In view of my aching head, hands and all my body in general, I thought it would release me from my torment. Soon before daybreak, my tormentor gave me a last chance to talk or else. What followed was a nightmare that I have relived so many times since, even forty five years later.

I have revisited this private hell in my dreams but this is the first time I have dared to describe it. One of the Robins brought a very large Polish cavalry army overcoat with visible scorch marks on its back. They told me to put it on. I remember taking a deep breath and holding it until I saw stars flying in front of my eyes. At that very moment I tried to commit suicide by holding my breath. My arms were twisted back and tied with something. The Robin was still talking and giving me a last chance. I had so much hatred in my heart that I wished I had a grenade in my hand. I would have pulled the pin out without a second's hesitation to take them with me. The collar was pulled over my head and I was bent forwards towards the ground. There was a massive explosion and something hit me like a hammer in the back of my neck. Then everything started happening as if in slow motion. He let go of the collar and I fell face down on the floor. I felt my body moving and falling as though into a crevice. I lost count of time. I felt something wet and warm against my neck and head. After a while I heard something that sounded like speech, but it was as if a Martian was talking, and I could not understand a word. Then somebody was talking in Polish but I still could not understand what the voice wanted.

The voice was asking me my name. I eventually started coming to my senses. I realised I was lying on the floor and there were faces above me, and it took me a while to get my thoughts back completely. Suddenly, I heard a piercing scream and saw a man grasping the window bars and screaming over and over again. I tried to get up, but I couldn't. Two men helped me up to a sitting position. The first thing I enquired was why the man at the window was screaming so much. They told me that he went through what I just went through five days ago and he'd been screaming ever since. They told me to rest for a while and they would tell me all about it later. I fell asleep and did not wake up until the soup arrived just before the fall of darkness.

When I woke up completely, I was told that the Robins had put me through a mock execution and that I'd came out of it quite well. My neck hurt so much it felt like it did not belong to me. I was rocking all over the place and could not hold my head upright. One of my fellow inmates, an ex-Polish prison guard, explained that in mock executions they use blanks they make themselves. They jammed a long revolver bullet in the door and used it as a vice to remove it from the shell. Then they pushed a ball prepared for spinning flax into the shell, instead of the bullet. Sometimes they used chewed-up paper pulp. The explosion propels the ball of flax and hits the victim in the neck with such a force that sometimes it dislocates the vertebra in their neck, so they often die through dislocated vertebra as if they had been hung. Well, whatever they used, it had the appropriate effect as it left me feeling sure I was dead.

The wet and warm substance on my neck was morning tea in which a sock had been dipped to help me to come round. In this way I was introduced to my new life in prison. My friend said we must first of all let everybody in the prison know who the new arrival was as they kept an unofficial list of prisoners. Their system for communicating with each other was ingenious but very effective. A slight tap on the prison's steel central heating pipes would carry sound many cells away, so Morse code was used - two knocks for a dash and one for a dot. Messages were sent at fantastic speed. The snag was the spyhole. If one of the warders heard tapping, they would try to locate the man doing it. My friend could even tap with his foot holding a small stone between his toes picked up in the exercise yard; he almost drove the Robins mad with his tapping. Our cell was designed to hold six prisoners as there were six beds folded up and secured flat against the wall during the day, but there were about 33 of us in it. There was no furniture at all except a big hardwood two-handed bucket near the door, which was our latrine at all times, and a washbasin. We were allowed approximately half a litre of water each per day. You could take your choice what you did with it. You could drink it, wash in it, have a bath in it, or whatever you wished. And, of course, you could sell it, as it was quite a saleable commodity.

The man in charge appointed by the guards was in charge of the water, bread, soup and tea. We were allowed 100 grams of bread a day. The Russian bread was sometimes made up out of several pieces, all joined together by a wood dowel some half inch square. At times there were a lot of arguments regarding the bread as sometimes it was weighed whilst on the stick. It was the charge man's job to pronounce the rights and wrongs in the argument and he often had to be wiser than Solomon to make a judgement. In our cell we had some seven or eight young Jews who had all attended the Rabbi's seminary before the war. I personally felt very sorry for them as they refused all non-Kosher food, so they were left with bread only, and you cannot go very far on four ounces of bread per day. They were all desperately thin, waiting for food parcels from home but were only allowed a one-kilo parcel a week. As the rest of us received no parcels, there was a lot of envy and some fights, but nothing serious.

Every night somebody was taken for questioning. There was a curious way of calling out the wanted man. The guard would stand at the open door and call out, "Anybody with a name that starts with the letter, let's say 'P'". Different men of that letter would call out their names and if someone replied with the wanted name, they were asked to give their first name and their father's name. If this matched they were told to come out, hands behind their back, face the wall and no talking. These prisoners often came back in the morning with black eyes, thick ears and knocked out teeth. In the two or more weeks that I was in that cell, I was called out twice. Both times I was closely questioned about the whereabouts of a young local teacher who I knew was an undercover agent of the Polish internal security, but I also knew that he'd gone west into German occupied Warsaw, as he had tried to persuade me to go with him. Quite a number of men in my cell, including myself, had assumed names to confuse the Robins as much as possible. Most men tried to protect their families who were resettled in the depth of Russia, including grandparents, grandsons and granddaughters.

After two weeks in prison I was told I would be sent to another prison, some 30 kilometres away for a confrontation with another "bandit". I knew that particular town very well and that the railway line to it crossed our part of the forest. At one point the train would cross the bridge of a very marshy river over which speed restrictions had been in force for some two years. Within half an hour of hearing the news, I got to know by the bush telegraph in the form of the pipes, that there was another inmate who would be coming with me. I didn't know him personally but, on receiving the message that I intended to escape, he replied that he was coming with me. On the day of our departure, we were both taken from separate cells into my hot room. This time there was no fire and it was quite cool. We were handcuffed together with a length of chain.

The Russians used chain handcuffs most of the time. We were marched to the railway station by five guards. I knew the town very well, but it is difficult to make a bolt for it when your right wrist is coupled to your friend's right wrist. The railway wagon in which we were travelling had no corridor and each compartment had two doors, one on each side of the carriage. We were under very strict orders not to talk. I told the guard that I loved Russian melodies and asked if I could hum at least one. He agreed, provided we didn't talk. Before the war there had been a craze amongst young students to communicate amongst ourselves in a secret code. To a stranger it sounded gibberish, so I decided to try a simple code on my companion. To the tune of 'Volga Volga' we started communicating quite reasonably singing out our Polish words to the tune. I told him there would be a bridge with very muddy banks where the train went slowly. As our right hands were handcuffed together, I proposed that I would hug his waist from the back, he would open the door, jump first and then I would follow him in a sort of piggyback fashion. I told him he must try to get up as quickly as possible after hitting the bog, as I would probably be drowning underneath him, as I would hit the bog first. He told me he was a cavalry man, a conscript, who frequently fell off horses, so a jump like that had no fear for him.

What amused us greatly was the fact that the guards were humming the tune and actually started singing with Russian words. Very soon after the train began slowing down to negotiate the bridge, I got cold feet about this crazy plan, but it was too late now to back out. My companion asked me to follow him to distract the guards. I didn't know what he meant, but I agreed. He asked the guards if they had got cockroaches in Russia. Before they could answer, my companion stamped his foot as if to squash something on the floor. I started doing it as well. The guards said they could not see anything, but started lifting their feet to look for the cockroaches. My friend told them there was a special breed of bug that was very fast and vicious and could attack personal parts of the body. I started scratching, followed by my friend and even the guards. If we had not been in such a situation, it would have been very funny indeed. One could talk the Russkies into doing anything – if we said that Polish horses could fly, they would most probably believe it.

Eventually the train started negotiating the huge bends and I knew that the river would be some 250 metres or so away at the end of them. I told the guards that I knew these bends and that the river was within a kilometre when my friend pointed to the ceiling above the luggage rack and shouted, "Look, they are gathering." I instinctively pointed as well. The guards jumped to their feet and turned completely round, leaving the other door on the inside bend unobserved, allowing my friend to calmly open it. We took a small run from the middle of the carriage and both leapt into the open space. We came out of the carriage like a bullet with me hanging onto my partner like grim death It felt like we'd jumped from about 1000 feet as, due to the marshy terrain, the railway line was raised about 6 feet. My heart missed a beat when I saw a concrete signal post rushing towards us, but we luckily missed it by a hair's breadth and hit a bush instead. It slowed us down dramatically, but also turned us forward onto our heads. As we were tumbling over and over, we hit the marsh and, as anticipated, I hit the peat ground first, but with my neck instead of the seat of my pants. I quickly took a deep breath, as I knew I would soon feel the full weight of my friend on top of me. The thud of the impact emptied my lungs with one rush and within seconds I had sucked up a considerable amount of filthy water. My companion was very agile and fit, and immediately pulled me out of the bog. Seeing my difficulty, he hit me very hard on the back and a fountain of water spurted from my mouth like a cork from a champagne bottle, and I was violently sick. Just as we scrambled to our feet, the first shots were fired from the train and we immediately dropped down with a splash. By now the train was coming to a stop with sparks flying from the stones packing the railway sleepers and the brake pads smoking, "Some bastard is shooting at us from the bank," shouted my friend, as we suddenly noticed a line of Russian soldiers advancing towards us. Apparently they were on a routine exercise and we had jumped smack bang into their laps.

We had to give ourselves up and our two guards soon had us back in the compartment where we expected terrible recriminations. The younger guard was asking how could we do such a thing to them after they'd allowed us to sing, and the episode had clearly shaken them more than us. We were just wet and a bit smelly, but they were absolutely devastated. Funnily enough, for the rest of the journey we became quite friendly and talked a lot. They said that if we had managed to escape it would have been a work camp for them both and they were absolutely terrified at the thought of it. The young man told us that his father and two uncles had been working on a collective farm when a bull died after swallowing some barbed wire. All three were accused of causing the death of the animal and sentenced to seven years in a labour camp and they never came back; they died within 2 and a half years. He said he was a young boy then, but ever since had developed a terrible fear of these camps. They really opened their hearts to us and even let us see our personal documents they were taking with us to our new prison. I could not read the Russian writing so they explained to us what was in them. My friend's case was not bad at all. He was arrested for being an officer's batman. My case was more difficult as it carried the double possibility of sabotage and banditry, and so my life expectation was not very great. They asked us with great uneasiness not to tell the Robins about our brief escape. As they were very simple peasant stock lads, we promised to say nothing. They were so grateful that they shared bread and a piece of sausage with us, which had been given to them for the journey.

However, on arrival at our destination, I immediately felt that my luck was running out. One of the three guards with automatic pistols who came to collect us was a local man, a known Communist, who had been released from prison on the day the Red Army entered the town. He was known as a large-scale poacher and a thief. He would go into the forest with a pair of horses and a special cart, then cut and down a fully-grown spruce or other pine tree or and take it away. The pines in our forest were so-called "peach pines" and were a very expensive commodity to lose. He was so skilled that it could take even a fully experienced forester a week or so to realise that the tree has been removed, when the moss covering the stump started wilting. This same man was an undercover NKVD agent who was looking for my father on the 17th September when the Red Army crossed the border. I knew straight away that my cover would be blown as he knew me very well. I later discovered he had accused me of blowing up railway petrol tankers on the day I was arrested some 30 miles away. This vital information was given to me a few days after my arrival, but it was unfortunately too late to avoid me from having a most painful experience.

On arriving, we were immediately separated and had to wait until dark for the questioning to begin. My new question master was a full Colonel, which was a bad sign. He had a quiet cultured voice and there was something about him that made my blood run cold. He turned out to be the most sadistic of all my inquisitors. A few years before the War he had been a primary school teacher in the southern part of Poland and had escaped to Russia after his Communist sympathies were discovered. At the very beginning I told him my real name, which threw him a bit, and he said that the documents in front of him belonged to somebody else. As I had decided to reveal my true name there was no going back. I was hoping that the general low standard of intelligence of the NKVD rank and file would help to confuse the Colonel as well. I told him that when my name was first taken I was asked to write it down on a document and, as the Russian alphabet was different to Polish, a mistake must have been made. He accepted this immediately, saying to his second in command, "Those sons of bitches", meaning the statement takers, "should all be sent back to school." But as he read on he started to smell a rat. My occupation, address, etc., were wrong also, When he started making sarcastic remarks such as, "Don't worry, we have got a special way to get to the truth and it only takes fifteen minutes," my blood froze. I didn't know what he was talking about, but I didn't like it. Eventually he said: "I will give you twelve hours to think it over and come clean".

My new place was not actually a prison. It was a pre-war police station with ten cells only, so I did not expect to be there long. After a full night of questioning I was taken to a single cell where I was to spend an uncomfortable day. I felt it was a nasty place but did not know why. There was something about it that gave me the real creeps.

About mid-morning the local NKVD chap came to my cell and began asking me where my father and another landowner were, saying that that he had got a special bullet for my father. He baited me for a good two hours until I felt I could stand it no longer. There was a metal folding bed secured against the wall, which he had let down and sat on, with his back against the wall. Suddenly I grabbed the edge of the bed and lifted it up with all my strength, trapping the rat against the wall as if in a pair of pliers. By pushing the bed towards the wall I trapped his head with the main steel angle frame. By violently pressing the frame with my shoulder I saw the iron cutting his cheek, eyebrow and forehead. The blood gushed out as from a pig in a slaughterhouse and he started howling for help. For some reason it took many minutes before it arrived. When I heard the door being opened I let him go and he fell to the floor. By that time he had urinated and opened his bowels.

To my astonishment, the Colonel himself rushed in with two other high-ranking officers and asked the wounded man what he was doing in the cell despite orders not to enter and interfere. That is when I saw how dangerous the bastard could be. Despite seeing the man's blood, he started slapping him about the face and head. I watched as the blood splashed across the white-washed walls. With a raised voice he told him that the Russians had spent a lot of money on him, including when he was in a Polish prison, and now he was disobeying orders. He said that if he carried on like that he would end up in a hedge as fodder for field rats.

Even after all these years, I can still see him pulling out of his pocket an immaculately pressed white handkerchief and wiping his bloody hands on it. Then turning to me, he said: "And I'll talk to you later", and walked out of the cell. He called the guard who dragged the bleeding man out of my cell. Later that day a piece of paper was pushed under my door. The unknown writer informed me that this NKVD agent had accused me of blowing up a train on the day I was arrested. Many years later, after the war, I met the man who had written it. He was a personal friend of my father's who spent the war with the Polish Second Corps in the Middle East, and in Italy with the British Eighth Army. As he had a perfect command of Russian he was employed by the NKVD as a sort of interpreter, and worked under an assumed name. He claimed to be an employee of the slaughterhouse next to the Police Station and a sympathiser of the Communists. He definitely saved my bacon on that particular occasion, as I knew how to defend myself. He managed to arrange for me to have one litre of soup so thick that you could stand your spoon in it. He also told me in the note to be careful of the Colonel. He didn't have to tell me that, I was scared stiff of the bastard.

I spent the rest of the day trying to sleep but to no avail. I was wondering if I would get another hot room treatment and was mentally preparing for it. By then it was December and the days were short. As soon as it got dark there was a guard at the door asking, "Anybody with the name beginning with the letter P?" It struck me as funny as I was the only one in there, but the system had to be observed and we duly went through the silly procedure of me coming out of the cell. I was taken to the interview room and there was my friendly Colonel with two officers who had visited my cell earlier in the day.

"Well, Galubczyk", he said. "Now is the time to sing the truth like a canary. Why the assumed name? Why the wrong address? Were you a scout master? Which school did you attend? Where is your father?

Why did he run away? Why? Why? Why?. To show what a good comrade I am, I'll give you a last chance to think it over and come up with the right answers." He explained to me that he thought that I was an intelligent young man and that I should know that sooner or later they would get to the truth. He then called for guards. Two of them, looking like all-in wrestlers, came in and told me to clasp my hands behind my back. Using a strong string like was used to tie sheep, they tied my hands very tightly and pushed a wad of cotton wool very tightly into my mouth. I thought to myself that my luck had finally run out and they were going to shoot me, but when he told them not to cover my nose I breathed a sigh of relief. After producing a woman's scarf, they tied it tightly around my mouth and chin so it was impossible to open my mouth or even shout. The night felt very cold as they took me outside and into the building next door, and by the time they eventually opened the door, frost and ice had started forming in my nostrils. I caught sight of a rail near the ceiling from which pulleys were hanging down on a large 'S' shaped hook. I thought, "God, they are going to hang me." Apparently it was a slaughterhouse and those hooks and pulleys were used to hang the dead animals' carcases in order to disembowel them.

The Colonel and his aides followed us into the building. They all had soft peaked hats on with huge red stars on the front of them. I still didn't know what was going to happen. Then the Colonel said to me: "Shake your head if you decide to tell the truth". The two wrestler-like guards put the rope around my wrists and started winching me up. I tensed my muscles to overcome my weight but to no avail. Eventually my feet left the ground and they tied the rope off. I felt my elbow and shoulder joints parting company and a terrible pain started that increased in intensity, and I felt as if my brain was splitting my skull. My weight was pulling on my joints and I wanted to be sick. I was thankful I had the cotton wool in my mouth otherwise I would have had to scream. I could not breathe through my nose and started feeling faint. I started saying "Our Father" inside, praying I would lose consciousness. I began seeing a mist in front of my eyes, in which sparks were flying like a swarm of bees. All the time the Colonel stood in front of me with a pocket watch in his hand. Eventually I heard him say, "Take him back to the room". I was dropped on the floor like a sack of potatoes and carried back to the interrogation room, as I could not walk. The Colonel said that it took had only taken fifteen minutes but that next time it would be half an hour.

He started questioning me about blowing up the train and brought in two peasants, who were unknown to me, but they both pointed their fingers at me and said, "It was him, it was him." Luckily, thanks to the note I received in my cell, I knew what to say. I asked the peasants for the date and if they were sure. "Oh, yes we are sure enough", they said. I asked the Colonel to have a look at the time and date when I was caught stealing potatoes. He looked very carefully at a document, turned to his two wrestlers who were still in the room, and said "Take those two sons of bitches into a cell. They have wasted enough of our time". The two peasants both dropped to their knees and swore blind that they were telling the truth. The Colonel rushed towards them and kicked them both viciously, before they were taken away. Turning to his companions the Colonel said: "That is all we can do in this case. We will have to refer it to a specialist unit at..." I didn't hear the name of the place as I was violently sick

After the hanging episode, I was left on my own for some 48 hours for which I was very grateful. I was in very acute pain due to my dislocated shoulders and elbows. My wrists and shoulders were badly swollen and I had a sensation of pins and needles in my arms due to inadequate circulation. I did try to bring my arms back to life by twisting my body from side to side and by swinging my arms helplessly from side to side like two red rags; but because of the acute pain I didn't do much of it. My Polish guard told me that I was due for a transfer but he did not know where exactly. The only thing he knew was that it would be east, into Russia. Many trains travelling east stopped to pick up prisoners or cattle wagons with people for resettlement. As it was only a single line railway the Red Army engineers had built some 300 metres of dual by-pass line there. The name of this place was Slonim, and it was the last station before the pre-1939 border between Poland and Russia.

I thought very intensely about the possibilities of escape. Due to having a very friendly Polish guard I had great hopes of it. I discussed the matter with him while he tried to massage my arms back to life. He also told me something about the Colonel responsible for my hanging. He said he was a sadist with a perverted sense of humour, who had already crippled a number of older men and had no hesitation in doing the same to young children. The Colonel boasted he always got results without further physical violence, and had got a young lad of eleven to tell him where his father and uncles were during one of his hangings. You could just survive his treatment if you were young and your muscles were still supple enough to recover. He found that women seemed to be more resilient to this treatment and after several attempts to get information from them, he stopped hanging women.

On the first day after my hanging, the guard told me that the Colonel had disappeared; he just had not turned up for work. I was hoping that somebody had had enough guts to stick a grenade in his mouth or crotch and had remembered to pull the pin out. By now my episode with the grenade was quite well known to everyone, but I did not dare tell my guard that it was me. The less people who knew about it, the better it was for me. Under torture some people might just spill the beans about me. About two days later my guard told me the Colonel had been transferred to the south where he had been a teacher before the War. By the look of things the local NKVD man, with a special grudge against my family, had been left temporarily in charge of the station. This news disturbed me greatly and I wondered what its effect might be. I didn't have to wait long for the answer.

In the depths of the following night, well after midnight, he came to my cell with another man. With them was a girl in uniform to take notes as he himself could hardly read even bold printed matter. He told me straight away that, one way or another, he would get the truth out of me and started accusing me of all sorts of illegal activities in the district. I denied it all and laughed in his face. He gave me the creeps, as the bastard was very accurate in both his assumptions and wild guesses. On the other hand I also learned quite a lot from him. He told me that during a dustbin attack which, unknown to him I was indirectly involved with, over 100 NKVD men died and some 150 were injured.

The Colonel who had lost his head in my grenade attack had been a top political commissar and had been promoted to General in the NKVD, just before his end.

He told me that my house was being used as a rest home for wounded men from the dustbin attack. I asked him to explain why they had cut all the fruit trees down and destroyed the beehives. His explanation was that it was an extension of the 1917 revolution and all those connected with landowners, the intelligentsia and the bourgeois had to be destroyed so as not to leave a trace of the past. His speech and explanations were identical to the explanations in the leaflets, thousands of which were distributed by the Red Army to the local population. All Communist propaganda in the form of slogans was, and still is, repeated by everyone parrot fashion. Immediately after crossing the border, the Red Army commissars displayed thousands of posters. Their slogans - "Long live this and that" – could be seen everywhere. Even now, as I write this in 1985, travelling throughout Eastern Europe you can see thousands of them displayed everywhere. If nothing is displayed in the village next to the railway line, the local party overlord can be, and often is, for the chop. So you see them posted everywhere. Most look identical; whether they are in Berlin or Vladivostok. The only difference is the language; as many are straight translations from Russian they lose their meaning and sound quite grotesque and ridiculous.

At the very beginning of our meeting he told me to sign blank pages, so the typist could fill in my statements later. He had a terrible inferiority complex and, to rub his face in the dirt, I pretended to write the name of someone supposedly important on the piece of paper and showed it to him. I knew he could not read or write but would not admit it. He immediately showed it to the so-called secretary and the silly girl started giggling as she read out to herself "Kiss my bum". I don't know where the girl came from but she obviously could speak and read Polish. When I joined three words into one to make a word of sixteen letters, he stared at the paper with a blank expression and commented that it must be the name of some nobleman as it was so long.

The giggling girl eventually whispered into his ear and told him what was written on the paper. At this, He blew his top and displayed his dissatisfaction in typical illiterate peasant's language, but it seemed to undermine his confidence in himself and soon afterwards he left my cell. Before he left, he turned to me and said that I must have heard a Russian saying, "You will live but you will not want sex". He said it with a very sarcastic smile and, to prove the point, he said he would leave the secretary in my cell so that I could have sex with her if I could, as she was a good Communist and would oblige.

I was a normal male of 16 and under normal circumstances I would have jumped at the offer, especially as the girl was shapely and good-looking. But unfortunately the bastards were right; it never entered my mind to make any kind of advances despite the girl kissing me on the lips. She stayed some half an hour without saying one word to me and eventually left. I am glad it was my first and last refusal to a shapely female. Mind you, I never was fortunate enough to be so openly propositioned again. These things may happen in a brothel, where I never had the inclination or need to visit. And now it is too late to contemplate such a possibility. I should say a better word would be "frivolity", not possibility. Before the night was out my friendly guard came in for a talk and I asked him who the girl was. He said he didn't know, she just turned up at the station and was billeted with the rest of the NKVD personnel. He asked me what had happened in the cell as the local Robin was livid and was swearing like mad. When I told him what had happened he said I was a fool as the Robin could be nasty. How right the guard was, but at that moment I was very satisfied I had made a fool of him.

The following night I was just falling asleep when my cell door opened and the same trio appeared, together with a burly man. They were dressed in warm clothing, which I noticed immediately, and I smelled a rat. What greatly amused me was the fact that the local Robin, who I had known before the War, took his peaked hat off as he entered the cell. This reminded me of the few occasions when he had called at our house to see my father. He would wait in the corridor with his cap in his hand for his turn. Locals would frequently come to my father to ask for his help in filling in forms, writing applications or similar tasks, as a lot of them were completely illiterate. Through force of habit he even observed this pecking order in prison, even though he was very much on top. It made me smile but I was very uneasy. I knew what this illiterate peasant could do and what he stood for. They, in many cases, were the most vicious animals on earth. They had many village feuds that in some cases had lasted for years without anybody knowing how they had started in the first place. Killings between them were commonplace. A favourite way for them to dispose of dead bodies was to feed them to huge pigs. Two or three of these pigs could devour a man's body in half an hour, without leaving any trace or remains. Police on patrols in villages were specially told to report any large angry pigs on premises, as it was a sure indication that a murdered body could be fed to them. I once saw a thick bull's leg bone being crushed and eaten by a pig in a matter of minutes. Before the War we had an unfortunate accident on our estate, when a man lost his leg. He had a high boot and a large sow snapped it off at his shin bone as if it were a candlestick.

In our district some horses were occasionally killed by hungry wild sows and devoured on the spot. I am not talking about the English bacon pigs of 70 to 80 kilos in weight, but old sows that could weigh up to twice that. Some small farmers were letting pigs loose in the enclosure around their house as a security precaution. Nobody in their right mind would dare to cross an open pigsty. This local Robin was under suspicion by the Police before the War of having committed many murders, but they could not prove anything concrete without a body.

He ordered me out of my cell but told me not to dress as we were going to his office. The office turned out to be the very cold slaughterhouse where I had been hung before. He and his colleagues all sat behind a makeshift table wearing thick felt Russian boots whilst I had only trousers and a shirt on. The cold was very intense and, on his instructions, the door to where I stood was partly opened to create a very cold draught. After some two hours standing there I was numb with cold and could not stop shaking. The pain in my bruised and swollen shoulders was increasing in strength until I could hardly bear it without screaming. But after about an hour it started subsiding and I felt no pain at all. My arms just went numb as though under a local anaesthetic. Their questioning went on and on. The same questions, the same denials, went on and on and on. After a while, I ceased to understand what they were saying. I felt as though I was transferred into another dimension and was looking on the scene from the outside. I was practically hypnotised by the Robin who was continuously making and smoking cigarettes. It was a scene worth watching as the tobacco was in the form of finely chopped tobacco plant stalks, and looked like a fine chopped rice.

It was a great art to smoke the damned thing, as I was later to find out in further prisons, but this was the first time I had seen the stuff actually being made into a cigarette. First of all you took an oblong piece of newspaper – Russian Pravda or Izvestia were favourites as you could make the paper into a pulp quite easily by chewing it. You then proceeded to make a sort of hollow trumpet, similar to a modern ice-cream cone, chew the edge and stick the outside edge to the main body. You then filled the trumpet with shredded tobacco and bent over the widest part into a star shape to prevent the sawdust falling out. You then bit off the sharp end like a cigar and lit the wide, crumpled end. The newsprint then burst into flames and you had to draw like mad to light the shredded tobacco. If you were not skilled or quick enough, the whole contents of your trumpet of red-hot tobacco ended up in your lap.

My inquisitor was regularly jumping up quickly and brushing burning tobacco from his lap. He wore Russian quilted trousers that were filled with cotton flock and fluted. After several hours of questioning and brushing himself down the inevitable happened. The cotton flock caught light and started burning. I should say smouldering. To start with he didn't notice anything. I was the first to notice smoke emerging from my side of the table. I realised what could have happened and started getting very excited about the possibility of him bursting into flames. I could see the smoke very clearly and eventually he started smelling burning cloth. At long last he jumped to his feet and started shouting, "Bring some water quickly!" I could clearly see a hole that was some 2 inches in diameter above his knee. His friend tried to put it out by beating the smouldering part of his trousers, but only succeeded in making some burning flock drop right inside them. This was quickly followed by a cry of, "You son of a bitch. What are you trying to do? Burn me to death?"

For a moment I thought they would start fighting amongst themselves. In a split second, I felt this was my chance to escape. I turned to the partly open door behind me and dived madly into the opening, hitting my head on the chest of a Russian Robin who was running in to investigate the commotion. I hit his chest unintentionally so hard I felt as though I had broken my neck. I bounced off his huge chest, fell backwards into the room and under the table. Picking myself up the best I could, I met the Robin in the doorway, pointing a machine pistol into my stomach. As the whole situation struck me as funny, I found myself hysterically screaming with laughter. This in turn enraged my investigator who picked up a chair and hit me over the head with it. I crumpled onto the floor and, as if in a dream, felt my hands being tied together behind my back. I saw the distorted face of my tormentor. "You son of a bitch," he screamed. "I'll teach you manners." Two of them grabbed me and stood me on the table. I didn't realise that one of them had secured the rope on a hook above. Unceremoniously they pushed me off the table. I felt a very sharp pain in my shoulders as my arms pivoted backwards and upright.

Before I could collect my wits I was left hanging by my arms again. I felt my arms and my shoulders coming out of their sockets and my muscles and ligaments tearing out of position. I could not understand why I felt no pain. Instead my shoulders were burning as though someone had poured hot water on them from the inside. I realised my shoulders must be haemorrhaging, hence the burning sensation. As they all started to walk out of the building the local Robin turned to me and said, "Now let's see you try and escape from this, you son of a bitch". I was left hanging in the darkness as they put the lights out. As my head was forced forwards and down I saw the moon shining on the floor through the small panes of glass of the window, forming squares of moonlight. After a while, the moon squares joined together and started to dance around me. Sparks flew from the light on the floor and came straight into my face. I felt warm and comfortable and realised I must be losing consciousness. I thought I was in my own warm bed at home under my enormous feather and down quilt. Semi-conscious, I had a brief moment of clarity and thought I must be completely losing my mind.

## Chapter 4 - Judgement Day at Orsha

I don't know how or when I returned to my cell, but I was roused from my stupor by a cold wet rag on my throat and face. My friendly guard stood over me and said, "Sorry, but I've got to put you on the train in less than an hour." He told me that I must have been hanging for well over an hour before they brought me into the cell. Cold compresses on my shoulders seemed to help me a lot. My shoulders were swollen and the colour of dark blue ink. The skin on my shoulders was so taut I felt as if it was going to burst. The swelling was so acute that it even split my shirt on the seams around my shoulders. With the help of the guard I tried to get up, but I could not. My body just did not belong to me any longer.

The friendly guard said he had heard the Robins saying they would kill me and feed me to the pigs. He said I must try to get onto this train or I would be dead for sure within a few short hours. After a further failed attempt by me to walk, my friendly guard brought a builders' deep barrel, put me in it, and drove me to the railway station some 150 metres away. In a very short time the train arrived and, after sorting out my documents, I was wheeled to one of the closed cattle trucks. The train guard unlocked the door and slid it open. The open door was filled with men standing shoulder to shoulder. Their spokesman said to the guard, "Don't be silly, we are already like sardines in here. There is no room for another person". But my friendly guard replied, "Look, you lot. He is injured and, if you don't take him, they will kill him in the next twelve hours."

The response was immediate. Kneeling on the floor of the truck, they grabbed my protruding feet from the high barrel and lifted me inside with them. I was lying on the floor in the semi-darkness, trying to understand what they were saying to me. This was the second time in the recent past I could not recognise my own tongue. Whilst trying to lift me by the arms, they spotted that blood and water had filled my shoulders. Thankfully, I was left alone for some time until I had regained enough strength to speak. In a very few words I explained about my arms. As luck would have it, one of the inmates was a qualified, middle-aged cavalry doctor who had set many soldiers' dislocated joints after falls from horses. He told the rest I must be left alone lying on my back, and he would examine me in a few hours.

Without grumbles, the others allowed him to use their very precious drinking water for my shoulders and I soon fell into a sort of coma or deep sleep. They later told me that it had taken more than 24 hours before I finally came round again. On examination the doctor found both of my shoulders and one elbow dislocated. He said that he was sorry, but if I wanted to have a chance of using my arms again, he must set them. I could not understand why he was sorry about helping me. I was soon to find out why when he called for some help and a few burly men held me down while he started setting my joints. I passed out several times before he finished the job. I was strapped with different kinds of clothing, which were given by the other prisoners from their precious bundles of personal possessions to immobilise my elbow and shoulders.

Some five or six days went by until I started taking stock of where I was and what was going on. The truck was some 15 to 20 feet long and some 8 feet wide. It had a sliding door on each side in the middle of the walls. There were two shelves made out of split saplings and on each shelf were 5 long grain sacks, filled with a handful of straw. These were the mattresses. There were also 4 solid, hinged vents, 2 on each side, slightly open and welded in that position so all we could see out was a bit of the sky. It formed a perfect scoop for rain or snow. There was a tortoise stove in the middle, with a chimney going out of one of the ends of the truck. Despite the days and nights being very cold and frosty, there was no fuel for the stove. As the so-called sleeping shelves or bunks were only five feet long, you could not stretch out without your legs hanging over the edge. The straw in the sacks did not cover the boards so you had to lie just on bare wood. There were fifty men in the truck so we were packed like sardines, with no room to lie on our backs and, because of my shoulders, I could not lie on my side. So for the first ten days or so, I slept in a sitting position or on the floor near an enormous toilet bucket. The stench was overwhelming as most of the men had diarrhoea. The worst moments were when the train driver used the brakes hard and the latrine bucket would spill. The floor became very slippery and foul. Once a day or so, the train would halt in open country where we could empty the foul buckets and get some water from a ditch in our two water buckets.

Food consisted of 100 grams of soggy bread a day and drinking water from the rain ditch. A lot of ditches and water holes were fouled up by previous trains that emptied their latrine buckets into them. They also rinsed their buckets into them as well, so no wonder we all suffered from acute dysentery after the first few days. Five days after I joined the train we had our first casualty when a young Jew died of dysentery. We immediately reported it to a guard. There was a very short stop at one of the stations and his body was just pushed out of the wagon. Most of us were so weakened by the disease that we could hardly move.

My good angel doctor looked after me like a father. He was forever looking in all the crevices between the boards, searching for spiders. He made a sort of sandwich out of them and we both ate it. He believed that a spider's web and bread was a cure for coughs and intestinal disorders. So he picked off all the webs very quickly, convinced that they were a cure for all. Furthermore, we both ate bread with the remains of soot from the chimney. I didn't know why, but we seemed to keep better than the others. On our very brief stops for water and latrine emptying he would scour the banks for some weeds, which we ate with our very small ration of bread. He hardly drank water and would not let me drink it either. At the end of the journey we were so dehydrated it was driving me mad. Once he announced that water we had found on a field stop was drinkable and we drank our fill. On another occasion there was a piece of ice from the rut of a horses cartwheel filled with frozen water. He begged everybody to refrain from drinking, but most of the fellows ignored him. A few of the men went down with pneumonia and soon started dying off. Every time a body was pushed out of the wagon, there was excitement regarding the dead man's belongings.

I am sad to say that some of the men behaved disgustingly and were practically fighting over a few meagre remains of clothing. There were a few real fights over stealing bread. Most of us would split our ration into two, three or sometimes more parts. It was the height of luxury to sit on a bunk, take a small bite of bread and chew it for a very long time. I have rarely tasted anything as good before or since. It was a crime for anybody to start talking about what his mother or wife would prepare to eat in the past, as everybody was too hungry to bear it.

The train sometimes stopped and stayed stationary for many hours at signals. We were grateful for it, as it was less draughty and a little warmer inside. The guards were not cruel to us, but completely powerless. They always had their masters with them, the masters of life and death. Some of them were ashamed of what was happening to us and our truck guard openly said he was sorry, but we should not be counter-revolutionaries and saboteurs otherwise we would not be in this predicament. Some of us had a bit of Russian money. I had ten roubles given to me by my friendly guard, so our truck guard used it and bought us tobacco from the guards' shop attached to the train. On being asked, he said he didn't know our destination, but it was somewhere beyond Minsk. Most of us had "Class 1 Case" status which meant "under investigation". I cannot exactly recollect how long it took us to get to Minsk, which was a very large railway junction with hundreds of sidings. They eventually shunted our train into a siding that was completely surrounded by a 3-metre high wire mesh fence.

Many guards with machine pistols stayed around the outside of the fence while they opened the doors and told us to get out. We had a long and exhausting parade while they sorted out our documents and destinations. In the compound there were two locomotive turntables and pits filled with water. On top of the water was a thin cover of some kind of oil. Russian railway workers came in to check the trucks' axles. Some of them were women. As some of our men could speak fluent Russian they told the women how desperate we were for clean water. One of the women climbed on to a water tower, turned the local water-feeding sleeve, and switched the water on. There was a mad rush to get water and within seconds all our buckets were filled, but to our great dismay we found that the water was foul smelling, with a film of oil on top. The process took nearly two days and I found myself placed together with another 41 prisoners in the last truck of the train. Unfortunately my friend, the Doctor, went elsewhere. After the War I found his name amongst the list of the exhumed bodies found at Katyn. I will always remember him with gratitude as he saved me from being a semi-cripple. Let the Lord rest his soul in peace forever more. He was a good man and very skilful in his profession.

I was feeling a lot better and by then my arms were unstrapped. Painful they were, but I felt better physically and mentally. Just before we got into our truck, I took a chance and asked one of the girls for some coal for our stove, as it was very, very cold. "You fool", she said. "Can't you see, there are tons of the stuff under your feet?"

True enough, there were masses of small pieces of coal on the paths. In my truck were mostly young men and, on my suggestion, we all rushed to collect the coal. Within minutes we had a few pails of the stuff piled near our stove. The girl knew the ropes as, without being asked, she threw an oily rag into the truck. "This is to start the fire with, good luck to you all", she shouted. We were given bread, 300 grams of it, for the whole of the journey. Other trucks were issued with 100 grams only. We deduced that our journey would last about three days. The railway workers had no idea what our destination was. One said it was most probably Orsha. The other added, "I hope its not Orsha, that district has very bad air. Two young men from my village died there from heart attacks. The Party said it was the air that caused their death." Poor beggars, they believed blindly what The Party said. They were a good bunch of people and felt sorry for us. Just before the train started they gave us a packet of 100 grams of shredded tobacco stalks.

Altogether we spent four days on this sideline at Minsk. Eventually, at long last, we set off. One of the prisoners in our truck was a Roman Catholic priest, who said it would be Christmas Eve in three days time. After one day on the move, our wagon was uncoupled and pushed to the side again. The door was slid open and we were allowed to slop out into a small hole in the ground, next to a signal box. The signalman had a good Christmas present from the party – the foul smelling contents of the huge buckets. My arms were getting better nearly every hour. One of the older men was massaging my shoulders and I was doing exercises myself very intensely. I still could not lift myself onto the top bunk, but I really felt that I was on the mend. Ever since we had left Minsk, we had had the luxury of a small fire which greatly improved our morale.

On the fourth day, the door opened when it was still dark and we were told to get out. I saw light some 200 metres away as in a town. When asked, a sleepy railwayman said, "It is Orsha". We formed a marching column in pairs and started off towards the light, surrounded by machine-pistol carrying soldiers and several dogs. These were queer looking animals, like Alsatians, but with their hair standing straight up here and there on their bodies. They were barking and snarling at us all the time for no reason. The guards, holding them on pieces of rope, would let the dogs sniff within inches of our bodies. This looked to me like a training session for the dogs and was very intimidating.

It was Christmas Eve and I was wondering what sort of hell was awaiting us in this Godforsaken part of the world. It turned out to be a very special kind of hell. I felt I had reached the point of no return. While crossing a bridge over the fairly narrow river with great boulders on the bottom, I was tempted to dive over the side and commit suicide. I felt I would not survive another hanging and I was prepared to die, but I felt my arms might let me down while jumping over the not-so-high railed sides of the bridge, and I didn't fancy being ripped to pieces by the dogs.

Soon after crossing the bridge, we started climbing a fairly steep rough road covered in slippery snow. It was a very exhausting climb. At one point the priest slipped and fell. Immediately the guards set a dog on which ripped his cassock from his back and bit him quite painfully on his arm and the side of his neck. Eventually we got to a huge gate with a massive stone building towering above us. It reminded me of a monastery on top of a rock. As I was later to discover, it was indeed an 18th century monastery which had been made into a top-security prison for counter-revolutionaries and saboteurs. We were let in through a small door in pairs and told to stand against the wall and be silent. Soon a very ginger man in a Robins uniform addressed us in

Russian. "Welcome to our hotel," he said. "There is only one way out of this place alive and that is through the gate you just walked in. There is no other way out alive so don't try anything. Behave well and you will be treated well."

There was one peculiar thing about the place, which was new to me, and that was the smell. I cannot describe it, but it was a sharp and sickly smell that left a nasty taste in the mouth. We were taken down below the building to the delousing room, which was a huge underground room with small vents on one side, and two large cauldrons of boiling steaming water. It was actually the boiler room of a sort of primitive central heating, as there was only one pipe of 3 inches diameter running through this part of the prison. On the floor in the room was a sizeable heap of string, the sight of which got me going. I felt as if a bucket of cold water had been poured over me as I could not stand the sight of it. Even now, after so many years, the sight of rope gives me a pain in my shoulders. There was also a long metal square box standing on metal legs. Before long we were told to strip naked. All underwear we had to throw into the boiling water in the cauldrons, previously tied in a bundle with a short piece of string from the pile on the floor. All outside clothing was hung in the square box on hooks. The stench of soiled underwear filled the room immediately.

The steam from the boiler was let into the box in an effort to kill millions of fleas, lice and all kinds of other bugs in our clothing. While our clothing was steamed, some four or five local prisoners came into the room with hand-operated clippers, and cut off all our hair. We were given a tablespoon full of some foul smelling jelly- like liquid, and told to rub ourselves down with it. This substance was corrosive and stung like hell, especially around the private parts. They kept us in this room in agony for a good ten minutes before opening the door and letting us into a so-called shower of very hot water. This consisted of a U-shaped pipe suspended from the ceiling with holes drilled in it. There was another pipe next to it, which was pouring out ice cold water. This was our first experience of Russia's version of a shower.

We were told to hurry, as the water would be turned off in five minutes. The effect of cold and scalding water was incredible. The stinging of the jelly soap increased to such an extent that some prisoners started to scream with pain. We were dashing in and out of the hot and cold streams of water to prevent scalding. All things considered, the pleasure overcome the pain, as it was my first body wash for nearly two months. In five minutes it was all over, and we were hustled back to the main room. We were kept there naked for another half an hour until our clothing was cooked. Some of the older men who had not moved around in the shower had blisters forming on different parts of their bodies through the effects of scalding water. Our underwear was eventually poked out from the cauldrons with wooden sticks onto the slatted table. One of the prisoners demonstrated to us how you get rid of excess water by hitting our bundle hard on the slatted table, a primitive Russian spin dryer. It seemed to work of a fashion. I was lucky enough to find my own bundle quite quickly. After 20 or 30 smacks on the slatted table, I decided I'd got rid of as much water as I could. I was glad to get into my damp but hot underwear, as the cold draught from the small windows in the ceiling was rather troublesome. We eventually fished out our top clothing from the metal box. It was steaming hot and very wet.

Whilst we were naked, the guards moved into the room in order to identify us. On identification, a prisoner was taken to the chief guard who had a blue marking pencil with which he wrote a number on the captive's forehead. He was licking the pencil before every single number and soon his lips and chin were completely dark blue. The markings were very intensive and hard to get off, as I saw some prisoners with numbers on their foreheads weeks after they had been marked. This was the first time that I'd come across such a strong marking from an ordinary- looking pencil.

While in the delousing room we heard a number of thumps which seemed to me like distant shots and I was wondering what they were. I soon found out that I was right. They were actually executing some unfortunates in another part of the dungeon. We were eventually ushered up to the first floor and stood in a long line. We were allocated to different cells by the numbers on our foreheads. Some of the remaining prisoners were taken to the second floor and some to the third. I was eventually put in a cell on the second floor, cell number 17.

On entering, the same stench hit my nostrils, and I asked, "What is that smell?" but received no reply. There were already 9 Poles in a cell of about 35 prisoners. "Who are you? Where are you from?" were the first questions that were thrown back at me by a big Russian with a sheepskin coat on. He was the head of the cell, an habitual criminal. On saying that I was Polish, he pointed out a corner of the cell and said, "You go there to sleep with your mates."

The bunks were similar to those on the train and there I met my countrymen. Amongst them were two Polish Jews. I was warned not to go near one of them as he was riddled with lice, which he refused to kill in the twice-daily killing sessions. He was a pitiful looking individual, hardly resembling a human being, who sat on the bottom bunk and scratched himself all the time. There were also three Finns and two Czechs, and I struck up an immediate friendship with one of the Czechs. There was something about his personality that I liked. He had been at Warsaw University when war broke out and was a Communist. At the end of September 1939 he decided to come into the part of Poland occupied by the Russians, and was caught crossing the border. He immediately got seven years hard labour for his pains and sent here for further investigations. They found a Communist Party membership card on him and wanted to know more about his friends in Warsaw.

I started calling him Pepic, a sort of slang for Czech. He told me that the two biggest problem in the cell were bed bugs, hence the smell, and Russian criminals. The criminals were stealing everything or taking everything that they fancied by force. "You will soon have your boots pinched," he said. I suggested that if we kept together, we could defend ourselves better. He said that it was difficult as they were very powerful and very ruthless. As soon as the lights went out I felt somebody grabbing my legs and taking my boots off. This really enraged me, but there was very little I could do about it as nobody was prepared to help. We were let out into the exercise yard for half an hour each day. The very first day I found a broken piece of crockery, which I picked up, so now I had some kind of weapon. I was working on the rest of the Poles to help me. My plan was simple. If they helped me to catch one of the Russian criminals in the dark, preferably the leader with the sheepskin jacket, I would sort him out. It took me some three or four days to persuade them to help. My Czech friend, one of the Finnish prisoners and a biggish peasant from my home town, agreed to help. This sheepskin jacket was originally the peasant's and he was furious, as they had beaten him up while taking it. After my boots were stolen I reported the robbery to a guard the very next day and he asked, with a sarcastic smile, whether I recognised who stole them. When I said no, but I could see where my boots were, pointing to one of the hooligans, he said that I'd have to get them myself.

What encouraged me with my plan was the fact that I was assured that the guards never investigated injuries in a cell. After I spoke to the guard, somebody tried to pull me out of my bunk at night, but I was kicking so hard that they let me go. A few nights later, when we decided to strike, I wrapped my hand in a piece of rag so as not to damage it, then waited for 'lights out'. We had been joined by a new prisoner, a Polish Corporal, who was a cavalryman. He had high riding leather boots and still had a Corporal's insignia on his shoulders. I explained the situation to him quickly and he agreed to help. He came from a prisoner of war camp so he had missed the de-lousing ceremony.

About one hour after lights out, the chief yob came to our bunk and told the Corporal to take his boots off or they would cut his legs off, producing a knife some 6 inches long. The soldier forgot my plan and grabbed his attacker's wrist with both hands and kicked him hard in the face with his heel. I didn't have full strength in my arms, but I managed to grab the robber by his ears and shouted in Russian, "Cut the son of a bitch's throat quickly." He started howling like a mad dog. His face was nearby so I dragged my piece of crockery across it as hard as I could. By then the fight was on the floor. I grabbed his ears again. We ended up near the main door next to the slop bucket. Without hesitation, I stuck his head into the bucket and into the liquid. I let him go when he went limp and the lights came on in the cell.

In the general fight somebody had cut the third thief's ear off and thrown it in the bucket. I had a feeling it was the soldier, but he didn't admit to it at the time. Four guards rushed in with their long truncheons and everybody got at least one whack. Unfortunately, as luck would have it, I got hit on one of my shoulders, which nearly knocked me out. The guards took the wounded men out and chased the rest of us onto our bunks. While walking out, the wounded thief, for some reason picked his ear out of the bucket and took it with him. That was the end of our trouble with the criminals. After half an hour or so, the wounded men were brought back to the cell. The fellow without the ear had a filthy rag wrapped around his head and he was still bleeding very heavily. The thief was very subdued and smelly, and didn't even threaten us with what he would do in the future. The exercise was worthwhile as we had no more problems with them after that.

As a matter of fact, after a serious and quite amicable talk, we agreed to a truce and they promised to be our friends from now on, and not to bother us any more. At that time I didn't realise what their friendship would mean to me. Quite by accident, I had found how to deal with Russian prison barons who only believed in the strength of arms and plain terror. So after this rough justice was dished out to the Russian Mafioso, peace broke out in my cell and a rather boring, everyday existence ensued. After the journey from the last prison in the cattle trucks, the new place improved our lot. Our breakfast of Russian bread was raised to 300 grams a day and the so-called tea was sometimes hot. The evening soup was still revolting in texture, smell and taste, but it contained pieces of fur-covered meat and the bones of some kind of fish. Well-stewed potatoes and cattle beet, like a sugar beet, gave the impression that the soup was thick.

There was great excitement one day when we found a poorly cooked cow's foot with some ligaments still intact. It was portioned out with immaculate accuracy on the scales made by one of the inmates. This consisted of a piece of stick with string tied in the middle, and strings with little cloth caps at the ends. The whole contraption was so balanced that two pieces of equal weight could be determined quite accurately. The actual weight in grams was not important, the importance being in the fact that all inmates got roughly the same weight. This operation could not be hurried but nobody cared; we had plenty of time on our hands. We soon learnt that the vast majority of inmates were of a political nature. Russians were real masters in adapting to new types of conditions and life. I learnt many tricks of the trade from them.

In one day in that cell I learnt more about personal adaptation and survival in any circumstances than I did during one month of a highly specialised survival course run by the army and senior scouts before the war. Within a few days we all became quite friendly and discussed our common cases and problems in general. We knew what was going on in the prison by different means of communication. These include tapping in Morse code and writing information very finely in the margin of newspapers, which we were allowed to buy. Pravda and Izvestia were the official mouthpieces of the Communist party and the Party made sure that the right propaganda was reaching everybody, including the inmates in their very vast population of prisons and labour camps. I was amazed to find that their favourite slogans were even displayed in prison. Our corridors and exercise yards were full of slogans, but I soon figured it out that they were aimed more at their own guards than at us.

We were even given washing facilities, which consisted of a very long trough with a solitary pipe of some 3 inches diameter over it. The pipe had small holes drilled on the underside through which cold water ran when a guard or trusty turned on the main tap. The water was a rather foul smelling substance that was polluted by our own toilets. The three storey toilets were really the height of Russian imagination and technical advancement. One side of the building was quite close to the edge of the rock on which the building stood. Right on the bottom was a fairly fast flowing, but narrow river. They built platforms against the wall on each floor of three stories. The platforms were just made of rough softwood boards lying on three or four pieces of railway line that were attached to a stone wall. The platform above was protruded more than the lower. The third was some 2 metres away from the wall. The seats were just a stout piece of wood log on which you could lean your posterior very carefully, so as not to get splinters in your bum or break the damn thing and fall some 15 to 20 metres into the river and rocks at the bottom. On the outside of each platform there was a narrow piece of Hessian to hide the sight of our backsides from the locals. All was well if the wind was kind but if not, the bottom levels were sprayed by the fall from the upper floors. In their wisdom the guards would close the bottom toilets, but not before the bottom floors were splattered from above. Whenever I had to go during our daily routine, I made sure that no more than ten men were occupying my platform. I didn't fancy going down with a bang!

While I was in the prison, there were a number of suicides committed by men jumping head first into the toilet. It would take a hell of a lot more for me to try and take this way out. My arms had got better very quickly now and I was in a better state of mind. Every night men were called out for a friendly, or not so friendly, talk with the Robins. Life in the semi-dark cell was taking its toll and inmates' behaviour began to suffer.

Darkness in the cells, despite four windows, was caused by the shutters attached to the outside wall, which meant there was only a narrow strip of upper sky that could be seen by us. The sight of those covers was very depressing, but by far the most troublesome aspect of this prison was the presence of millions of bedbugs. These ladybird-like insects were very vicious and every morning we would wake up with our bodies stung as if by nettles. We killed a few thousand of them in the cell, along with other blood feeders like lice and fleas. Twice a day, it was a cell rule that everybody had to kill bugs for half an hour each time. Within a minute or so one's thumbs were covered in blood, as we used our nails to kill the vermin. Bedbugs gave a very unpleasant odour, hence the particular smell when I arrived at the prison. The first extermination, half an hour just after breakfast, was particularly unpleasant. Many lice would attach themselves onto our eyelashes and eyebrows during the night. So we would take a freshly delivered paper and try and brush them on to it. After a few others had taken their turn, there were about 200 lice on the paper. They were shaken into one spot and, with great ceremony, a lighted match was placed under the heap and the amazing performance would start. After a few mini explosions, when blood filled lice would explode in the heat, the paper immediately would solidify with blood and stop burning. The bodies of the lice would pop like cracker-jack fireworks and the paper would be completely red with blood. Even after so many years, the thought of the sight and the smell makes me feel sick.

Generally we got quite friendly with the Russian inmates. They had a fantastic sense of humour but, when cornered, could be very serious adversaries. The Russians and Poles had a mutual respect for each other. Both sides knew no quarter would be asked for or given in a showdown between us. The episode of the ear in a bucket saved us from further serious abuse. The Russian criminal element was very well organised and the guards were reluctant to tackle them openly, calling them hooligans, as many of the guards had been terribly mutilated by them.

Like the real Mafia, they had a code of silence which they very strictly observed, so the guards were powerless to find out anything. Furthermore, the guards accepted, and actually looked forward to, gifts from the Mafia. The best clothing, boots, etc., were taken off a new batch of prisoners and given to the guards for their favours. We had one Russian Mafioso for two or three days in our cell who had killed a guard by biting through the main artery in his neck. These so-called hooligans were the aristocracy of prisons and labour camps and liked to be called Mafia. Often they would sacrifice an individual in unbelievable violence to bring general terror to other prisoners and guards. They would have a sort of general ballot as to who was going to be sacrificed amongst themselves. The chosen person would then simply murder a guard in the most bestial way, knowing very well that they would be topped for it. In this way they could spread untold fear. There were two ways to get on with them. To either submit to their outrageous behaviour of stealing and violent robberies or to be even more violent and outrageous to them. Luckily we adopted the second option and gained immediate respect from this band of wild animals. They would demand to be transferred from cell to cell at will, so you had to be careful how many of them would suddenly appear in your cell.

This story and warning about the Mafia was given to me by one of the Russian political prisoners whose brother had served three years in a labour camp. On hearing the terrifying story about them I called their leader, Ivan, for a talk in the corner of the cell. I told him that our bunch and several in the prison belonged to the Polish undercover Mafia and would not be spat on from a dizzy height. He said he understood and would co-operate. To my amazement he asked me the very next day if two of his men could come in for a day for consultations. In order not to outrage the bastard I said yes, but told him they would have to watch their step. True enough, they came in the next day and sat quietly in a corner, talking in whispers.

We found them very useful in obtaining many things such as tobacco, soap or even extra food, and started getting half a pail of thick soup daily. I even got painkiller pills and some horse ointment for my shoulders, which cured my arms completely and proved to be the perfect deterrent against bedbugs. During my stay in the cell I was called out twice for night questioning, which was conducted in quite a civilised manner. There was such a massive increase in the prison population at that time, the Russians rekindled the old idea of trial by three – that is three NKVD Officers dishing out sentences. This was the norm for different misdemeanors. Crossing or attempting to cross the border got 3 to 7 years; stealing from the state meant 7 to 15 years or a bullet; and any charges of counter-revolutionary activity, sabotage or banditry were punished with a bullet in the base of the skull. The exercise yard in the prison was very uneven, like a building site and we were told that we were walking on the mass graves of executed prisoners. So I took special notice during the brief exercise period of what was going on in the yard, and saw two pits that were being filled in by still steaming quicklime. Under them was a layer of bodies. This task was exclusively carried out by the guards. Despite the snow and extreme cold the lime pits were always steaming, I felt somewhat uneasy looking at them, knowing full well that I was a possible future occupier of one of them. I could not see the bodies in the main burial pit, but soon realised that they were covering them with quicklime to prevent disease spreading out. However, to be frank, I was far too preoccupied with the day-to-day life in my cell to worry too much about it.

I think it is worth mentioning the fact that we had a prison doctor, who immobilised broken limbs with a handful of reeds and ordinary string.

Any other ailments were treated by a general purpose medicine from a blue bottle. A nip of liquid out of this bottle was a cure for everything. The preparation was boiled wormwood and it had an extremely bitter taste. This quack in the NKVD uniform was very proud of the fact that his mixture cured anything, from cold to dysentery. He also performed operations under local anaesthetic and a good gulp of strong vodka. Some inmates prayed for a large boil so that they could get a gulp of that strong vodka. The Russian yobs were regular visitors to his surgery and in some cases, came back quite drunk. One guard told us that the doctor made a fortune stealing vodka and selling it to prisoners. I was told there was a still in the prison's boiler room, but I was not fortunate enough to taste the final produce.

For some peculiar, and I suspect, twisted reason I was looking forward to my birthday on 17th January. I didn't expect to get a cake but was instead treated to a night of questioning on 16th January. The Interrogation room was underground at the furthermost point from the cells. By looking at the massive walls I realised they must be completely soundproof. The questioning was conducted in quite a civilised manner, but after an all-night session I felt completely drained. The main theme was to establish my identity. They even confronted me with some stranger but frankly I could not place him at all. He seemed certain who I was. I asked the Robins why there was all this nonsense about who I really was, and he told me that we Poles caused such confusion with our lies about names and addresses that they were trying to establish the truth. I returned to my cell and just lay on a bunk, trying to assess my position. I didn't like their unusual politeness and finesse in questioning. In the morning confusion somebody stole my bread ration. At about midday, the Russian Mafioso assured me it was nobody from his lads and he had already requested some extra bread from the guards and he would personally reimburse me later.

True enough, my bread came with an exceptionally good double portion of soup that evening. I rubbed some ointment on my shoulders and settled down with a full stomach for a change, but for some reason I couldn't sleep. I could not forget the face of the stranger who'd been so insistent he knew who I was. The man knew so many facts about me and I just could not remember him at all. I had a feeling I had met him somewhere before, but I could not place him. I spent the whole night turning over in my mind every page of my past association with the Russkies.

The next day we heard on the grapevine that ten men from our corridor had not returned from the night's questioning. In the afternoon I did not go to the exercise yard, as physically somehow I could not bear it. When they returned, the inmates told me that the guards were shovelling quick lime into a freshly dug long trench. So obviously quite a few people had been despatched during the night. I spent the whole day and evening in torment as I had a premonition that something was wrong.

The guards came and took three or four men for questioning. I was expecting to be called, but to my surprise they did not want me. Absolutely exhausted, I eventually dropped off into a shallow restless sleep. Everybody was sound asleep when the solitary light in the cell came on. I jumped up so quickly that my head smashed into the bunk above, and I hit my head so hard my ears started ringing. It was very unusual to be called out for questioning that late at night. The guard was unusually grumpy and seemed half asleep and I smelt vodka on his breath. He must have been at a party the previous night. Both myself and another inmate, the cavalry man who been involved in our fight with the hooligans, were called out. Despite the no talking order he turned to me and said, "This is it, they are going to shoot me tonight". I told him not to be silly, but I felt uneasy myself. At the end of the corridor there were more guards waiting each side. When we reached there we were given the usual order "Face the wall, no talking, arms behind your back".

I was quickly grabbed by the wrist and my arms were immediately tied behind my back, but the cavalryman started fighting like mad. I tried to kick the bastards but I had no boots on. They eventually over-powered him and dragged him down the stone steps. In the struggle one of the guards trod on my bare foot and it hurt like hell. They took me to a very strange, spartan room on top of the landing, which was part of the old monastery, sombre and foreboding. It had been made into a top security room and, instead of a friendly monk facing the Abbott, it was I who stood there facing three Robins, sitting with piles of folders behind the table. I was desperately trying to put my scrambled brain together. What the hell am I doing here, facing these three heartless butchers? It all seemed so unreal. I was aware of the soothingly cool floor on my bare feet and gradually realised there was some other evil presence beside the three Robins, and true enough there were two framed portraits of the most evil men on earth. One was Lenin, the founder of the most evil ideology this earth ever had the misfortune to face. The other was Stalin, the most bloodthirsty butcher on earth. Even wild hoards of Tartars in the past did not manage to produce a monster that carried out genocide of his own people on such a massive scale in the most atrocious possible way. On his orders, millions of unfortunate, so-called counter-revolutionaries whose only real crime was to be born a Russian, built the White Sea Canal with pick and shovel. It is said that under each barrow of earth dug up in the construction of the canal, at least two men were buried. I stared at the self-appointed, perverted idiot hanging on the wall and wished he had barbed wire around his neck. Through fear of assassination he had ordered Beria, his chief of security and secret police, to organise the murder of all high-ranking officers whose only sin was in having a greater than average I.Q. He then planned and arranged a non-aggressive pact with Hitler, with the partition of Poland in mind. At that particular moment, the hatred in my heart bordered on insanity, and I believed that the final phase of my saga had begun.

I asked for my hands to be set free as my leg was itching from the close attention of the bedbugs. The man in the middle said with a smile, "Not at the moment, dearie". He was busy making a cigarette out of the shredded tobacco. One of his assistants pulled out a packet of huge cigarettes called Bialomore and offered him one. He refused, saying they were not strong enough, and continued making his cigarette. Eventually it was done and, after a good bout of coughing, cleared his throat and began. He first checked my identity and said, "You are accused of counter-revolutionary activities, sabotage and banditry, and hereby the power of three judges sentence you to be executed by shooting. The sentence is to be carried out as soon as convenient." The last part somewhat astonished me. Convenient to whom? Them or me? I was grabbed by the guards under the arms and taken out of the room. I was led down some very wide granite steps into a very long room that resembled a chapel. At the end there were the remains of what looked like an altar. A few metres from the bottom of the stairs we stopped at a massive solid door, with one big spy hole in the upper part of the door.

## Chapter 5: 23 Days Awaiting Death

The door frame seemed to have been put in as an afterthought and it did not match the rest of the wall. The door was opened and I was led into a narrow room about six feet wide. There was a high window near the ceiling at the end of the corridor, underneath which were three nails with some Army coats hanging from them. One had a Polish Army insignia on it. I soon realised that the rusty marks on the walls and doors were dried blood. The last door on the right was partly open and there I was pushed inside a small room. There was no furniture and on the concrete floor was a smelly sack with a few handfuls of straw in it and a wooden slop bucket. They slammed the door hard and it felt as if a coffin lid had been nailed on the top of my head. Despite no visible heat source, it was not too cold. I lifted the sack and immediately saw several hundred bedbugs, huddling together for warmth. Through the sack I squashed as many as I could, and it made the cell stink to high heaven. I tried to collect my thoughts. How long are they going to keep me in here? How much time have I got? By then it was time for morning tea. I found a badly mutilated, once enamel mug behind the slop bucket. The guard opened the door some 6 inches wide and told me to put my mug out, which he filled with tea. He had a foot against the door so I could not open it suddenly. My 100 grams of bread was pushed through a slit in the door. The spy hole cover was not too tight, so I could move it to one side and look at the small slit of sky visible through the window in the corridor.

I spent most of the day staring out of the spy hole until my swollen ankles would not hold me up any more. I was so lonely and vulnerable I felt like crying, but my eyes were dry. During the night there was some screaming and swearing coming out of the other cells and the frequent sound of shots being fired. To my great delight I found that the cell opposite me was occupied by my Czech friend from the main cell. He told me that in spite of him having an identity card of the banned Communist Party in Warsaw, they stuck him in a condemned cell, as they didn't trust the western Communists. We both managed to jam our spy hole covers in the open position so we could see each other's one eye. During the next ten days, we spent many hours talking through the hole. Sometimes it was easier to lie on the floor and talk into the slit in the bottom of the door. One day we saw an inmate from our block being led into the corridor. A coat was put on him and he walked out to his death. We heard the shot soon afterwards.

My friend, Pepic, was shot on the eleventh day of my joining death row. I soon found it was no good resisting as the guards were huge with long sticks and chain handcuffs which they used to beat the prisoners senseless before getting them into the coats. We decided it was undignified to be beaten into submission before you die, so when Pepic's time came he went off with dignity. As a matter of fact he was singing a rather sad song about his beloved Prague, which he taught me before he died. I cannot remember all the words now but I remember the tune to this day.

The execution Army coats hung so near to my door that I could have touched them if I could have put my hand through the spy hole. I examined them visually for hours as if hypnotised. They had dark scorch marks just under the collar on the back. I tried to visualise how those wearing them briefly must have felt in the last moments of their lives. How did they behave? Did they say anything? If so, what? How did the people who were pulling the trigger feel at the time? Who were they and how were they chosen to do this grim task? I tried to talk to them but all my attempts were met with complete silence. After the first three days in the cell my door was open and I thought, this is it, but to my surprise the guards brought a parcel for me with my few belongings from my old cell. The Russian Mafioso cell boss had sent me this parcel which included my boots, horse ointment for my shoulders, a little tobacco wrapped in newspaper, a few split matches and a note written in Polish, which he had dictated. I was really touched by this gesture. During our first meeting we had had a rather violent confrontation, but he had kept his word that we would be friends for as long as we lived.

I could never understand these people's mentality. They could be so very violent and vicious, but when you met them on their own ground and won, they decided that you were worth their respect, and they would then do anything to help you. Days and nights were going by with nothing at all to do and this began to have an effect on me. Mentally I was kept quite alert until my friend's death. I desperately tried to communicate with the next occupant of the cell opposite, but he was completely mad and was banging on his door continuously, screaming and shouting. In a way I was relieved when, after only two days, he was despatched.

The cell opposite stood empty for a whole day. The next prisoner was Russian and I felt sorry for him. He was crying most of the time and told me his story. He was a university student from Moscow studying engineering. Some of his pals had been attending secret meetings with a Russian Orthodox church priest for religious services in a private home on the outskirts of the city. He was eventually persuaded to go to one of these meetings, for the sake of his grandmother who was very religious. During the second meeting the house was raided and he was caught escaping through the gardens. They beat him to a pulp to reveal the name of the priest, who was a complete stranger. Furthermore, they found in his locker an atlas of the world with the Polish/Russian border marked in a thick line. His explanation that he had bought the atlas second hand in a campus shop was not accepted and he found himself in prison, with me as his neighbour. Just a few days before that he had found out what they were doing in the dungeons and that broke him completely. He had gone through a mock execution just before they brought him in and he was completely devastated by it. I tried to comfort him as much as I could, and this temporarily took my mind off my own situation. From the time I arrived in the cell, I had been making marks on the wall with my mug to count each day. I had 16 marks when my crying companion was taken out, shouting to me, "Please pray for my soul". There and then I knelt in the filth of the cell and said very slowly the Lords Prayer. I was so deeply absorbed in the prayer I did not hear the shot.

At that moment my faith began to falter. Why, oh why Lord in Heaven, do you allow these men to go to their death? I felt in the depths of despair. Why the hell do they keep me alive in this hell-hole? I was hoping my turn would soon come as I felt at the end of my tether. After so many days of misery with hardly any sleep, I felt I had had enough. Every few days the guards would let me out to slop out my bucket into the hole in the floor at the end of the small corridor. I often wondered where on earth this hole disappeared to. Once, I started banging on the door for them to let me out, as my bucket was full. After quite a long time the guard came and shouted through the spy hole, "Shut up, you son of a bitch. What do you want?" It was another ten minutes or so before he opened my door. He held the handcuff chain in his hand and said, "Come out you son of a bitch". I grabbed the slop bucket and threw the whole contents of it in his face. He sort of fell backwards against the opposite cell door, letting go of the chain. As quickly as I could, I grabbed the slimy chain and wrapped it around his neck. He was a very strong man with a neck like a bull and I could not quite manage to break his neck before I felt the other guard hit me with his chain. The pain was almost unbearable but I would not let go. Whilst struggling we both slipped on the slimy contents of the bucket and fell to the ground and only then did the other guard kick me in the temple on the side of the head. I had a sensation of falling into a bottomless hole. I heard a high-pitched buzzing in my ears.

When I came round I was laying face down in the cell with a burning sensation on my face and neck. For a while I could not move and I felt something on the small of my back. After a long time, and after several attempts, I rolled onto my side. I found the slop bucket on my back, as the guards must have thrown it into the cell after me. The burning on my face turned out to be hundreds of bed bugs feeding on me. I was brushing and killing them with feverish urgency. The revolting smell overcame the smell of the contents of the slop bucket over me. I sat up against the wall and started vomiting violently, which seemed to go on and on. I was still in this state when they brought the evening soup. Despite my state I knew I had to eat it if I wanted to live. It took me most of that night to eat my soup. When the morning tea came I still had some soup left in my mug. I told the guard that I had no empty mug. His reaction was, "We feed you too well, you son of a bitch." But to my amazement he gave me the tea in another mug. I told him that the bed bugs were eating me alive. He said he would see if he could do something about it and left.

An hour or so later, the main door opened and I started counting the guard's steps. There were nine steps to my cell. If the guard took less than nine, I knew that my time was not up yet, and it was some other unfortunate who was going to be shot. Through force of habit I counted the steps. Seven, eight, nine. It is me they want this time and, as incredible as it seems, it gave me satisfaction to know that all the vermin on me would die in the quick lime. To my amazement, a hand appeared in the slot at the bottom of the door with some cotton waste on the palm. "Rub yourself down with it", the voice said. I grabbed it and put it under my nose. The strong smell was very familiar to me. It was iodine. The small bundle of cotton waste was well soaked with the liquid and I rubbed myself all over, the main target being my neck and armpits. The stinging pain gave me pleasure that at long last I had some kind of disinfectant on me. So many days without a wash were taking its toll. The guard opened the spy hole and whispered, "It is a pity you didn't kill that son of a bitch, the guard. He is a proper bastard. We are all afraid of him."

He stopped at my door for quite a while and talked to me. He told me that the guard I attacked shot himself in the left hand a week ago whilst killing a prisoner and that was the reason why they had not killed me on the spot. I begged the guard for another mug of tea as I wished to wash my face. I was indeed given another mug of it and told to wait and he would see me later. He kept his word. In a very short time he came back with some jelly soap on the ends of his fingers. So after 17 days buried in the cell I had one litre of tea to wash in and some liquid soap. Using cotton wool with the remainder of the iodine on it, I used the soap and tea to give myself a wash. The jelly soap stung slightly on my bitten body, but it was heaven to me. The guard told me he was going off duty soon but would see me the next day. When I asked him why he was doing it, he said that it was not right to keep men in these conditions. He was not a Party man himself and he was only doing what he was told.

My next neighbour was completely mad. He was cursing Stalin, Beria and the NKVD in such a way that it was scary to listen to him, and I felt I could not hang onto my sanity much longer. After two days or so I asked my kind guard to do something about him. His answer was,

"Don't worry about him, he will soon go to the lime pit as he has killed a Robin". He was right, they shot the madman a few hours later.

The next few days I spent mostly walking around my cell, desperately trying to keep my sanity. I still kept marking days on the wall and tried to recite a square table and poetry from my fading memory with various success. Anything that would keep me sane. It is impossible to describe my feelings at that particular time. One has to go through such a nightmarish experience to understand what it is like and I am quite certain no reader would be prepared to do just that.

My talkative guard told me that the sentence of my new neighbour, a student from Moscow, had been commuted to 15 years hard labour, and he had already been sent up north. But the guard could not understand what was happening with my case. I was the longest-serving prisoner in death row and they must have forgotten about me. That afternoon I counted the marks on my wall. There were 22 of them and I settled down to another restless, nightmarish night. Despite being prepared to die every time the main door clanged open, I would wake up from a slumber for the inevitable counting of the steps. During the night a commotion in the corridor woke me up. A prisoner would not put his Army coat on and they were beating him up. I stood up, jammed open the spy hole with a piece of chewed-up bread, and tried to see what was going on. As soon as the unfortunate was overpowered and taken out, the solitary light went out. Once again death row became quiet.

A man in a cell near the door started singing a sad Russian song. Through my spy hole I could see a small slit of sky through the window in the corridor next to my cell. For the first time I saw a piece of moon shining very bright. The combination of song and the moon had a devastating effect on me. I thought about my mum and dad and wondered if they too, at this very moment, were looking at the same moon and thinking of me. And for the first time since I arrived in the condemned cell, I could not prevent the tears. They came like an untamed flood and I could not do anything about it. I sobbed quietly and uncontrollably until the moon was gone and only the reflection was left.

The clanging of the door woke me up again. I was standing against it. You can sleep standing up you know. It was the morning and my guard was on duty again. While giving me tea, he whispered, "They will come after you and very soon". He could not say anything more as the other guard was nearby. I braced myself and decided to go with dignity and not be beaten like a dog. The corridor fell silent after the distribution of tea and, after a long break I started saying my prayers.

For days now I had started losing faith in God and did not pray, but as I was about to meet my maker I decided to make peace with him. I was still praying when the clank of the main door brought me round. There were nine steps and an order, "Come out, face the wall and no talking". I shuffled on my swollen legs out of the cell. I fully expected to be told to put the coat on. Instead the guard said, "Come out, they want you upstairs". As I could hardly move, they took me under their arms and helped me along and up the granite stairs. I was led into the same room where I had heard my sentence, with a guard on each side holding me up. Three NKVD Officers behind the table all smoked cigarettes. The one in the middle could not have been much older than me. He told the guards to let me go and I crumpled down onto the floor. He stood behind the table and said, "We revised your case and your sentence was commuted to 25 years of hard labour, with a further 10 years of losing your citizenship rights." I then heard him saying to the guards, "Take him for delousing. He smells like a pig".

All my senses seemed to drain out of me. When I came round I was lying on the landing and my friendly guard was bending over me, squeezing cold water on me out of a snowball in his hand. "You must try to get up and I will take you out of this place." He helped me to get up the stairs, and to the outside door. The bitter cold hit me in the face as we were near the exercise part of the yard, next to the lime pits. There was a pair of Russian high boots lying in the snow. The guard bent down and picked them up, stuffing them under my arm and saying, "He will not need them now where he is", referring to their original owner who was now lying dead in the lime pit. Whilst passing the exercise yard I heard someone ask my guard, "Where are you taking him?" "To be deloused," was the immediate reply. I suddenly realised that the questioner was the fellow who lost his ear in the cell, as he had a slight stutter. We eventually arrived at our destination. The inmate with the hair clippers had one look at me and said, "I'm not touching him. He's too lousy." Two chaps out of the boiler came to have a look at me and decided he was right. They filled a huge wooden oval container like a bath and told me to get in. I undressed and got into warm water. They also gave me a full handful of jelly soap. The effect of the last hour's excitement and the warm water had its effect and I passed out again. When I came to I was still in the tub and the chap without the ear was pouring hot water over my head, which had been shorn short by then. When I came to completely I realised what power those prison Mafiosi had. They could move around the prison at will and do what they liked. There was another surprise waiting for me. When I eventually got out of the tub he handed me a bundle in which I found a double ration of bread wrapped in long johns. These were dirty but freshly boiled and free of vermin. I was asked by one of the boiler attendants if I wanted to sell my own boots as they were pre-war Polish and still quite smart. My feet were so swollen that I could not put them on anyhow so I sold them for five roubles. The dead man's boots were much bigger, so I put them on.

I could not believe my good fortune. Here I was comparatively clean with new underwear, tucking into bread and having a huge cigarette to follow. To me it was like a dream, more than a dream, I was absolutely amazed. I could have easily been lying in a pit by now, with quick lime sprinkled over me. I was still in a daze when my guard eventually took me upstairs into the cell. There was no number of the cell on the door, but I couldn't care less, it seemed like a five star hotel room to me. I was immediately surrounded by the Russian Mafiosi and their leader said, "We heard about you Jozef Jozefovich (my first name and father's first name). You had a bad time, but you are amongst friends now. We will look after you. Is there anything you want?"

I asked him to get me some tobacco and gave him two roubles for it. I said I was very tired and wanted to sleep. They gave me a place on the top bunk in the corner. Before lying down I crossed myself. On seeing it, he told me that he knew about God as his granny was very religious and told him all about it. He said he had forgotten how to pray and would I teach him how to, even in Polish, as there was only one God.

That was what his grandma had told him and he always believed her. I started saying "Our Father", but fell asleep immediately. When I woke up I had two rations of bread of 300 grams each, as I had slept for nearly 48 hours and my bread had been saved for me.

I still could not believe my miraculous escape and was in a daze. I was told by the Mafia boys that our resident Robins were being replaced by a different bunch and it was my good fortune for the change. There were very few cases where prisoners were reprieved, and I was one. My body swelling started improving considerably and very soon I came to the conclusion that where there is life, there is hope. Things could not get any worse than what I went through. A few days more and I started getting my cockiness and self-assurance back. I told the yobs to lay off one of my countrymen and to my amazement they left him alone.

I soon got into the routine of cell life again and became more and more aware of the goings-on around me, but my 23 days under sentence of death left their impression on me, and even now, after 45 years, I still feel the effects of them. Many, many times I live through a private hell in my dreams. These nightmares usually drain me totally and leave me feeling jumpy and nervous. The worst part was the fact that I could not share my anxiety with anybody. Nobody could understand my point of view. When once or twice I tried to speak about it, I was told not to be so silly, it happened a long time ago, and it is high time you got over it. This is very easy to say, but impossible to do. It was and is, and will always be, in a pigeon-hole in my brain, and one I cannot erase.

Since I finished writing the last episodes of my story, I have had great difficulty in picking up the threads of further thoughts. I had to take a break of some two weeks to recover from the painful memories. My nightmares returned briefly and they were as scary as ever before. But I feel better now, so let's go back to my vermin infested cell. The Russian hooligans were rather active but luckily they were very cautious of me. They still thought I had cut the chap's ear off in my previous cell and nearly drowned the other in the slop bucket. I quickly guessed that admitting or denying the rumours would be to my disadvantage, so I made no comment regarding the incident. We found that more and more Polish nationals were arriving in the prison and, as a result, even the Russian Mafiosi had to sit and take notice of our presence. Most of my countrymen had already been through hell and were prepared to defend themselves in a rather violent way if need be. To my delight, one of my countrymen was involved in a struggle with a guard who fell down the stone stairs and broke his neck. The news and rumours went through the prison like a fire. The Russian yobs immediately changed their attitude to the Poles. That is where I heard for the first time a Russian saying, that having a fight with a mad Pole is like having sex with a beehive. You can manage some of them, but there are too many of them to fight off and they have got a nasty sting. After the guard's death, the violence and robberies practically stopped for a while and we were treated with respect.

Soon after I asked the guard if I could be temporarily transferred to another cell and to my astonishment he agreed. I went to my first cell for a day, No.17. It had changed a lot. Most of the inmates were gone but the Mafia boss was still there. He treated me like a long lost brother and gave me a small piece of pork fat and a head of garlic. I was particularly glad of the garlic as I had started suffering from scurvy, and garlic was one of the most effective cures for it. I chewed it to the best of my ability, but my gums were badly swollen. There was no pain involved, but you could remove your teeth with your fingers as the diseased gums did not hold them firmly.

One day some idiot found out from my documents that I was a medical student, so they made me into some kind of doctor. Even the guards were seeking my advice on all kinds of ills, which amused me immensely to start with. But I soon found that it could be to my advantage. In this way I soon cured myself of scurvy as the guards were supplying me with garlic and onions. My new standing in the eyes of the guards sometimes resulted in real comedy. One day a guard came with a badly swollen face due to an abscessed tooth. There was a very strong anti-Semitic feeling among the Russians and the guard said that he didn't trust the prison doctor-cum-dentist as he is a greasy Jew and could I help. I didn't have the heart to tell him that I was not a dentist so I agreed. I told him I needed a dentist's pliers and some surgical spirit. After a while he came back with ordinary pliers and said the doctor had drunk all the spirit so he couldn't get any. I told him that the inmates made spirit in the boiler room and it would be suitable. He eventually managed to get about half a litre of the stuff through the prison Mafia. On the way back to the cell he visited the surgery for 100 grams of spirit and borrowed the dentists pliers from the doctor, who was three-quarters drunk. I told him it would hurt but it didn't seem to worry him. We had a drink to start and he knocked back about 200 grams, eight or so singles, and became quite merry. I only drunk some 75 grams, but was very soon as drunk as a parrot, due to my general state of health. I practised the grip of the pliers on some bread sticks and eventually came the crunch moment, as the guard gradually became more and more agitated. I realised that there was a great risk of infection as it was such a large abscess, but I could not back out now. He lay down on a bunk with his head hanging down so I could get to his top tooth. I had to push his swollen cheek and gum away with my finger to see the ruddy tooth. Eventually I managed to get hold of it and tried to remember what I had been told by the surgeon during my stint as a hospital dogsbody. He had let me pull a few teeth out during post mortems.

I was afraid I might crush the guard's tooth as the pliers were very smooth, but to my amazement there was a slight crunch and the ruddy thing popped out like a cork from a bottle. He yelled out like an Irish banshee and promptly sunk his teeth into my finger. I was bitten so hard my finger started bleeding. I dipped a piece of cotton flock in the spirit and stuck it into the gaping hole left by his tooth. The guard was so keen to call me a son-of-a-bitch that he was spluttering blood all over the place. The smell of the pus from his wound worried me a lot. It smelt of gangrene and I thought he would never recover from it. When he didn't turn up for duty the next day I felt, this is it, I'll never get away with it. To my amazement he turned up for night duty and said the swelling was nearly gone, he was free of pain and very, very grateful. To my astonishment and delight he produced one pocketful of garlic and another of onions. Some of the goodies I exchanged for tobacco, as by then I had become a habitual smoker, despite the fact that I had only smoked the first cigarette of my life on 17th September, 1939.

He was telling me that his mate went to the prison doctor with a toothache and it took him two weeks to pull out bits of the tooth, as the ruddy drunkard must have crushed his tooth. My fame spread very quickly throughout the prison and I started holding a sort of surgery. The most troublesome sort of epidemic was with boils, small, medium and large ones were appearing on all parts of the body. Every cell throughout the prison had a sufferer with boils. They were vicious and very painful and I had several myself. I lanced them and started getting willing customers from other cells. The prison quack used some kind of bradawl to let the pus out and, as he was mostly half drunk, he was not too gentle to squeeze the rubbish out. I used a piece of glass to cut the heads off boils but it was not very satisfactory. I asked the guard with the tooth, for a razor blade. He said he had never heard of one but he had a very old open razor, which was originally his grandfathers'. The razor was indeed very old, but I was delighted with it as I could open a boil practically painlessly. When he asked for it back I told him it was stolen. He looked very upset, as it was a formidable weapon in anybody's hands. He and a few of his guard friends made a very thorough search in the cell but found nothing. During the search I had held the blade all the time in my hand, including when I was stripped naked.

From the first moment in that place, I started planning to escape. I didn't know how, but I felt I must get away from this madhouse or else I would become a raving lunatic. I had literally scores of ideas but nothing concrete. As my cell was situated on the second floor I did not think that the window would be feasible, as there was a long drop from the foundations into the river below. In my quest to find a way to escape, I started watching everything very carefully. Out of our toilets I started observing the river and by moving the Hessian, the opposite bank of the river. One thing struck me as peculiar, that the river still flowed even when there was a severe frost. When asked, the guard told me that this part of the river hardly ever froze and there was a spring some 150 metres up river, which kept the river ice free. I immediately thought of escaping by jumping from the window. The height was considerable – some 60 or so feet – but it was better than staying in this hell hole. I started examining the security of the bars in the windows. I found they were upright, not welded and were secured not with cement, but with ordinary mortar, which was soft and quite easily removable.

I managed to get a sort of prison made knife and started chipping away at the base of the bars. My activities amused my Russian friends greatly as they thought I had taken leave of my senses. My plan was simple. If I could suspend myself some 3 metres down the wall from the window, I could push hard away from it with my feet and project my body away from the wall enough to miss some rocks, which were protruding on the way down to the river.

Despite thinking I was mad, the Russians co-operated fully. They took turns to stand guard at the door and spy hole, and made noises to divert attention from time to time so that I could chip away louder. I made good progress and exposed the bottom of the first bar within two days. The top of the bars were quite easy; just a matter of pulling hard and it would just crumble out of its soft mortar. The authorities never gave it a thought that some lunatic might try to get out of the second floor window with a 60-foot drop, but to me it was a feasible thing to try. So between killing the vermin, my crazy surgeries and trying to get out, my life was very busy. Fortunately, the authorities seemed to forget about me and there were no more calls out at night for questioning. There were still more Poles coming into the prison and very soon we were a vast majority. This fact subdued the Russian Mafia to such an extent that robberies were, at least for the time being, a thing of the past.

The mentality of this breed was very peculiar. They were great believers in violence and brute force, and yet they could not take it themselves. Even the threat of violence was enough to cool them down, so they needed to be reminded, from time to time, of the new pecking order. This was sometimes rather painful, like the time when one of them had his fingers crushed. The door was slammed shut by the guard while a big Pole held the Russian's hand against the door frame. This rather drastic measure was taken after deep thought and consultations amongst the Poles. We had held a sort of council of war on what to do next to keep these animals off our backs. Due to the charges against me, the fact I had spent a record 23 days in a condemned cell, my 25 year sentence, plus my ideas to subdue the bastards in the cells, meant I was at the top of the list on the war council. We soon found that even the guards had a great respect for us, mainly because of the fortunate accident (for us), when the guard broke his neck falling down stairs.

The guard happened to be an unusually nasty bit of work, who would inform on his mates. I spoke to my countryman involved in the incident, who had been a Polish sailor on leave when the war broke out. He swore he never hit the guard, but tried to steady himself after tripping on the top of the stairs. When we were asked about the accident, we decided to stare at the enquirer, say nothing and occasionally wink. It was enough to send wild rumours right through the prison and beyond. One day a group of Russian Hooligans came from Minsk prison. They had apparently heard that Orsha prison had been taken over by the Poles and were determined to put it right and sort us out. They were all smartly dressed in sheepskin jackets with high riding boots and were all very well fed.

I still dealt with a fair amount of boils. One of the Poles spread rumours that I was pretty handy in all kinds of operations, including castration. These spread like wildfire throughout the prison and they grew to crazy proportions. Within a very few days of their arrival, the chief Mafioso asked me in the toilet queue if it was true that I had castrated a couple of chaps. I did not say yes or no, but with a wink told him that this was only a rumour and I would never do such a thing to my friends. I said it was true I lanced boils and occasionally took a tooth out, but that was all. The expression of horror on his face had to be seen to be believed. He was utterly petrified and would not turn his back on me whilst standing in the queue. Telling me how friendly he was to us Poles, he stuffed something into my pocket. Later in my cell I found it was a good 50 grams of tobacco, which was very valuable in prison.

The inmates in the prison were forever being transferred from one cell to another and the following day, two of these yobs came into my cell. One of them had a real reputation. His face looked like a badly designed quilt; some signs of quite fresh and old scars criss-crossed his face, arms and chest. He was a well-fed cocky bastard, full of self-assurance and importance. He came in with a sizeable bundle of personal things under his arm and straight away started looking around for the best bunks. I could see what sort of fellow we'd got and decided to put a dampener on his fire by telling him that his bunk was near the slop bucket. I was sitting on the middle bunk with my feet dangling some one metre from the floor, and he came over to try and to stare me out. He had large protruding eyeballs and a vicious expression on his face. It took a good minute of staring before I decided to act, kicking him in the solar plexus with all my strength. The strike was spot on and he fell backwards towards the row of bunks fixed on the opposite wall. He hit his head on a bunk and went out like a light. Two of my cell Russians leaped up to lift him and tried to revive him. One of them screamed at me, "You son of a bitch, you killed him. He has stopped breathing." I realised that by such a kick I must have moved his heart practically into his throat. I must admit that for a moment I panicked. I jumped off the bed bunk, sat astride him and, with all my might, smacked his face a few times with my open hand.

Then general panic broke out in the cell. One Russian started banging on the door like mad. When two guards rushed in they came to the conclusion I was in the process of killing him, sitting on top of him and smacking his face. Out came the chain handcuffs and a guard hit me two or three times over the head and back. They eventually pulled me off him and dragged me into the corridor. Despite the pain my adrenaline was flowing high and fast. I jumped up to my feet and screamed at the guard, "You son of a bitch. If you hit me again I'll cut your eyes out". The other guard said to him, "Leave him alone. He'll do it. He's mad." Two or three more guards appeared and tied my hands behind my back, took me along the corridor, down the stone staircase and into the dungeons. The punishment cells were made below the building and in an old tomb where sometime in the past monks placed the coffins of their leaders into the wall. I was led by a piece of rope like a dog. Despite my hands being tied the guards wouldn't come near me. One of them went forward and opened the steel door to one of the so-called cells. It reminded me of the door on a baker's oven. I had no time for further thoughts as they grabbed me and threw me head first and face down into the hole in the wall. The door slammed behind me and I heard disappearing steps along the corridor. The stench inside was overpowering. I must have brought some bedbugs with me from the cell as I felt them biting me after I was left alone.

I was lying in a very uncomfortable position, face down on fine rubble with my head pushed into the depth of the tomb. After an hour or so I felt a very acute lack of oxygen and started hallucinating, which scared me more than anything else. I was wondering how long they were going to leave me in this hell-hole. I must have gone to sleep or passed out, as the noise of the door opening brought me around. Someone started pulling me out by the feet. They then tried to stand me up, but my legs were completely lifeless, so I had to be supported by somebody under the arms.

The comparatively fresh air started bringing me around. I felt something very soft on my face and realised it was the fur of a sheepskin jacket. I realised that two Russian Mafiosi were holding me up. I believe there were some five or six of them. Some of them were holding fairly stout split wood sort of logs. I could not grasp what they were saying to me, but I did understand somebody screaming, "You sons of bitches. What are you doing here?" One of the yobs replied that they had been told to turn me around, as I couldn't eat like this. I realised that the questioner was the same kind guard who took me out of the condemned cell and into the boiler room. The Punishment cells must have been near the death row and the guard had heard the noise. He had a stout chain in his hand and told them to go upstairs. They sat me against the wall and I was left alone with the guard. He told me not to be so stupid and not to antagonise everybody because if the authorities did not kill me, the yobs would. "You wounded one of their leaders and they are out to get you", he said. "They could have killed you here like a dog. Nobody would be any the wiser. You are soon due to be sent to a labour camp and if you are wise, you will get there in one piece."

He told me how powerful these hooligans are and said that even the prison chief was very cautious of them as they had friends on the outside and it was nothing for them to kill or report anybody for counter-revolutionary activities. The guard was not strong enough to defend himself against such a serious trumped-up charge. Apparently the yobs were making representations to the prison authorities to have me killed or let them do it and most probably they would have succeeded if he hadn't come at the right time. He told me that the guards thought I was mad after spending so long in the condemned cell. There were rumours amongst the prisoners that I had castrated at least one man and the hooligans were afraid of it more than anything else. The yobs were looking forward to being sent to a staging camp on the way to proper labour camps, as there was no segregation between men and women prisoners and they did not want me to turn them into eunuchs.

The guard told me his wife's mother was very religious and secretly went to an underground Orthodox Church. He did not dare go himself as the church meetings were full of spies and they would soon report him. He said that if I thought it was a hard life in prison, I should try the labour camps, as he had been a guard there for five years before being posted here for a rest. Telling me more, he said he had been sent to be a guard for some past misdemeanours, but did not tell me what he had done. He continued speaking for a long time as if he was trying to confess his sins to me, and asked me what I was really in for, as the counter-revolutionary activities in my papers meant nothing in this regime.

To this day I do not know why, but there and then I told him the truth. I said the Communists had raped my country and I was only trying to defend it. When I mentioned the episode with the grenade it amused him greatly and he said, "It's a pity you haven't managed to kill all the bastards, then we would all have peace and quiet." I was very touched when, before taking me back to my cell, he blessed me with the sign of the cross and said, "God bless and have strength to survive. This gangrene cannot survive forever." I have often thought since then of his description of Communism. Gangrene is perhaps a more suitable name than cancer, as sometimes the best flesh of society rots away with an unbearable stench.

I was very surprised to be taken back to the old cell and even more surprised to see the hooligan who had caused me to spend two days in the punishment cell. He was sitting on the bunk near the slop bucket with his boots off which were standing on the floor. I don't know what made me do it but as soon as the cell door slammed behind me, I picked up his boots and threw them into the slop bucket. He grabbed them out and said to me, "You crazy bastard. You could have had them for the asking, as I was fed up with them, and they are a good pair of boots." I didn't say a word, but jumped on my bunk and went to sleep.

The excitement over the previous two days had caught up with me. I felt drained and very tired. I did not worry that he might attack me while I was asleep as there were many of my countrymen around me. Eventually I woke up and amazingly found my adversary at the window, chipping away at the mortar. He said that he knew about my plan and that if I was crazy enough to try it, he was crazy enough to help me with it. He said that he was not a spy or stool pigeon and that he would help me. And help he did. He had a very stout knife made out of a thick steel blade from a band-saw, which he had acquired in Minsk prison from a fellow prisoner who had once worked in a sawmill. The steel in the knife was hard and tough and he soon released the bottoms of all the bars in the window. My next step was to acquire some kind of rope for my escape. That is when the hooligans excelled in their adaptability. Many scraps of material, such as shirts, pants, etc., were pulled apart, thread by thread and twisted together, again and again until they were made into a fairly thin, but very strong sort of rope.

Frankly, I could not believe that a flimsy thing like that would hold my weight, but it did. The whole of the cell was involved in pulling apart and twisting and twisting and twisting. My own shirt and other parts of clothing went into this rope. We even got some linen shirts from other cells. Then suddenly we had unexpected help. Some two metres of rope were sent to us from the boiler room gang. By now I had an ample amount of rope and I started preparing myself mentally for the big jump. The window was small, but plenty big enough for me to go through. But there was still a need to remove the outside shutter, which was blocking our view and my way out. It had been badly fixed to the outside wall with nails. The makeshift knife was soon used to pull most of them out until there were only two left. Whilst my new helper was forcing the nails out his mate was holding the shutter with one hand to prevent it falling. Suddenly the unexpected happened and the damn shutter went clattering down the wall. On its way down it knocked the other shutter immediately below our window and that also went down the side of the rock. It clearly upset the guard dogs somewhere below, who started howling like hell. I was told later that an elderly chap had fainted whilst sitting on the toilet as part of the shutters fluttered sideways and hit the board that he was seated upon. The inmates inside the building thought that the whole structure was coming down and a general panic ensued.

The prison guards went completely berserk, as they didn't know what the hell had happened. The prison was under NKVD control and the guards, although conscripted into their fold, were members only through necessity, having been ordered to do so. A few lower-grade NKVD officers occupied administrative positions, carrying out tasks such as censoring, segregating inmates, deciding who went to which labour camp, etc.

After this incident with the shutter collapse some 40 proper NKVD officers descended on the prison and started to re-organise matters. To start with, and to demonstrate who the bosses were, they executed over 60 people, including a few members of the Russian Mafia. On the first night they took for questioning the Mafia boss and shot him on the spot. They also took me for further interrogation and accused me of being the head of the Polish Mafia. I followed the Russian hooligan into the interrogation room and then saw him being led out with his hands tied behind his back. He was shot a few yards from me, on the stone staircase leading to death row. For a while I thought that my number had really come up that time, but to my relief and surprise they took me back to the cell. In the morning two huge NKVD officers came into the cell to check on the window. As it was pretty high they brought a stool with them to stand on. This was not quite high enough, so one of them got hold of the bottom of a couple of the bars in order to lift himself up. The fixed top of the bars held him for a second or so then he went sprawling backwards off the stool, still holding them in his hands, and onto the floor. As he jumped up he looked at the two bars in his hands he exclaimed, "Well, son of a bitch, I never thought I was that strong". The comedy of it all would surpass even the best Irish jokes and stories. He actually believed he had torn the bars out of the window opening, when really they had come out so easily because they had been set into the stone wall with soft mortar instead of cement.

A few years later I was told that the tradesman who had originally set the bars was probably given cement to do the job but most likely sold it on the black market and used mortar instead. Even today there are many buildings in Russia, Poland and other so-called Socialist states built with inferior materials because the original workmen sold the proper materials on the black market. Their brand of Communism could not exist without dishonesty due to the control by The Party of all consumer goods. A black market in the construction industry is supplied by workers pilfering materials to sell on to enable them to feed their families or to buy vodka. In such a society, if you need something for the home, you go to a building site and ask the chief engineer, foreman or just a workman. You can buy baths, pipes, taps, washers, boards, etc. Anything that is used on the site is available at a price. If one cubic metre of a certain concrete calls for, say, four bags of cement, but the workman has a customer waiting for three bags of cement, then only one bag goes into the mix. Never mind the quality, count the quantity, which was exactly what the Party ordered.

Many years after the War, in a then Communist Poland, the wife of a friend of mine accidentally broke the plastic top of a sink tap. I said I'd get a replacement. "Where the hell are you going to get it?" I was asked by my friend. "There is nothing like it on the market. But don't worry, I can get it myself in a few days," he said, putting a screwdriver into his pocket. All kinds of people, including doctors, lawyers and teachers, walk around with screwdrivers to enable them to unscrew bits and pieces in public places and take them home with them, so that they can replace breakages in their homes. Apologies but, rightly or wrongly, I found it appropriate at this point to deviate from my story to explain this consequence of the Communist system. Their engineers and architects are not exactly idiots, but the whole rotten system does not necessarily mean that what was designed is actually built. Hence the shoddy bars in my prison cell.

Needless to say after this incident, I had to abandon my attempts to escape. My night-time visit to the interrogators scared the daylights out of me and I now became preoccupied with trying to heal the side of my face, which had been badly scraped when I had been thrown into the punishment hole. It was covered in a large scab with pus underneath. I asked for a visit to the doctor as I knew he had a big bottle of iodine concentrate which he used freely on all cuts and abrasions. Just before I went to see him, I managed to rip off most of the scab on my face, exposing some not so healthy flesh. True to form, on seeing this, he painted the wound with the iodine with the help of a paintbrush. The pain of this treatment was very acute, especially as he also splashed the stuff in both my eyes. Before I had gone to see this quack, I had tried to get some spirit from the boiler room to disinfect my wound, but was told me that the NKVD had closed down the still and had also shot two inmates running the operation. The NKVD officers had no need to drink this illicit stuff like ordinary guards as they could get the real thing in special shops, which had been set up in the prison for their use only. It was impossible for an ordinary member of the guard to go and shop there, as a special identity card was needed to do so.

## Chapter 6 : 9 days in Lubyanka Prison

At this time our daily bread ration was cut to less than 100 grams. Other conditions started getting a lot rougher as well. Suddenly news spread throughout the prison that a massive transport was being prepared to go into a region of the Arctic Circle where, in the River Pieczora delta, there were many labour camps or Gulags. The next day there was great activity by the guards in the prison checking identities of the inmates. Spurred on by old lags in the know of what lay ahead there was very intensive trading within the cells for all kinds of warmer clothing.

After my brush with the hooligan from Minsk, he had given me three good warm shirts that were in great demand, but I did not succumb to the temptation to sell any of them. By now I was the proud owner of a rather filthy Polish Army overcoat, which was very long and quite warm. I was greatly tempted to exchange my open razor for a sheepskin coat. Luckily I did not succumb to this temptation as we later found that all coats of this type were taken off the prisoners just before we boarded the train. The NKVD man on our landing heard that I had a razor and I got pretty badly knocked about with a chain over my back and legs in an attempt to make me give it to him. The bastard didn't know that that wouldn't work and only the threat of hanging by the arms would have made me give it to him. I was still having nightmares about my previous torture. Luckily, for unknown reasons, they did not hang prisoners in that prison.

Since 1940, I have spoken to many ex-prisoners and came to the conclusion that this type of hanging was a speciality of the ex-teacher from Ukraine who I had the very grave misfortune to come across earlier in my story. After doing some research, I came to the conclusion that the pervert must have heard about this type of punishment from someone who had served in the Austrian Army, where it was also widely used.

I very nearly exchanged my razor for a Polish Army bayonet with a 10 inch blade which one of the Russian Mafia had in another cell but I was worried about how I was going to smuggle it onto the train so it came to nothing. Eventually lists were made and transport became imminent. One day, very early in the morning, the sounds of dogs barking and howling woke us up. With morning tea a guard arrived with a long list of names. Practically all of the inmates of my cell were called out. We were counted, re-counted and then formed into long columns five abreast and then surrounded by guards carrying automatic pistols and accompanied by many guard dogs. The guards' commander, a far-eastern man with very slanted eyes, gave a short speech in pidgin Russian to the effect that anybody attempting to escape would be shot without warning.

It was the second part of February 1940 and the cold was very intense. Inmates were tapping their feet on the ground whilst waiting for the order to set off. Eventually the order came to move. Guards armed with pistols also carried long truncheons to keep us in order. Their weapons were hanging from shoulder straps around their necks. Eventually we moved off towards very massive railway sidings. Our train was at the furthermost point from the prison; on the line next to it were sizeable heaps of coal and split wood. We were counted out at fifty inmates per cattle truck. Just before we were ordered in, we were told to take in some coal for our fires. There was a mad scramble towards the heap of coal and wood. We grabbed what we could in the shortest possible time and rushed back into the trucks. All the Poles amongst us began to sing our National Anthem and we all crowded towards certain trucks to be together. While waiting in the queue to get aboard, I was grabbed by the arm by one of the Mafia lads and asked again whether I wanted to trade the Polish bayonet for the razor. I agreed and as I had the razor hidden in my personal bundle I handed him the lot and he gave me his. This exchange was very profitable for me as in his bundle I found 200 grams of tobacco and 600 grams of bread. He couldn't claim a fairer exchange as he was pushed into the next truck by the guards. We found that the trucks were fitted out in an identical manner to the trucks I had travelled in the past. The majority of men in my truck were my countrymen and being quick thinkers, most of us had some coal stuffed into our pockets.

Before our sliding door was shut, we heard a burst of automatic gunfire aimed at an escaping Polish prisoner. To our delight the ricocheting bullets hit some of the guards. One, just outside our open door, was hit in the forehead and neck, which severed an artery in his temple. Blood started pumping out of his temple onto the snow. For some unexplained reason, I jumped out of the truck and by putting pressure on the side of his head stopped the bleeding. One of the other guards set a dog on me and it sunk its teeth into my leg. At the same moment it was hit over the head by another guard and was killed. Another blow from a stick went onto the bewildered dog handler who promptly went out like a light. The guard with the stick turned out to be an NKVD officer who had seen the incident of the wounded guard and my attempts to help him. He levelled his pistol at two other guards who were going for me. "Back off you sons of bitches, can't you see he's trying to save the soldier's life?". I remember thinking that I must be getting very slow and not taking an opportunity to escape under the trucks. Later on I found out that the original escaper who had started this affair had been shot dead...

The wounded guard was conscious and pulled out of his pocket 100 grams of tobacco and a large box of cigarettes and gave them to me to say thank you for saving his life. By this time the truck door had been shut and I was left with the wounded soldier on the ground. At long last a medic arrived and took over from me. While I was showing him where to press to stop the bleeding, the knocked-out guard came round, and, thinking I had knocked him out, levelled his pistol at me, practically touching my nose with its short barrel. Before he could press the trigger I ducked down onto the chest of the wounded soldier. As he fired the gases from the barrel knocked the hat off my head and burnt the skin on it. If I had any longer hair, it would have set on fire. The bullet from the gun went into the floor of the truck and I could clearly see the splinters hanging from the wooden floor underneath the truck. The incident was seen by the NKVD officer who screamed at the Sergeant in charge of the Tartar soldiers, "Take that son of a bitch soldier away or I'll shoot him myself". The sliding door of the truck was opened and my mates rapidly pulled me inside. My ears were ringing like hell from the gunfire and I bolted to the back of the truck as I felt I had experienced enough excitement for the moment. After a very short while the steam engine was hooked up but before we set off I was told that the NKVD man wanted to see me. My heart raced when I saw an NKVD Major standing at the open door. He said that he had come to say thank you for saving one of his soldiers. He had heard from the prison guard that I was some sort of doctor and thereby appointed me to be a medical orderly in charge of the transport entitled to double rations. He also handed me a package wrapped in newspaper, a 100 gram packet of tobacco, a box of 100 cigarettes and a sandwich wrapped in newspaper, made by his wife that morning. It was made with Pork fat and wrapped in a page of 'Pravda' newspaper. It was absolutely delicious.

In the semi-darkness of the cattle truck we immediately started sorting ourselves out. The allocation of places on the bunks was very important and we made a rota for fire duties. The weather was so cold it would have been easy to have our stove burning red hot, but we had no idea how long we would remain locked up, or whether we would get any more coal for the fire in the future. All the tobacco and food I had was distributed amongst everyone in the truck and I settled down to examine my prized possession, the Polish Army bayonet. It was of the newest design, ten or so inches long, and sharp on both sides. I kept looking around the truck, as the thought of escape had never left me. I noticed that It was made out of narrow boarding, fixed to metal frames with bolts. If we could only take the bolts out, we would make a hole big enough to slip through. It was no good trying to get through the sides or the roof, as they were always under observation by the guards from specially constructed platforms at the end of each of the trucks. Nor could we simply slide the doors open, as they were secured from the outside. Therefore, we needed to escape through the floor, but there was one serious snag. If we tried while the truck was moving, it would result in certain death under the wheels of the train. The way I was feeling at that moment, though, I was prepared to try anything which offered even the smallest chance of survival. One of the boys noticed some kind of unevenness in part of the floor and, on careful examination, we found it was riddled with bullets, which had weakened it considerably, loosening two or three of the bolts.

We decided to form an escape group of 11 and all of us were determined to find a way out. My bayonet turned out to be a godsend and, within a short time, one board was quite loose but in order to escape we had to remove all the boards. An engineer from our group had counted the bolts that we needed to remove, which came to nearly 100. The amount of bolts didn't worry us, as we had countless hours ahead of us. This didn't stop one of the fellows, who was as restless as I was, getting a massive blister on his palm through chopping constantly at the boards with my bayonet.

As I lay on a bunk watching the fire, I spotted a piece of coal escape from it and burn a small but deep hole in the floorboards. This immediately gave me an idea. Why not burn the bolts out? I discussed the possibility with my friend Ted. He immediately put it to the test by placing a red-hot piece of coal near a bolt. Sure enough, it rapidly sunk into the board. The only drawback of this method was that it gave off quite a lot of smoke, but luckily the truck was so draughty that the smoke and smell disappeared instantly through the holes and crevices. This was a very effective method of removing bolts but agonisingly slow, especially for Ted and me, who had fire in our bellies and were impatient for a quick way out. We had even discussed starting a proper fire on the floor and burning a hole big enough to slip out, but we realised that our escape would have to be carried out while we were stationary, otherwise it would mean facing instant death under the wheels of the train. All our efforts to find out where we were going came to nothing as the guards were under very strict orders not to reveal our final destination.

On the third or fourth day, while the train was stationary, the guards called me out to attend an injured Mafioso, whose face and arm had been badly slashed. I said I needed a curved needle and a sterile thread in order to stitch him up. The chief guard was very amused by my request and said, "You stupid son of a bitch. Where the hell am I going to get that?" He promised to do something about it, however, and had the train stop in the next town. I set off with two guards to a disgustingly filthy sort of barn that they called a hospital to ask for a curved needle, but a man wearing a once white jacket was even more amused by my request than the guard. He said they had plenty of these needles but in Moscow or Leningrad, not here. Instead, he told me, used an ordinary needle to close wounds and created a curve by turning the sharp end over with a pair of pliers.

By then nothing the Russians said surprised me, so I asked him for a demonstration and he duly obliged by taking me to a large room with some 20 beds, and showed me a post-operation patient with what looked like a double rupture and appendicitis on both sides. The poor fellow had been carved up like a Christmas turkey. When I asked why he had so many cuts, I was told that in Russia so many people had appendicitis on different sides, they made a sort of Caesarean cut to make sure they got the damn thing out. To my absolute horror I could smell the stench of both bedbugs and gangrene. After trying to pump me for some professional information, the man in the grubby white coat proudly said he had attended medical school in Moscow but added, "I never finished school because of the war." "What war?" I asked him, surprised. "Haven't you heard?" he asked, "there's a very bloody war against the Polish capitalists and landowners and all proper doctors had to gone to defend Mother Russia along with the storm-troopers."

Poor fellow, he was so brainwashed and confused that he hardly knew what day of the week it was. While walking around this so-called hospital, I actually managed to pocket a few things, including the newest looking scalpel I could see, and some kind of brass microscope insert with broken glass in it, before being hurried back to the train by the guards. I had been given two straight needles, a metre of linen cotton and more thread. I managed to heat and bend the needle into a curved shape and was ready to sew up the Mafioso. Unfortunately, I blunted the needle while bending it, but even so eventually managed to finish the job and received a whole loaf of bread and a tin of sardines for my troubles. Sharing a loaf of bread amongst 50 men was easy, but to split a tin of sardines amongst the lot was very difficult. All I was left with at the end was a small amount of fish oil but I was very grateful for it.

We were on the move for some two weeks when I had my second call – a real emergency. One of the trucks contained women prisoners and a few of them were pregnant. One of them, a Russian girl of about 21 years of age, was on the point of giving birth. She told me her child was the result of being raped by a soldier. She was very pretty and looked so frightened. As I had no experience at all in the matter, apart from what I had read in books and learnt from lectures, I was more petrified than her. I was also very dirty.

I told the chief guard that I must have hot water so that I could wash myself, and so he arranged to stop near an isolated signal box. There was an enormous fire inside the box together with a rather sleepy signalman, who closed the line by reporting a major breakdown to his superiors and then bolted like a rabbit when he discovered what was going on. The chief guard on our train shouted after him, "send your wife to the box", but the signalman claimed his wife was a cripple and so could not come. There was a pail of lukewarm water on the stove and I washed my arms and hands as thoroughly as I could with the soap. I was just in time. As soon as we transferred the girl into the signal box, she went into the last stages of labour. To my great relief, the baby boy popped out a few minutes later, easy as anything. The only thing left for me to do was to separate him from his mother, which was quite a simple, straightforward operation. The signalman was summoned by telephone and given the baby to hand over to the local Party's nursery so that it could be brought up in the Party way of thinking. At the time there were, and indeed still are, many centres in Russia where the state takes control of individuals from birth to the grave. Many babies from Poland went this way, taken by Russians and Germans alike. After this nerve-wracking event, I jumped back into the truck and off we went again. The following day I was called to see the Mafioso that I had previously treated. He had developed a big lump full of fluid where I had stitched him up and it needed treating So I opened up a stitch and saturated the bad spot with iodine, the only disinfectant I had, hoping it would heal.

Whenever we stopped at a station with goods wagons on the sidelines, our guards would open them and look for anything they could loot. Huge cisterns were their favourite targets and one day there were feverish activities as they found a whole cistern of alcohol. This left them very happy for a number of days as they filled all available containers with this very strong alcohol. I asked for an enamelled pail of the stuff to use as a disinfectant and was given it as the chief guard seemed very anxious to keep the prisoners in reasonable health.

One time we were given a large barrel full of salted pork and I was given the task of distributing it pork amongst the men. Being taken out of the truck practically every day gave me an ideal opportunity to find and pick up all kinds of things, so I became a human magpie. I would pick up anything that might be useful at a future date with no idea of what it actually was. Among the rubbish I found on the line was a huge steel nut. I could not see any use for it immediately, but I picked it up just the same. My friend Ted got very excited about this find and soon showed me why. He heated it in the stove until it was red-hot and then dropped it over one of the bolts in the floorboards. To our delight, it practically burnt right through the timber. Following this treatment the bolt with the nut on it could be pulled out quite easily. To be truthful, I was tempted to escape on occasions whilst outside the truck but stopped myself as I felt that I could not let my mates down, especially Ted, who was so keen on escaping with me. He was a young man of about 20, very tall and blond with blue eyes. He had a been given seven-year sentence for attempting to cross the border between the Russian occupation territories and Germany with some friends, which nearly cost him his life. All had been arrested while taking shelter in a barn after the farmer, who was an active member of the Communist Party, called the Russians. Ted had been only at Orsha prison for ten days, but had heard so many stories there about the labour camps that he was determined to escape if at all possible.

After two weeks of hard work on the bolts in the floorboards, we could remove a section that was large enough for even a big man to go through quite easily. We were very excited and waited impatiently for a big railway junction with a longer stop, but the damn train crawled very slowly, with many long stops at signal boxes. At one point we stopped for two days in order to help clear wreckage from a head-on collision between a train full of prisoners and another that contained supplies. Most of the prisoners were dead and we had to use heavy digging equipment to bury them in the frozen surface. The other train was packed with dried bread in big sacks and, needless to say, a lot of this found its way into our trucks. Under the supervision of the Russian engineers we re-laid the line and moved very carefully across it. At last, we were on our way again.

Time on the train seemed to drag by very slowly and I spent many hours talking to Ted, discussing ideas of escape. We also got friendly with a Russian called Olekk, who was on his second trip to the labour camps. He had first been imprisoned for getting drunk and hitting one of the leading hands at the collective farm he worked on. For that he got three years in one of the labour camps in the north. During his first stint he killed a man in an argument over a bread ration and was sent on trial to Minsk, where he got ten years and a further seven years loss of citizenship rights. This type of punishment was quite fashionable in Russia. It meant that you had no right to vote, you had no right to any identity cards or permits or reliefs. During this time, they just pretended you did not exist. Olekk was absolutely petrified of going back to the camps, as the almighty Russian hooligans who ran them abused human dignity every day in every way. Male and female brothels were openly run with full approval of the guards. The female barracks were located inside the main camp, surrounded by barbed wire, and were turned into massive brothels, mainly for the use of the guards and the Mafiosi. He despised the Mafiosi more than anything else, because he had been abused, raped and robbed by them on several occasions. The more stories we heard, the more determined we were to escape. Olekk watched our activities very carefully and, guessing that we were planning to escape, begged us to take him with us. It was very difficult to trust anybody in the circumstances, even our own countrymen, so we were reluctant to agree, but I knew he had the courage we needed. I had chosen to include mostly young men to go with us who were determined to escape and had the guts to go through with it.

There was another Russian lad, a friend of Olekk's, who ignored all our attempts to converse with him. He acted like a cornered animal and hardly ever came down from his bunk. We felt desperately sorry for him, but we could not afford to jeopardise our plans by taking him with us. One night, one of the young Polish lads woke me up in a panic pointing to the floor. To my absolute horror I saw someone's upper torso protruding through a gaping hole in the floor. I immediately woke up Ted and we both jumped from our bunks onto the floor. Olekk followed us, screaming at the man in the hole, "You son of a bitch, what are you trying to do, kill yourself?"

There was no time to lose, so we grabbed the man, who I now realised was the Russian recluse, and tried to pull him out with all our might, but the freezing wind was gradually pulling him out of the truck. Seeing this, Olekk stopped yelling and grabbed him as well, and we very gradually managed to start to pull him upwards. Then suddenly, there was a mighty pull as the man's feet touched the track and he was pulled out of our grip and through the hole to his death.

Olekk had given out an almighty scream as he tried to grab his friend's collar, and in the process his own arm seemed to bend the wrong way. We heard a small thud, and felt the vibration of the truck when the wheels ran over the unfortunate man's body, squashing him like a ripe apple. I felt quite sick at the sound and we quickly replaced the floorboards. Taking stock of the situation, we realised that the young Russian had probably intended to commit suicide. Olekk was very distressed and crying and told us that his friend had been hell bent on taking his own life. Apparently he had been raped by a whole cell of hooligans at Minsk prison, and was determined to stay out of the labour camps, where rapes were a daily routine, at any cost. We were now in a great dilemma about what to do next. If the guards came in the morning for the count we were in danger of being sunk. We felt that they couldn't but fail to notice the partly removed floor and that would be that. Our dreams would be gone completely and forever. In desperation we mixed some bread, saliva and ash from the stove, and then pushed the pulp into the holes in the floor to try and camouflage them.

To our delight, many inmates joined in and that was the time when we chose our escape group. Once our work had been done, we anxiously waited for the morning's head count. To our relief only one guard climbed inside. Due to overcrowding, the count was difficult at the best of times and with some diversions it proved impossible. He counted us two or three times, and every time he said there were more of us than there should have been. Eventually he got fed up and left, desperate to get back to his heated truck, saying, "You son's of bitches somehow multiplied last night."

At long last everybody could breathe freely, and we had a general discussion about what to do and who was going to escape. We all agreed that the first places should go to the younger inmates, as older men were less likely to be abused sexually by the mob. There were 11 of us who qualified for this, and we had a number of discussions and heated arguments regarding our final plans. It was eventually decided that we 11 would go first, and then lots would be drawn between the others to decide the order of exit from the truck. Finally, everything was fixed and ready. After this came days of anticipation, whilst we waited patiently for a long enough stop in the sidings for us to make our escape. After the unfortunate suicide, we were all suspicious and mistrustful. Every time somebody climbed down from their bunks to go to the bucket, practically everybody sat up and watched anxiously. Olekk was our navigator and watched all station names to try to figure out where we were. At the moment we seemed to be going due east and, as if through spite, the ruddy train was only stopping briefly for coal and water, and the head count was always done in the middle of nowhere. One of our inmates was a Roman Catholic priest and we all prayed with him for a nice quiet siding on a dark night that wasn't bathed in bright moonlight.

Our next stop was in the sidings at Minsk, but there was no question of escape as we were ringed by a number of guards with dogs and automatic weapons. Sentry boxes were placed on each side of the train and searchlights were trained on us all the time. We wondered what was going on until we saw the guards bringing over 200 inmates from a local prison. They then packed us all into the train like sardines, with 70 or so men to each truck. One of the guards told me, "You'll be glad of the crowd. Where you are going, you'll need a crowd to keep you warm. You are going north beyond the Arctic Circle."

To my horror I found out that the NKVD man from Slonim, who had been so keen to finish me off, had joined the train as a labour camp guard. I was summoned with my bag to dress the hand of the guard who had damaged his fingers in a sliding door and, to my delight, it was my old adversary who was suffering with a squashed and badly lacerated hand. He had already been attended to in the local hospital, but an unqualified doctor had applied bandages too tightly and the flesh had swelled up, making the dressing very tight and painful. After examining his hand, I told him that he was in danger of getting gangrene and losing his arm. Alarmed by the news, he got into a panic and begged me to do something about it, offering me 100 roubles to patch him up. Whilst bargaining he spotted a small diary I kept inside my shirt and told one of the guards to take it away. After this unfriendly act my price went up to 300 roubles, and I had a nasty surprise for him. I mixed about one litre of 95% pure alcohol with iodine, telling him it was a special sterilising liquid, and stuffed his hand in it, bandage and all. The howl of pain could probably be heard a kilometre away and he took off like a mad ferret, racing up and down the train swearing like a maddened bull. I quickly made myself scarce and went back to my truck. Within an hour they took me to the chief guard who had my diary on his lap and was wearing a very stern face. He said that it was obvious that I was a spy and that he had no option but to hand me over to higher authorities for investigation. I was then handcuffed and spent about four days in the guards' truck chained to a sturdy hook.

Once we set off again our progress was fast, as we soon arrived in Moscow, where we were pushed deep into a marshalling yard. I was picked up by the local NKVD guard and marched to the main goods station, where huge fluted marble pillars supported the roof and very large mirrors on the walls created an incredible visual effect. My head started spinning at the sight and I almost lost my balance. Within some ten minutes they had handcuffed me inside a dustcart and we were off to Lubyanka prison. Once inside, my hair was shaved and I was sent to have a shower. To my amazement I was even given a brick of boiled sweet-smelling soap. After over two weeks without even a decent wash the shower was heaven. Afterwards, I was given a heavily starched prison uniform that chaffed the inside of my legs so that they became sore within minutes. I was put into a cell which was small and solitary, but it was clean and smelt of disinfectant.

A clean-shaven, smartly-dressed guard smelt heavily of aftershave. He read out the prison rules and instructions, even though they were clearly displayed on the inside of the door. The folded metal bunk against the wall was to be up at all times, until the cell lights dimmed twice in the evening. When I was called out I had to stand facing the wall with my hands behind my back. There was no talking and all guards and officers had to be addressed as "citizens". I looked around the cell. It was whitewashed, and had a very small window near the ceiling, caged on the outside, so only a small slit of the sky could be seen from the inside. I remember it was about midday and outside was sunny with masses of cumulus clouds. I watched them hurry by with great envy, wondering which way they were going. After a while, by the position of the sun, I figured out they were heading west and suddenly I felt very lonely and vulnerable. All afternoon I walked up and down the length of the cell. By now my chafed legs were very painful, so I took off my trousers.

Eventually the short winter day came to a close and I could no longer see the sun from the window. A small low-wattage protected bulb above the door dimmed twice, so I dropped my bunk down and lay exhausted. The complete silence got on my nerves but I didn't have long to worry about it. Within an hour of the lights dipping, I had been called out, and was being escorted through a number of long corridors and into the room of my interrogator, which was both huge and incredibly clean. The floors were highly polished with beeswax and behind a very large, carved oak desk sat a Robin NKVD Colonel. He was smartly dressed and had charcoal black hair with dark eyes to match his complexion. He started by asking questions about my personal details, checking the answers with my papers in front of him.

Eventually he leaned back in his chair and, holding my very dirty diary in one hand, asked me, "And what is this? Well Galubczyk, I want to know the truth about this. Why are there so many names in it? Who gave you a pencil and notebook? Who were you going to give it to?"

When I didn't reply, he said in a very quiet and rather cultured voice, "You do know that we shoot spies, don't you." "Yes, I know", I replied. "I've seen enough men shot." He asked me where and under what circumstances. When I told him all the incidents I had witnessed he suddenly started shouting like a maniac, calling me a liar and told the guards to bring others in. Within a few moments, three more officers walked in and sat behind the desk. That was the beginning of my all-night questioning. They wanted to know everything about me. Who my father was? Where was he? Where was my mother? Where were my brothers and sisters?

I soon realised that, despite having my documents in front of them, they knew very little about me. On arriving in prison they found the 100 roubles I had got from the guard and the other 200 I hid in the truck before I was taken away. Where did I get 100 roubles from, they asked, and what did I want it for? There and then I decided to have a bit of mischief with my pet guard, the one who had got me into this trouble by having my diary seized, so I said that I had collected the money from other prisoners in order to bribe a guard to leave our door unlocked. When I was asked who the guard was, I replied, "I don't know, but he's got a bad hand." The Colonel wrote everything down and I signed the statement.

Daybreak was already showing through the heavily barred window behind the desk when I was eventually led back to my cell. I felt completely drained, both mentally and physically, but started taking stock of the previous night. I began to regret my statement regarding the accursed guard, as I felt there might be some further implications. But what the hell, what is done is done. One thing made me uneasy, however. Those interrogators were a different breed of people. They were still ruthless, but much more subtle. I suppose that's why they worked in the Lubyanka, the HQ of the NKVD in Moscow.

As it was daylight my bunk had to be up, so I lay on the floor and tried to sleep. For a long time I could not get to sleep through thinking of the previous night, but finally tiredness took over and I slept through the whole of the day. Eventually, the sound of my door opening woke me up. It was already dark and I was being summoned for a second night of questioning. It was then that I felt a deep hunger, as I had been given nothing to eat since they took me from the train. I found that I could not talk because my throat was so rough. It felt as if I had a handful of sand stuck inside it.

I croaked that I wanted some water and the guard gave me a big enamelled mug of real tea, very hot and strong. All four NKVD officers were given tea as well. Popping in their mouths a small lump of rock sugar, they started sipping the tea very loudly through their teeth. To my amazement I was given a piece of sugar and so attempted to drink my tea in the same way as they were, thinking 'when in Rome do as the Romans do', but I would definitely not recommend it. I burnt my lips and throat pretty badly, to the delight of the Robins. "Teach this son of a bitch how to drink tea or he will kill himself before we can shoot him," laughed the chief Robin. The remark amused them and they all howled with laughter. "You don't sip your tea loud enough," said the guard. "The louder you sip, the cooler the tea becomes before it hits your lips and the sugar lasts longer behind your teeth. I can drink three mugs of tea with one lump of sugar," he said proudly.

The general attitude and appearance of the Robins somewhat unnerved me. They were clean-shaven with clean and pressed, well-cut uniforms, cultured voices and the whole experience scrambled my mind into a lump of confused jelly. But, nevertheless, despite appearances the main stamp of the NKVD was still very much there. As always, they persisted in asking me the same questions and continued to insist that I was a spy. When they suggested that I must have been spying for the Germans, it threw me off-balance completely. It didn't make sense, as I knew how friendly they were with the Germans, with whom they had signed a non-aggression pact before the War. When I pointed this out to them, the chief said, "Some friends when they hug each other, hold knives in their hands at the same time".

On my nightly routine visits to "the office", as I called it, I gradually noticed that we passed some no-go areas, where I saw some inmates I had met before with unshaven heads. I wondered what crimes they were being accused of and whether their fates were more certain than mine. My all night visits to the office were very, very tiring and I would fall asleep so deeply when I returned to my cell, I started wetting my trousers before I could use the enamelled slop bucket. On top of being very uncomfortable, my bladder was always tight and under great pressure. After I had burnt my lips and throat with boiling tea, I had asked for cold water but was told that the Volga's water was bad at the moment, so I could only have tea. The chief asked me when I had last eaten. When I told him I had not eaten since leaving the train, he ordered the guards to bring me a plate of soup and a chair to sit on. The chair was especially welcomed as my legs were badly swollen.

The chair I was given was some sort of antique with a straight back and upholstered seat. I could not take my eyes off the pictures of Lenin and Stalin on the wall above the heads of the interrogators, boring right through me. I just could not keep my eyes off Stalin, who was in a peasant style army tunic, buttoned up tight on his neck. The Colonel in charge spotted this and asked me what I was staring at. Foolishly, I answered that the collar of Stalin's neck was too tight and he seemed to have a swollen face. As a result the Colonel got up, strolled behind me, and then suddenly grabbed both my ears and lifted me clean off the chair. Pulling my head hard back he calmly said, "Look at him. He is the next world saviour. The Romans managed to conquer Europe but he will conquer the whole world." Since then I have often thought about these words. Perhaps he was right and this gangrene of might will spread all over the world, like the bubonic plague. He held me up for a good 15 seconds, which seemed like an eternity to me, but eventually let go when a guard came in with a huge dinner plate of soup and placed it on my lap.

My ears were rather painful and I felt blood trickling down my neck. The plate was unbearably hot and was burning my thighs. In desperation I pulled a piece of old vest I had wrapped around my throat as a neck-tie and slipped it under the plate. The Robins didn't even notice, I did it so quickly. The smell of soup was overwhelming. It was a fairly thick vegetable soup with small cubes of fried pork fat floating on the top, and smelt absolutely delicious. A cast aluminium spoon was in the soup and there was no steam rising from the plate. I learnt well before the War that hot fat stops soup from steaming, so I picked up the spoon very cautiously. The steam immediately went up like a cloud. As my lips were still painful after the encounter with the boiling tea, I very cautiously blew a few times on the soup and brought it to my lips.

Remembering the guard's tip, I sipped hard and loud. Despite all precautions the pain was very intense and on the spur of the moment I exclaimed, "Oh, son of a bitch". The Colonel barked, "Who are you calling son of a bitch?" I quickly said, the cook who made this soup so hot. On that they all burst out laughing and the atmosphere improved until a further guard entered and handed over a piece of paper to the Robins. After examining it, the Colonel said to me that they had found the bribed guard and asked whether I would repeat my accusations to his face. I realised there was no way out and I had to stick to my story, so I said, "Of course I will", not even dreaming that they might bring him into the office. After a while the Colonel summoned the guards and barked, "Bring him in". To my amazement my pet guard walked in with a chair in his arms. He was told to sit some four feet from me.

Meanwhile, I was concentrating on consuming as much soup as quickly as possible without burning my lips. My badly bleeding ear was dripping into the soup on my lap and I heard one of my interrogators whisper to the Colonel, "Tough little bastard Pole. Are they all the same?" It gave me a great deal of satisfaction, as I was determined not to show any discomfort. Soon one of the Robins started reading my statement aloud and watched the blood drain away from the accused man's face. Suddenly, I saw him jump to his feet and braced myself, as I knew he was going to attack me. Automatically I raised the soup plate off my lap, so as not to spill it, and saw his fist flying towards my head. At the same time, I threw the heavy bowl of very hot soup into his face. His fist and my soup hit their opposite targets roughly at the same time. I felt a sharp pain underneath my ear and saw thousands of stars buzzing around me. When I came round I was lying on the floor with a guard standing over me, but there was no sign of the accused. I could not grasp what the guard was saying to me for a while, but eventually I came to my senses and looked around the room. Both chairs were overturned and there was congealed soup on the parquet floor. I wiped my hands across the congealed soup and licked them. The soup was cold and tasted better than ever. The guard said to me in a whisper, "Don't worry about the soup. I'll bring you some to your cell later."

Daylight was coming through the windows, so the night birds had flown and I was taken back to my cell. On the way I felt dizzy and unsteady on my feet as if I was drunk. The hard punch on the side of the neck must have stopped the blood from flowing properly to my brain and I felt really dreadful. Soon after, true to his word, the guard brought me some soup in a large container, which looked like a tin with a wire handle fixed to the top on both sides. The soup was as thick as porridge and smelt really good, but I was too tired to eat. I lay on the floor and immediately fell asleep. My aching bladder woke me up and I just made it to the bucket. My soup was still standing on the floor. I immediately started eating it like a starving dog. The soup was cold and good. I heard the door spy hole being opened and somebody observing me for a while. The door eventually opened rather quietly and a woman guard handed me a sizeable lump of bread. She said I was on the inmates list now and would be getting what I was entitled to regularly. She asked me what had happened to my ears and did I want a doctor. I'd enjoyed my feast of cold soup and bread enormously, but when she told me she had already dimmed the lights, I knew they would soon be calling me again. I hurried up as quickly as I could, and lay down on the bunk with the last piece of bread and some soup still in my mouth.

I woke up to feel somebody's finger in my mouth, raking the remains of the food out of it, and saw a middle-aged woman in a white coat above me. She said she was a doctor who had come to attend to me and was raking the food out of my mouth because she thought I was choking on my vomit. I replied that being so hungry, I was not in the habit of giving my food up this way. We had quite a talk and she asked me if I was a White Russian (the north-west part of Russia is called white Russia). When I said I was a Pole, she replied, "Oh, there are quite a few of your countrymen here, but they are all a lot older." I saw a glint of pity in her eyes and she asked me quietly if I was a Roman Catholic, and I replied, "Yes". After examining me and dressing my ears, she said, "They will heal OK." but added that there was not a lot she could so about the bad bruising on my neck and shoulder blades, except rub my neck with surgical spirit. Whilst attending to me she got a small Crucifix from her bag and gave it to me, saying that it would help me to get through hard times.

When I eventually had a chance to examine it in detail, the Crucifix looked as if it had been stamped out of aluminium with the figure of Christ faintly outlined on one side. I kept it on me always until I joined the S.O.E. in England, when it was taken away as they wanted to change my identity, and was destroyed along with all my other documents. But that is another story and, God willing, I might write about that at a future date. At the moment I am getting long in the tooth and so I do not know if I have enough time left to finish the complete story of my life. It was very important to me to put something down on paper, for the sake of my sons and my grandsons, even if I do not see it in print. The bunk had a very thin straw mattress but I slept like a log. Before I fell asleep I thought for a long, long time about that lady doctor. During our conversation I called her "Madam", and her eyes filled with tears. She told me sadly, "Nobody calls us women in this way any longer in Russia. When I was a little girl I remember my mother being spoken to with respect, but now it is not allowed," and that was when she gave me the Crucifix.

Since then she has often been in my prayers and thoughts. A great lady with some trace of humanity left in her veins. Thankfully, I was left alone that night and it gave me enough time to recharge my mental and physical batteries.

## Chapter 7 : Escape from an Arctic Gulag

Altogether I was in Lubyanka Prison for nine nights, eight of which were spent in the office with the Robins. Very little was said about my throwing the soup over the Robin guard, but further statements were taken regarding the bribery, with the same boring questions and the same parrot fashion answers. The prison food was pretty good in the circumstances, especially as I received some extra soup and bread from the girls who were employed as guards. I felt a bit ridiculous for a few days, as the pain in my neck meant I could not keep my head upright, but I had suffered this injury before so I knew I would be OK. On the tenth day, two guards like big bears came into my cell and handcuffed me with chains around my hands and feet. For a while I felt rather uneasy, as I didn't know what was going on. One guard put me at ease when he said sternly, "If you make any attempt to escape we will shoot and we never miss. Do you understand that?" Then there was a return journey to my goods sidings, this time in a lorry marked with the NKVD insignia.

To my complete astonishment my original train was still there, and they even threw me into the same truck I had arrived in. My friends' delight was overwhelming, and within a few minutes we again started to discuss our escape plans. Our transport chief guard called me to his truck and told me very strictly that I had made very serious accusations against one of his guards, but luckily nothing was proved because the 200 roubles I had mentioned was missing. When I told him that I could show him the money if he promised not to confiscate it, the chief guard threatened to send me back to prison. I replied, "Yes please, as the conditions there are better than the train", I took him to my truck, after he promised not to confiscate it, and showed him the hidden money. When I produced it, he called the accused guard "a proper black-marketeering son of a bitch", and told me, "For Christ's sake, shut up and don't say anything about it or you will never leave these sidings"

I was taken off duty as a felczer (unqualified doctor) and told, "You must have done something nasty to the guard's hand as he had to go to hospital in town for three days, especially when some bastard scalded him in prison."

Apparently, my pet guard did not admit that I'd thrown the soup over him. As I did not want to antagonise him further I let it be and said nothing. Within 24 hours, and after being manoeuvred to and fro on the sidelines for hours, we were off again. Our train grew in size to the extent that we could see two steam locomotives pulling masses of trucks when we cornered the bends. Another huge train with two engines was following us a half a mile behind and so we all realised that our destination was the Arctic Circle, and the infamous labour camps. Russian inmates who had travelled on this line before said there were great distances between major stations, so we began feeling very anxious regarding our escape plans as they were solely dependent on a long stop on the sidings of a large station. With the limited vision we had from the truck, we tried to observe the landscape and the night sky. While the train was negotiating bends we could see the North Star from time to time and we knew we were travelling nearly due north. We managed to get some coal and coal-dust from the side of the line when we were ordered out every other day for the head count.

One night there was great excitement as we heard gunfire somewhere in the front of our truck. Apparently a few inmates had broken out and were spotted very early by the guard and shot dead. I was called to help the Russian medic but there was nothing anybody could do. One of the escapees was barely alive with a bullet through his chest. While examining him closely I found a real treasure – a small Russian Army issue compass. Needless to say I pocketed it immediately, as I was worried about how I was going to find my bearings after our eventual escape, and possession of a compass was essential if we were going to make any progress. A map was another must, but there was no chance of pinching one, as even the guards didn't have one. Soon monotony began to get us down so we kept busy and fit doing press-ups and sit-ups, despite the overcrowded conditions. Our Russian inmates thought we were mad running on the spot for hours, but with temperatures still well below zero and plenty of snow on the ground, it kept us warm as well as fit.

The monotonous rattle of the train began to irritate everybody and gradually more and more heated arguments developed, making it increasingly difficult to keep our bunch of hooligans in order. Almost every day there would be a fight in the truck and so the iodine and spirit left in my first-aid bag came in handy to treat the injuries. Unfortunately two Russians took a shine to it and got helplessly drunk on the surgical spirit after stealing it from my bag. All hell broke loose when the guards found them drunk during a head count. One of the drunks spat on the guard and a fight developed. Eventually the guards managed to overpower them and the drunks received a pretty vicious beating with rifle butts and pieces of steel piping. One of them lost most of his teeth and was bleeding for hours afterwards. Eventually we stopped at a fairly big station, called Vologda, and decided to make a bolt for it, despite there being plenty of guards around. We quietly opened the floor and were about to jump on to the line when there suddenly appeared the snarling head of a dog. A second dog appeared seconds later and we had to abandon our escape bid. We closed the hole as quickly as we could and heard some guards crawling under the truck. We speedily tried to save the situation by rubbing some dust from the stove into the slits between the boards. It worked like a dream as the guards decided it was just falling dirt that upset the dogs and we were soon on our way again.

Staring out from the trucks we noticed the scenery was changing dramatically. We saw fewer and fewer houses on the side of the tracks until they disappeared altogether, and we could no longer see the woods. The winds grew very strong and icily cold. In a bid to keep warm and prevent the draught, we tried to patch the gaps between the boards. A lack of food also started taking its toll. A prolonged deficiency of essential vitamins meant that some of the inmates started to suffer with scurvy. Their gums became pale grey and swollen and eating, especially our ration of dry bread, proved rather tricky. The suffering individuals had to suck their bread as biting it was impossible. Hunks of dry bread were often covered in a green-grey mildew, which gave off a cloud of dust when tipped from the sack onto the floor.

One day we felt the train lurch to the right and we discovered we had started travelling due East. Kotlas was our next stop, but we only stopped long enough to take some provisions on board and two additional trucks were attached to the front of the train. One contained water and the other was full of coal. We were given the task of loading provisions and frozen coal onto the open truck with just two or three shovels and a crowbar. As a result, most of the work was done with our bare hands, which was very dangerous as the frozen coal could split your fingers. A number of inmates died in the following days due to gangrene, which could spread very quickly, and I was once again used as a kind of doctor. While at the station I became quite friendly with two locals employed as railway maintenance crew who spoke openly under the noses of the transport guards. When I asked why, they said, "Oh, those sons of bitches want some garlic from us so they have to keep friendly." It seemed that many of these men were ex-inmates of the labour camps who, after they had served their sentences were kept there. They told us that once a prisoner is sent up north, he never returns home alive. Some of the ex-prisoners become guards, some stay and get married to women ex-prisoners, but none were never allowed to go South again.

I asked them for some garlic but they wanted something in exchange so, after a quick consultation with Ted and Olekk, we took a long sheepskin coat from one of the hooligans in the truck. It didn't take me long to persuade him. I just told him that he could either have his coat or his throat intact, but not both. In exchange for the coat we got garlic, a huge sack of dry bread, a litre of spirit and about two kilos of frozen meat. This was obviously part of a dog as I could clearly see a bit of fur on the leg. It took us a few days to part cook the meat on our fire and then we ate it half raw.

The locals told me the markings on our truck showed we were destined for the last stop at Vorkuta, which was situated at the very tip of the Ural Mountains. Apparently, the scores of camps in that region were completely open to the elements. "You'll soon find that even God doesn't go there because it is too rough," one of the locals told me. After a lot of bargaining, we got a filthy quilted jacket, a piece of flint, part of a broken small file and a dried piece of tree fungi to make a fire with. But my most treasured acquisition was a page from a school atlas showing North Russia. It was very sparse in information but it showed enough for me to know where we roughly were. There on the top of the page was the tip of the Ural mountain range and Vorkuta just west of it. As for our chances of escape, the locals told me, "Don't even think about it. You will never walk across the tundra."

Now the tundra is a sort of desert that is found around the Arctic Circle, as well as to the north of it, where trees do not grow due to the icy winds and plummeting temperatures. There were a lot of my countrymen who thought they could do it, warned the local, but scores of them had frozen to death. As soon as we finished loading we were on our way again, travelling north-east as fast as the train could manage. On every stop dead bodies were thrown out of the trucks onto the sides of the line and just left there for the wolves to eat. The guards laughed about this, calling the bodies 'wolves' fodder', and, indeed, we saw packs of wolves running close to the tracks as if they were following us. The guards would often open fire on them for fun and killed or wounded a lot, which were immediately torn apart by the rest of the pack.

In our truck casualties started mounting quickly due to the spread of dysentery and gangrene, caused by frostbite. Thankfully our escape group kept reasonably well. Every bit of garlic we got was rubbed onto our meagre dry bread ration. Traces of garlic were also massaged into our gums with fingers and we tried to keep reasonably fit. More than anything, the crazy thought of escape kept us alive. Some of the other inmates, however, lost all hope and the will to live. They would just curl up on the floor and die quickly and quietly. There was no struggle for life, just an acceptance of their fate and a wish to die quickly. I had the unpleasant and revolting task to declare them dead.

When we travelled through Ukhta station without stopping, we were convinced that our last hope of escape was gone. Then one night, without any warning, our train suddenly stopped and started shunting to and fro. We quickly realised we were being pushed somewhere onto the sidelines. The excitement in the truck was incredible. Our escape group sprang into action and forced their way near the stove on the top of the loose floor. All our precious belongings were gathered and put together, including our warmest clothing and a small kind of rucksack that I had made out of the garlic Hessian sack. Soon the daylight came and the sun was so low we could see the very long shadows of the trucks and people walking around them. Two- wheeled hand carts were being loaded very high with all kinds of primitive furniture. There were stools, chairs, tables and long benches made out of clean, freshly worked wood. I realised we were at Pechora, famous for its furniture factory. We watched the activities all day. The furniture was loaded into the trucks, which were then locked and sealed with a piece of wire.

All the prisoners doing the work looked quite well fed and most of them had sheepskin coats on. I recognised them as being hooligans or members of the Russian Mafia. In our truck we had three Mafiosi left and we made contact with the outside through them. Two of the bastards were in good condition, but the third was on his last legs. I persuaded him to ask for help from outside and true enough, they recognised their kind immediately and told him to lower a mug or container out of the window. I lowered the biggest mug I could find in the truck on a string and within a few minutes there was a tug on it to signal that it was ready.

As it was getting pretty dark I did not bother to be careful how I pulled the string and felt a terrific explosion near to my hand, which became momentarily paralysed, like it had been hit by an electric shock. There was a big thud on the roof of the truck and I immediately realised what had happened. A guard had seen the mug and fired his rifle. Luckily the bullet missed my hand but hit a steel ventilator flap. The vibration momentarily paralysed my whole arm. The ricocheting bullet then hit the roof and went fizzing outside, whining on the way like hell. Ted finished the operation by getting the mug in. It contained some smelly kind of liquid with a few pieces of bread stuck in it. The stench of rotten fish was overwhelming. "What the bloody hell is this?" shouted one of the Russians. I knew only too well – fish soup. "It is refined cod liver oil, I shouted. "For Christ sakes don't throw it away." We took the top off our lid stove and in the dim light I began to distribute our precious food supplement. Everybody got a piece of dry bread with a teaspoon full of oil on it. Consuming it was another matter.

Even smelling it made some of the inmates violently sick. This added to the unbelievable confusion that filled the overcrowded truck. Somebody's stinking vomit hit Olekk on the neck and he in turn vomited violently on to his neighbour. It took a lot of control, but somehow I managed not to be sick and swallowed two pieces of dry bread soaked with oil. Even in this tragic situation there were some comical scenes. One Russky shouted, "Oh, son of a bitch, I just swallowed my teeth," and everybody burst out laughing. Apparently he bit the dry bread with his scurvy-infested teeth, which then fell out and he promptly swallowed them. I told him he would have to go to the toilet with a piece of rag to find them again. When he asked me what he would do then, I promptly replied that he could swallow them again to subdue his hunger, which was met with screams of laughter. "You stupid son of a bitch," he said. "I suspected you were mad, now I know you are." Well, what else could I have said in the circumstances; a stupid question deserves a stupid answer!

By now, we could hear the guards patrolling on the outside with their dogs. A few of them had climbed up onto our truck and stood on the lookout platform, having a smoke. We were wondering why they had picked on our truck's observation platform. The answer came late in the night when we heard a guard say to his mate, "Come up and warm your hands on this chimney. Those sons of bitches thieves must have nicked a lot of coal if they still have a fire burning." We decided that the following night our stove would have to be put out so as to get rid of this special attention by the guards. But it wasn't just our chimney they were warming their hands on. There was a brazier ten metres away where some of them were burning furniture. Despite all this, we decided that the following night must be the moment of truth. If we don't escape then, we would not escape at all.

The following day, bribed by the Russian Mafia outside the train, a guard opened our door and a whole sack of nearly fresh baked bread was thrown into our truck, along with a few packets of tobacco and one page of Pravda to make cigarettes with. We also got two bottles of fish oil with rotting fish floating in it. At the same time our chief guard came to ask if there were explosive experts in our truck. I immediately put my hand up and volunteered with Ted. We didn't know what it was all about, but decided to see if we could find a way to make a break for it. We were taken some two kilometres across the settlement, past the huge furniture factory, and out to the bridge across the river. Downstream the ice had broken up in a temporary thaw and the pressure of water had picked up huge slabs of ice, which rode high against the bridge. There were also huge icebreakers made of timber logs upstream of the bridge and two Russian Army engineers were standing on the bridge standing next to two barrels. When we came close one of the Russians explained, "It is quite simple. What I want you to do is to make the stuff in the barrel into a small ball, stick a detonator in it with a fuse, go on the ice where we tell you, light the fuse, place the explosives in a crevice of the ice and run like hell."

They intended to use plastic explosive with the consistency of soft plasticine to chip the mountains of ice so that it could flow under the bridge without damaging it. Really it was quite a stupid idea as the other side of the bridge was frozen solid, but that was their idea. The plastic explosives were put in two barrels covered in some kind of foul smelling liquid. The putty was rather loose and we could not make large balls to start off with, so we were told to mix it with sawdust brought from the nearby factory. Despite long stretches of under-nourishment we were still agile and it was a fairly simple task that we enjoyed in a way, especially as they gave us a good lunch of bread, one salted herring and a large onion. We were given half an hour to eat and allowed to go into the furniture factory boiler room. There, to our amazement, we found a countryman brazing broken handsaws from the machine shop. I immediately asked him for a knife and he handed me one made out of a band-saw blade, sharpened on his grinding wheel. I hid it inside my sock along with five detonators. The Pole also gave me four boxes of Russian matches that I stuffed under my shirt. It was getting dark when the guards called it a day and we were given a litre of soup each, full of fish bones.

The two Russians in charge of explosives were very pleased with us after we had made a big hole in the mountain of ice. Ted and I slipped and fell a few times but were only slightly bruised. After the meal and before they took us back to our train they told us to strip naked. Boldly I put my knife on the bench with my trousers and they found nothing on me. Unfortunately they found explosives on Ted, hidden in his crotch, and knocked him about pretty badly. They said they were going to attach the report to his documents and he would be charged with the offence at our destination. I didn't take my socks off and got away with my contraband.

We regretted having lost the explosives because it would have been nice to make a big bang later on, but we were given a loaf of bread each and marched back to our truck. We told the rest about the factory boiler room with the Pole working there and the massive yard where timber was being stacked. My heart started pounding and the adrenalin started flowing in anticipation of our escape bid that night. I checked and re-checked all my belongings. My weapons were the original bayonet and my new band-saw blade knife. For all I knew, we would most probably have to fight our way to freedom and made plans accordingly. The guards were mostly armed with automatic pistols called papashas, which were great from close range but inaccurate from a long distance. Before making our escape bid we checked that there were no guards warming their hands on our chimney, which there weren't as the boys had put the fire out. I was to go first and Olekk last. Carefully we removed the remainder of the floor and descended into the bitter cold outside. To my horror, I heard a commotion inside the truck as somebody shouted, "Guard!" twice, and I froze in my tracks. Carefully poking my head out from under the truck, I investigated but, as I couldn't see or hear anything, I gave the rest the OK to come out. They started jumped out onto the snow covered track like rabbits out of a bolt hole and soon all 11 of us were crowded near one of the single axle bodies, and I could see more people popping out. After a while we heard the floorboards being replaced by two partly disabled Poles who had stayed behind.

I found out that the shouting had been by the Russian hooligan whose coat we had bartered. He tried to call the guards but Olekk had killed him swiftly with a knife. Ted and I were shaking uncontrollably, partly because of the cold, but mostly through nervous tension. We must have crouched there for nearly half an hour before our next move. Our plans to get out of the truck were so well thought out that we had forgotten to plan what we would do when we eventually got out. Eventually Olekk, Ted and I jumped the distance between our line and the next and crouched under a goods truck. The light from the brazier some 30 metres away seemed to search us out and we crouched behind the massive truck wheels and waited for a chance to jump under the next train. The only thing we could hear was the squeaking the guards' boots some distance away. Suddenly, there was a bark and a guard shouted, "Halt or I will shoot." Immediately there was a long burst of automatic fire, some screams and the yelping of the dog. Seconds later came a massive burst of gunfire, the ricocheting of bullets and the screams of men. It seemed to go on forever but must have only lasted some fifteen seconds. Finally, someone screamed to stop firing and an empty drum of bullets rolled under our truck and nearly hit Olekk in the face.

Rattled, he ran on all fours and hid under the next train. One of the dogs spotted him and rushed past us, running towards Olekk. We saw the guard drop to his knees on the side of the truck and open fire from the hip. Bullets whizzed past us just a metre away. Inevitably a few bullets hit the wheel and ricocheted around us. Ted clutched his chest and fell next to me face down onto the snow-covered sleepers. The guard crawled under our truck, past us, and under the next train searching for Olekk. As soon as the guard's torso had disappeared under one of the trucks we heard a thump and saw his legs kick straight and lay still on the ground. Olekk had killed him with a knife thrust to the throat. My concern was for Ted, who still lay motionless on the ground. I lifted his head carefully up and saw some blood on his face. My very cold hands brought him round and he opened his eyes. He seemed to be short of breath and said he felt numb on the side of his chest. A ricocheting bullet had hit there and knocked him out. By feeling the hole in his outer quilted jacket I probed with my finger and found a hard lump in the quilting, which we found later to be a flat bullet. The guards appeared from all directions and started pulling corpses from under the truck next to us. They had killed 13 or 14 escapees.

They brought the brazier over to give them some light, very near to the wheels where we were hiding, and we could feel the heat from the fire. Some of the guards were only an arms length away from us but they ignored us completely. They were very agitated and swearing as they tried to determine the truck we escaped from but, as the floor had been replaced, could not find it. We decided to stay put where we were and wait until daylight. The transport medic came to examine the bodies of prisoners and spotted us. The blood in my veins ran cold. But luckily for us he felt there is honour amongst thieves and he said nothing to the guards and whispered to us, "Keep still and be quiet or they will kill you." The body of the dead guard was carried away and I saw in the dim light of the fire the knife was still sticking from the top of his chest. Apparently the medic was too squeamish to pull it out.

Silence eventually fell upon the scene of carnage and we started to feel very cold indeed. The temperature was well below freezing and I knew that if we didn't move before light we might freeze to death. I had quilted Russian trousers on me and Ted had a quilted jacket. At one point Ted even suggested jumping out from under the train so that they could kill us quickly, as that seemed preferable to dying slowly from exposure. So we decided to try to get away by moving very slowly. Ted's chest wound also affected one of his arms, so he laid on top of me in a piggyback fashion and I started crawling very, very slowly between the lines. It must have taken me more than an hour to cover just three metres. I could only use my elbows and toes to move along, but cross we did without being noticed. We found Olekk uninjured and skinning a dog's carcase, which had been shot, and he decided to keep it for food. It always amazed me how quickly the Russian lads could adapt to new circumstances and how strong their survival instinct was. We had managed to crawl under another train on the next line before daybreak and felt a bit safer. To my astonishment, Olekk was wearing a quilted hat, which he had taken off the guard he killed.

Even before daybreak we heard many steps around us and in the grey daylight we saw many civilians servicing the trucks. At one point

Olekk got up from under the train and started mingling quite openly with the others. Within an hour he brought us a big hunk of bread and some kind of smoked fish. He also made contact with a gang of prisoners loading furniture into cattle trucks and it was Olekk's suggestion that we should hide in this truck and travel south by train instead of attempting to walk. His reasoning was quite simple. There were no roads and we had no chance whatsoever of walking more than 20km across the tundra before freezing to death. So we got into one of the trucks that was partially loaded with furniture and had a good look around before making a final decision. While in the truck we saw a long line of handcarts being loaded into the cattle trucks and Olekk suddenly suggested that we should go to the factory with the gang of prisoners and empty carts. We didn't have the nerve for that, so he went alone.

Before he went, I told him about our countryman in the boiler room and he said he would do his best to contact him. He got back safely some two hours later, helped to unload the cart and went back again. On the second return he joined us in the truck and revealed his plans. He said he had made contact with local Mafiosi who promised to help us in our escape, and spent the following night planning our next move in detail. He urged that at least one of us must go to the factory with him the next day. Ted and I drew lots and I lost, so I set off to the factory with the working party. I nearly died of fright when we were counted at the gate, but somehow all went well and I found myself in the boiler room. The Pole turned out to be an army Sergeant sapper who was very willing to help. He would have liked to go with us, but knew his escape would be discovered immediately as he was always wanted there. He explained that he and a helper had stripped the clothing from the dead bodies of the prisoners that had been killed under our truck when their bodies were brought in for burning. There were Russian quilted jackets and trousers for us, which were ideal to keep warm.

I lost my nerve and did not go with the first lot of furniture back to the train but, to my amazement, Ted arrived back on the return journey. We kept out of sight between the mass of machinery in the boiler room. Somehow the Russians had adapted a steam locomotive to propel all the machines in the factory. Ted brought with him the interesting news that my NKVD guard from Slonim was looking into every crevice on the sidings searching for me. His hatred towards me was at least as great as mine towards him, and he had offered a reward for our capture. The last load of furniture was eventually ready to go and we decided to head back. I told Olekk about this special adversary of mine and his reaction was swift. "Well, let's kill the son of a bitch when he comes near our wagon."

We had to change our hiding place as our original truck was now filled with furniture and sealed. The new truck was a lot better but it had a partially burnt floor in one corner, covered with steel plate. While transferring to our new truck Ted accidentally kicked an empty tin used for carrying soup by the prisoners, which started off the dogs' barking. A few guards came out with a smouldering brazier to investigate. To my horror my NKVD man was there with two other guards, discussing our escape. He was certain that some prisoners were still alive and hiding. There was a change of guard and one of them was preparing to go when his restless dog sensed our presence nearby. Luckily, it was ignored by his handler.

Meanwhile, my special guard had decided to climb into the wagon for a closer look. Like a fool he took his automatic pistol from around his neck and laid it on the floor of the truck, so as to have both hands free to climb in. In a flash Olekk grabbed the gun and hit him over the head with the short butt. Without a sound the guard fell backwards onto the truck. For several minutes we didn't dare to move. Then, to our horror, we heard the groan from the wounded guard. Olekk thrust a knife into my hands and whispered, "Go and finish the son of a bitch off or we shall all be dead." I looked down from the truck door and saw he was moving slightly. I jumped down and looked closely at my bitter enemy. For some reason I just could not bring myself to stick a knife into his throat. Seeing his helpless body lying on the snow-covered ground, my hatred somehow melted away and I could not force myself to kill him. If he had sprung to his feet suddenly, I would not hesitate to finish him off, but not like this. I had a close look at his head. Seeing how hard Olekk had hit him I could not understand how he had survived. What saved him was his Red Army issue quilted soft hat.

All this type of headgear had a soft peak on the top, like German helmets in the First World War. His head was split and was bleeding, but that soft peak saved his skull from being smashed. We had a rather hurried conference as to what to do next. Olekk was quite adamant that we should not let him go free. He said that Ted and I didn't realise what those bastards stood for and how vicious they were, they never forgave or had compassion for anybody. Once you were in their bad books you were as good as dead. On my insistence we pulled him into the truck to decide later what to do. He regained consciousness in 20 minutes or so and Olekk started a conversation with him. When asked who he was and where he came from, he started pouring his hatred out to Olekk about the Polish bourgeoisie. At the time he didn't know that I was in the truck and could hear him but, as he spoke with a white Russian dialect, I understood him perfectly. He said that he could not trust anybody as somebody had shopped him for black marketeering, selling goods from the Red Army stores of confiscated items, and that as a result he'd been sent to the North as a guard.

The meagre brazier outside went out completely and in an hour or so it started getting light. We heard a cart being dragged outside and suddenly our wounded guard screamed, "Comrades, help, I am being murdered". Olekk sprang on him like lightning and stuffed a piece of rag into his mouth. Luckily the men with the cart did not hear him. They came back with a further load and Olekk told them we had got a machine pistol and two drums of ammunition, and started to try to barter it for some provisions. The bargaining was short and very lively. The leader of the working party said they would bring the supplies back with a further load of furniture later in the day. Sure enough, they brought quite a variety of supplies consisting of fresh and dry bread, fish oil in bottles, some smoked fish and a small bag of coal. On the suggestion of the working party leader we stripped the wounded NKVD man of his brand new clothing and left him dressed in some very old rags that we had got from the boiler room.

It was fairly dark when Olekk said to me, "Well, now is the time to get rid of this son of a bitch," pointing to the NKVD man. He said that nearby was a railway tank partly full of surgical spirit and we had to throw him inside. It was a difficult job to drag him under two trains and up the steel ladder on the side of the enormous tank. Eventually we opened the top round flap and dropped him in. I slammed the very heavy cover down and that was that. Since then, I have often wondered if he was ever been found. The liquid of surgical spirit is usually used for preserving flesh tissues, so if he was found he would have been well-preserved. Olekk told me not to worry about it as guards and prisoners frequently fall into the cisterns while stealing alcohol. Apparently a lot of distilled alcohol is being transported this way and the local guards periodically check all tankers on the very massive sidings.

Eventually we settled down in the corner of the truck with furniture packed all around us, so that our hiding place would not be discovered. As they hadn't finished loading our truck we had to spend the night in very cold weather with the doors wide open. After a seemingly endless night, the same work gang came with a new load of furniture in the morning. In their wisdom they also brought a big open tin of tea from the factory. Without asking anybody's permission, they lit the empty brazier outside and put our tea on the fire. It was well into the afternoon before it boiled and it was very welcome.

During the day guards came and went and were ignored by everybody. To Ted and me it seemed so unreal to be hidden in the truck under the very noses of the heavily armed guards. Olekk busied himself with cutting the meat off the guard dog's carcass into thin strips, so that they could freeze. Frankly, I was not very keen on dog's meat, but Olekk said it might save our lives. Eventually our truck was packed solid, the doors were shut, then wired and sealed. Olekk was a master of improvisation and took complete charge of us. I had total confidence in him. He said that the biggest danger while on the sidings was that we might freeze to death. To combat this he said that the only way out was to combine our body heat together. So we stripped to our underpants and huddled together under any covers we could lay our hands on every night. While stationary at Pechora, waiting for the train to form and go south I was very nervous in case somebody from the local gang of prisoners spilt the beans to the guards, but luckily nobody did and we started moving south.

The truck's ventilators were fully open so we could observe the fields from the moving train. The driver was rather rough and used his brakes rather viciously a few times so the packed interior was forever shifting. The cold was very intense and no amount of clothing could stop us from shivering. We had two tins with us and we made a few holes around one of them and made it into a kind of mini brazier. We then shaved and chipped the wooden furniture for a mini fire. The small amount of smoke was rapidly sucked out through numerous slits between boards and out of sight ventilators. We could only put one tiny piece of coal on at a time, as it gave off dense smoke. We were only able to do this when the train was travelling so as to make sure that its movement would suck out the smoke quickly. Hour after hour we sat around our fire, keeping our hands on the top of it. Periodically, we took off our boots and kept our feet and hands near the fire at the same time. The most, unpleasant times were when we needed to go to the toilet. Even this problem was quickly resolved by Olekk, who tore small pieces of cloth from our spares items of clothing, and we threw them out of the ventilator once they had been used. I was all for throwing the carcass of the dog out, but Olekk was adamant that this would be a folly, so he cut all the flesh into thin strips about 6 inches long and laid it near the big gap of the sliding door for freezing. The flesh would freeze solid in a very short space of time. I packed some of the meat into my Hessian haversack and we cooked some on the fire. We found that the bones would dry fairly quickly and burn well, giving off a lot of heat but no smoke.

Olekk's Russian was different to mine but we could understand each other very easily. He could not understand how and why before the War we were allowed to travel from place to place in Poland without permits. Apparently even in peacetime the authorities in Russia had a phobia regarding spies. Every stranger was a spy and that was that. He told us that political officers would tell them that the working masses in Poland were exploited by the kulaks, bourgeoisie and American agents. Even in those days they had a mania regarding the USA. Olekk was a barely educated man and he could not understand why Russia was completely surrounded by the enemies of the people. Everybody who did not agree with their system was classified as an enemy of the people.

He was horrified when I told him about our 1000 hectare estate. He was shaking his head in disbelief and actually ignored me completely for a few hours. He said that even comrade Stalin or Beria did not have so much land. There was another sinister fact of life I discovered in that cold, Godforsaken truck. Every time Olekk mentioned the name of Stalin or Beria his eyes glazed over like the eyes of a cornered animal about to be killed. He argued that the showcase court cases of high-ranking officers proved that even in Russia there were bitter enemies of the people hiding everywhere, even in the Military. Whatever brain Olekk possessed, it had been washed clean and bleached. Our stories eventually had such an effect on him that one day he said that he now knew that there were more enemies of the people than he thought at first. His attitude to human problems and his way of thinking reminded me of my great-granny; a very religious person who believed that whatever happened to anybody was God's will. In Olekk's eyes everything that happened in life was the Party's will. He was rather uneasy when we talked about religion and could not understand what it was. He could not understand why his dear grandma and granddad had an icon hidden in the loft and spent many hours praying to it.

He said that his granddad nearly died when his house caught fire and dashed to the loft to save his icon, while his grandma taught him how to pray and cross himself. Despite his loud protestations, I once caught him crossing himself in the Orthodox manner and he said shyly, "Well it can't do any harm, can it?."

When I asked him how old his grandparents were he said sadly, "Oh they are quite old and I think that by now they must have been taken for the "sleigh ride". As I had never heard that expression before, I pressed him for further details. Apparently, when a person gets old and a burden to their families, they are sent to sleep on top of the bakers stoves in the houses, then dressed in a huge sheepskin coat, put on a sleigh with a horse and taken out for a ride in the forest. Then suddenly they are pushed off the sleigh and the sheepskin coat whipped off. Olekk explained that it was quite quick and painless as the temperature is usually at least minus 40 degrees. The tradition was illegal and you could get fined 100 roubles if caught doing it. You were also forced to pay for the coffin if the body was found, but he said the Russians were clever and waited until there was a pack of wolves in the district to eat a body. To him, this was quite simple and natural, but Ted and I were shocked at the revelation of this type of euthanasia practised in Russia.

We soon adapted well to our new conditions hiding amongst our furniture. There was an adequate amount of food to survive, although our water started running out. Luckily, drifting snow blown through the gaps in the floor formed long ridges which we scraped eagerly and turned into water. Ted and I were very perturbed about how the hell we were going to get out from this prison, but "something will turn up" was Olekk's philosophy. We were, however, all anxious about where and when the truck would eventually be opened. There were sliding doors on both sides of the truck, but they were sealed from the outside, which meant there was no way we could open it from the inside. We suspected the name of the truck's destination was written on the outside, but we could not see it.

One night the train stopped for a while, so the engine could pick up some water, and we could see a railway man on the outside of the truck with an oil lamp in his hand. Without hesitation, Olekk asked him what it said on the outside of the truck. The man, on hearing the disembodied voice nearly had a heart attack and said in a shaking voice, "Moscow". This upset Ted and me as we knew it would be very difficult, if not impossible, to escape unobserved from the massive sidings there as there would be much higher security. Olekk didn't seem to care and said: "Well, we'll have to kill a guard or two to get away, so what? But don't worry, thieves will rob our truck for sure, well before we get to Moscow."

A few times on the journey we saw people around the train, but a guard would fire his rifle a few times and they kept away. Eventually, the train stopped at a big junction off Kotlas and we were pushed on to a sideline next to a northbound train with prisoners on board, so the guards remained vigilant to stop thieves from stealing from our train. We were in a great dilemma about what to do about the fire, but the cold was very intense so we had to risk it. One of us was always waving a piece of rag to dispel the smoke and I personally prayed for something to happen. Eventually, the prison train next door departed and we heard somebody carefully opening our sliding doors. "Oh, son of a bitch, it is full of furniture," said a voice from outside. "Oh hell, I don't want furniture."

While they were talking, Olekk pushed through the furniture to the thieves and told them, "Hey, comrades. Get me some tea from the tearooms in the station, or even some water." The very startled man said, "Where the hell did you come from?" "Never mind that," replied Olekk. "Just get some tea I will give you a padded jacket for it." It was a brave thing for Olekk to do, and oh, how dearly he paid for it.

The man departed hastily and Olekk was pleased with himself. "You see, I can arrange anything," he told us. We heard somebody whistling and I saw two men ducking under the train next door. Olekk rushed to the door and, poking his head out, said, "Here comrades". I was standing on a stool no more than four feet away when there was a thump and Olekk's head practically disintegrated. A split second later there was loud report of a fired rifle and his body fell limply out of the truck. Ted and I huddled together, afraid to breathe. The two railwaymen had reported the incident to the local guard, who ambushed us and shot Olekk through the head. They pulled poor Olekk by the legs and disappeared with his body under the tracks next door, followed by the guard with the rifle. At that moment I wished we hadn't exchanged the automatic gun for our food at Pechora. I would have killed all three of them without worrying about the consequences.

## Chapter 8 : Two On Our Own

The shock of the incident brought tears to our eyes in a flood. The two of us were left on our own with no idea what to do next. Very reluctantly, I realised that it was up me to get us out of the predicament. I was now thankful for my long conversation with Olekk about Russia. There was one thing I was certain of, that passes were needed for any movement in Russia, even for visits from one village to another more than ten kilometres away. In view of this, I decided that we must avoid contact with all human beings. It was vital to get our proper bearings so we both looked for the North Star. We became very thirsty and so eventually slipped quietly out of our truck and self-imposed prison, and scraped some dirty packed snow between the railway lines to quench our thirst – a most depressing thirst. Within a few hundred yards, we found a frozen river and railway bridge running due east-west. Despite our legs feeling weak and stiff, we crossed the frozen river quite easily and followed the track due west. Here we found what looked like a yacht club and decided to have a close look at it.

There was a metal chimney protruding from the roof and a round patch of clear snow around it. This showed that there must have been a fire lit there quite recently. The door was held shut by two pieces of wire twisted together, which indicated that there was nobody in the building, and so I carefully undid them and we walked in. The intense heat and stench of sweat hit our faces. A large tortoise stove was lit in the middle of the room, with its centre ring taken out. In the very dim light of the stove I could see a wire cage around the stove full of steaming rags for the feet and, to my horror, some Red Army padded hats hanging by the stove to dry.

The wooden floor was quite squeaky, despite us moving very carefully. Suddenly, Ted grabbed my elbow and put his finger to his lips. We froze to the spot and listened. My heart skipped a beat when I heard the gentle snoring of more than one man nearby. We decided to beat a hasty retreat and Ted opened the door, which he thought was to the outside. To our horror we found ourselves in another room with moonlight streaming into the room through the window. There were several pairs of skates and sticks propped against the wall. It was then I realised that a Red Army unit was occupying the hut. I now recognised another smell – the sharp odour of stale vodka from the breath of sleeping men. They must have had quite a party. We were just on the point of departing when we heard someone swear outside the door, and realised it must be a soldier returning from guard duty. We swiftly moved to the darkest spot in the room, crouching next to the skis and hoping for the best. Only then did we see a row of machine guns hanging on one wall with rounds of ammo stacked on a lower shelf. The very cold returning guard went into the sleeping quarters and started calling somebody by name. His replacement came through wearing his long Johns, dressed near the fire and headed out of the door, twisting the wires together to secure it. So, to our horror, we found ourselves trapped inside the building with the Red Army asleep in the next room. My brain tried to override the panic I was feeling and soon a solution presented itself quite nicely. The bedroom door opened and two sleepy individuals came through. One, without a moment's hesitation, started urinating into the tortoise stove. The stench upset the other, who said, "You lazy son of a bitch. Can't you go outside to do that? You will suffocate the lot of us." He went to the door and tried to open it, swore again and put his shoulder to it, and it opened with a bang. Without going outside he urinated through the partly open door and they both went back into the dormitory. We decided to make ourselves scarce immediately, but the thought of meeting an officer coming to inspect his charges froze the blood in my veins. I was determined not to be captured alive, so I took a machine pistol and grabbed a magazine off the shelf. In my haste I knocked the next magazine onto the floor. An enormous bang echoed round the hollow under the floor. Immediately a very low voice shouted, "Shut up you son-of-a-bitch and go to sleep." His unanswered advice still rang in my ears when we rushed out of the building.

For the moment we had to crouch low to get our bearings from the North Star and spotted a guard some 50 metres away in the direction that we wanted to go. So we made quite a big detour and found our railway line. Only then did Ted show me three pairs of fur Red Army issue gloves. He also pulled out of his pocket a partly drunk bottle of vodka. While I was practically dying of fright in the hut, that bastard was calmly robbing the Red Army of their equipment and booze. We were making good progress walking on the frozen dyke next to the railway line. The line was fairly highly elevated so I climbed up to take a look around and saw the sparsely lit town of Kotlas. As the stars in the sky started to dim to foretell the coming day, we started looking around for somewhere to spend daylight hours. I realised that having a good lookout was essential in the circumstances. Unfortunately, Ted was short-sighted, so it was left to me to observe any possible danger. Soon after daybreak, we heard the steel rail track humming quietly, announcing the arrival of an oncoming train. We hid in a stack of reeds and found it nice and cosy. Whilst waiting for the train to go by tiredness struck both of us with its full force. In the previous 12 hours we had lived through traumatic experiences, losing our friend and finding ourselves trapped with the Red Army, and now it all started to catch up with us. As we had got into the stack in a hurry, we didn't protect our hide very well from the cold so we decided that at the next big stack we'd make ourselves a proper hide and stop for the day. The train, as if for spite, stopped just outside our hide at the traffic signals. I saw a long train, consisting solely of cattle trucks with side vents and mini chimneys sticking out from each one.

I spoke to Ted but got no answer. He was sound asleep. As the freezing air bit my face, I realised that unless we got warm we would be dead in an hour. A sharp penetrating whistle from the locomotive woke me up and the train started laboriously moving off. I hadn't even realised I'd fallen asleep for a while and, now the train had gone, I woke Ted up and said we must move on. After a while, and a few slaps on the face, Ted eventually came to and we started our walk again, even though all our muscles were stiff and painful.

Ted wanted to stay and rest but I could see a bigger stack in the distance, so we increased our speed as much as we could. We were some 200 metres away when we heard an oncoming train and, with our last reserves of strength, sprinted towards the stack. However, what I thought was a reed stack turned out to be a railwaymen's hut, made from upright railway sleepers. We crouched behind and, to my astonishment, it felt quite warm to the touch. There was no sound coming from inside, so we went in to see what we could find. In the middle was half of a huge steel drum, full of burning slabs of peat. The heat was very intense. There was no chimney, only a narrow slit in the roof through which the smoke and fumes were escaping. A huge samovar was boiling away on the side of a big wooden barrel of water. Hanging from the strop on the wire, we saw a large piece of half-cooked and half-burnt meat and two huge loaves of bread were spiked onto nails sticking from the wall. I decided there and then to stay put and, if necessary, to hold the railwaymen against their will. After all, I was now armed with over 120 rounds of ammunition. Outside I could see a broken platform and a set of wheels on two axles. I realised that this was a lightweight hand propelled inspection unit, which railwaymen used to inspect or repair the track lines.

Ted busied himself with his sharp knife and was cutting into the meat. We could not bite with our sore gums, but just swallowed huge lumps of the meat which turned out to be only half-cooked, being carefully not to upset our teeth. Suddenly, we heard some noises on the line and saw the maintenance men coming back on a spare trolley. They were pumping hard on the double-armed propelling shaft of the unit. One of the men jumped off near the hut, and three others carried on down the line, towards the station without stopping. The man who got off, stamped his feet outside and walked in. He didn't see us at first in the dim light and started undressing, taking off a belt, which was laden with tools, from around his huge waist. He dropped it on the floor with a bang and noticed the meat was nearly all gone. He swore in an agitated voice, muttering: "Those thieving sons of bitches are at it again." Looking around the hut, he spotted Ted fast asleep and rushed towards him with his arms outstretched. Almost immediately, he stopped dead in his tracks. I had my gun pointing directly at his gut. His arms dropped to his sides and the shocked look on his face reminded me of someone who had just woken from a nightmare.

"Comrade, there is no need for that. I will not hurt you," he said. As soon as I opened my mouth to speak, he knew who we were. "You Poles are mad," he continued. "There are scores of you on the run and some are half naked for this kind of weather. We don't see the spring here until May, and many of your friends are freezing to death. If you are serious about escaping, I will tell you all you need to know about how to survive. I would have escaped from this hell a few years ago, but where can I go?" he shrugged. "If I go back to my village I will be back up North within days. I served my sentence of seven years and now I have got to stay here for another five years. You see I lost citizen's rights for seven years and, with no papers, I am less important than a dog." It appeared that we were very lucky to be still alive, as he told us that one kilometre further along the track was an underground bunker full of soldiers with sniper rifles, who would shoot to kill anybody approaching illegally, without warning.

"They shot the deer that you ate from a great distance. Some times they shoot pure white foxes, which are very good to eat, and they sell me the skins," he said with a smile. "I can cure the skins myself and sell them back to them in exchange for different goods." He was very talkative and would not stop chattering. Shortly, my eyes started to close, I was so tired, and he suggested I should have a sleep. Pointing at two railway sleepers that were fixed flat near the lower part of the hut, he said, "Get your friend on one and get up on another. You will be safe here."

The railwayman enquired anxiously where I had got the gun from and when I told him, his reaction was, "I said you Polish sons of bitches are mad. Do you realise you pinched the gun from the barracks of the Red Army who guard all this district?" We pushed the half-asleep Ted on to one of the shelves, and I climbed onto the other and within seconds I was asleep too. Loud arguing voices woke me up. For a moment I could not think where I was and very nearly fell off my railway sleeper. The voices outside were agitated and the makeshift door opened slowly. Our friendly railwayman Misha came in backwards, followed by two Red Army men in full uniforms. They kept on arguing about money they wanted for the carcass of a dead fox. The railwayman would not give them the demanded amount because the carcass was badly damaged by a bullet and it had been left frozen for too long. The soldiers' heads were so close to my shelf that I could have grabbed their hats with an outstretched arm. I took the safety catch off my gun and was preparing to have a shoot-out, but luckily for all concerned they never looked up above their shoulders. The only light was coming from the peat fire, which by then was covered with white ash, but even so, it was fantastic luck that they didn't notice us. Misha stuck to his guns and would not budge from his original offer. Eventually, they struck the deal and, true to Russian tradition, each of the soldiers got a bottle out of their pockets and drank most of it in a few minutes. Misha went out with them and brought in a whole deer's leg, saying, "Those sons of bitches are getting very greedy and wanting too much for the carcases. But never mind, I've got some venison for your journey."

Misha said he agreed to stay in the hut and keep the fire going because he was a bachelor. His mates would be back in the morning, so we would have to leave by then, especially as there was an informer amongst them. Ted and I slept fully dressed and were sweating profusely on the high shelves and now we had climbed down, I found that my legs would not support me and one of my shoulders was hurting. Ted also felt rather knocked about. Good old Misha came to our rescue again.

"Well, you will just have to stay here. If need be, I'll throw the son of a bitch informer under the train," he said. "We are all fed-up with him anyhow, and have been considering doing just that for some time. But it might not be necessary, I will try and send him on a job further down the line." When we took our sweat-soaked clothing off, Misha fished out a piece of boiled, sweet smelling soap and gave us a small empty tin to bathe in. So Ted and I had the unsurpassed pleasure of using warm water, a piece of linen as a flannel, and some soap to wash ourselves properly. I couldn't even remember when I last had a proper wash, most probably in Lubyanka prison. Some ingrained dirt had formed a thick skin, like on a snake, and was impossible to shift it all in one go. Despite this, all the exercise was well worthwhile, as it improved our mental attitude and morale.

Misha got an attack of verbal diarrhoea and would not stop talking. He taught us survival tips that became invaluable in the weeks to come.

He said that the sparse population in this part of the world were very sympathetic to escapees and would always help if possible.

It was well into the next day when we heard the maintenance trolley approaching. Misha was watching the line coming from the town, and when it was close he told us excitedly that the informer was not on the trolley. When they stopped outside, Misha went out to speak to his mates. He came back and said that the informer was ill and had gone to the doctor in town, and that the rest of the gang were willing to help us. They then came in and greeted us with great excitement. For a time they all talked together and I could not grasp what they were saying. On hearing about the pains in our limbs, they all agreed that a good rub with pure spirit would do the trick. As they had none in the hut, one of them volunteered to go back to town five kilometres away and fetch some. One man took off the extra rag cladding around his boots so he could walk better and set off to town to buy the spirit. Ted and I then tried to get the circulation going in our painful bodies. Some rags dipped in hot water from the samovar were used to rub our numb limbs. The man with the spirit arrived before long and they rubbed us down with the stuff, bringing great relief to our aching bodies.

The rail workers gave us some of their long johns and long-sleeved vests. Clad only in underwear, Ted and I climbed onto our bunks and slept very soundly. The Russians were great tea drinkers and must have drunk gallons of the stuff while we were there. We had two more visits from the guards, but they talked to the gang outside. We spent another night in the hut and every moment awake was taken up by Misha's talking. The Russian lads had a great sense of humour and told us hundreds of jokes about the NKVD, militia, collective farms, etc. I found that, generally, the Russians were very helpful and jolly people. They hated any kind of authority and were very brave. As for helping us, they would have certainly been shot if we'd been caught with them, but they couldn't care less. Misha warned me against walking near the railway line, as there were many patrols on the line, or near it. He told me to just keep the line in sight and, some 40 kilometres away to the west, there was a water point where engines took water and coal on board. If we went due north from there, we would find a large village consisting wholly of ex-prisoners, who were usually very friendly.

So very early, whilst it was still dark, we set off from this friendly hut. They all advised me against taking the gun, so I left it behind with Misha, who planned to say he'd found it and then sell it back to the Army boys. We started due north for some 800 metres and turned due west again. We were lucky that there was no recent snowfall on the ground and the snow was well packed and firm. The temperature when we set off was minus 18C, which the gang said was a mild day. We were determined to cover the distance to the station in one day, so we pressed on as quickly as we could. By the time it started to get dark, we were near our goal, which was clearly visible in the distance. There was a big structure where coal was stored, and after a brief rest and getting a bearing on the star, we struck due north. Soon after, the wind got up and started blowing hard. The temperature dropped noticeably and, after some hours of rapid marching, we started slowing down. The wind whipped up the snow and was very troublesome. It practically stopped our breathing, despite us placing pieces of rags in front of our faces. We were straining our eyes in case we could see some light on the horizon, but there was nothing, and began stumbling over even the smallest unevenness of the ground. The terrible pain in our limbs returned with a vengeance and I started believing we would never make it. I had to fight very hard to not just close my eyes and go to sleep, as we would have quickly frozen to death.

We started punching each other on the arm every minute or so to keep ourselves awake and alert. It was well past midnight when I saw some sparks flying into the air. At first I thought I was imagining things but after walking another few metres, I saw a dark shadow right in front of us. I rushed a few more steps and collided with something hard. It was some kind of building with a sparse covering of reeds on the outside. We started looking for a door feverishly and eventually Ted found a simple wooden cleat which, when pressed down, opened the door. It turned out to be a typical Russian sauna or bath house and in the corner was a pile of still warm stones and a dead fire underneath it. There was a kind of chimney above the fire making some ghostly noises. We were too tired to eat, except a few bites of bread so we sat down next to the stove and fell into an uneasy, nightmarish sleep, apprehensive of what the day would bring.

I woke up from my uneasy sleep as something kept pushing me on the chest. When I opened my eyes the first thing I saw was the sharp end of a Dutch hoe thrust menacingly near my throat. I raised my eyes very slowly to see who was holding this nasty weapon. To my great surprise I saw a round, kindly-looking woman's face surrounded by an abundance of grey hair. The face and hoe somehow did not match. The woman said in a cultured Russian voice, "Where did you come from and what do you want?" As soon as I explained our intrusion a smile appeared on her face and she said, "You Poles never give up, do you? And which camp did you escape from?"

I felt there was no point in keeping anything a secret so I told her the truth. She said that the nearest labour camp was some 100 kilometres away and all the Poles must have escaped, as there must have been at least 30 going through this village. She herself was an ex-secondary schoolteacher who had settled in the village because one of her sons had served his sentence in the nearby labour camp, and she came to join him when he was ordered to settle there after his release. Her husband had died in the camp through heart failure. "A lot of men are dying through bad hearts," she winked. All deaths in the camps were described this way by the authorities, whatever the real cause. There was a single line rail into the village, and there were a few large buildings where they stored grain of all kinds. A lot of this came from the Polish territories. She was a very intelligent woman, well educated, with a very flexible and clever brain. All the first day was spent on talking on different subjects, and she eventually wanted to talk about life in Poland and religion. She remembered the Revolution very well and described the terrible slaughter of all the Intelligentsia and the Russian Orthodox Church clergy. Russia, she told us, had moved the clock back at least 100 years and would have difficulty in catching up with the West, if indeed they ever could. The Communists tried very hard to stamp out religion, but all they succeeded in doing was to drive it underground, and she was convinced that the Russians' belief in God remained so deep that the authorities would never succeed in destroying the Church. At least once a week, she lit a candle in front of an invisible icon, which was well hidden in the house, and had heard that there were secret seminaries where priests were being trained.

We drank tea and chatted all day, and enjoyed some salted pork and meaty stew. It was too dangerous for us to go to her house as there was a Red Army unit guarding the grain and they were all on the lookout for the crazy Poles who had escaped from the labour camps. Her real name was Olga but in conversation we called her "Mamushka", meaning "mother". She was very knowledgeable about Russian geography and knew that there was a huge lake that barred the way to Finland. Her sons knew the lake pretty well as they took grain to a port there, and had told her it was frozen. It was some 100 kilometres across and very dangerous as it had been mined by the military.

The main fuel in the house was peat bricks and some of them were stacked up in the bathhouse, which was warm and cosy. Early in the afternoon, there was a knock on the door. Two Army boys wanted a bath but she sent them packing without opening it. As soon as it got dark she said we could come into her house, but we must be careful and quick. The house was a ground floor only building with an enormous brick stove in the middle, which was used to cook and sleep on during the bitterly cold winter. The heat was overwhelming. Ted and I noticed a small space under the stove that we could use if we needed somewhere to hide in an emergency. We tried it out by managing to squeeze into it, feet first. Olga had a small kind of hurricane lamp which helped her prepare lessons for the local school, where most of the pupils were illiterate members of the Red Army. We talked well into the night as she was helping to plan the next leg of our escape.

Well after midnight we heard her sons returning from their trip and we dashed under the stove in double time, despite her assurances that it would be alright. There was a lot of thumping outside the door and the two men walked in and kissed their mother in greeting. She asked them about the trip and one of them said, "Those crazy bastard Poles are running around the tundra everywhere. We met three of them half frozen and brought them on the truck to the edge of the village." She listened and said very calmly, "Two of these people you call bastards are in the peat store," pointing under the stove. Their mouths dropped wide open in disbelief. One of them bent down and put his hands into our hide. He touched my head and, as a joke, I growled like a dog.

"Oh, son of a bitch", he screamed, pulling his hand out. The old girl told him off severely for swearing and said, "Come out lads. You will be safe."

Then came lots of tea and, of course, more talk. They were very amused and quite surprised regarding our adventures so far. One of them said that they knew Misha, as one of the boys had spent nearly two years with him in a slave camp. "He is a fine fellow, who will never betray anybody to the authorities, especially Poles. We all have a lot of sympathy for you, as thousands of Poles were brought up North to the camps. You are not very good survivors in the camps as you always fight the hooligans, but you are very good at running away. There must be hundreds of your countrymen running around everywhere. You cause a lot of problems for the army and some of them are very angry with you."

They agreed to get us some skis and showed us a route map to the lake, which was 360 kilometres away. We all agreed that we should be able to cover the distance on skis in six days. Then there was another 100 kilometres across the lake, which they confirmed was mined on the far western side. The Finnish border on the other side of the lake was only some 150 kilometres and would be a piece of cake on skis. "For your efforts so far you deserve to escape so we will help you all we can," said Boris, the eldest son.

They brought us skis and camouflage suits as soon as it got dark and one of them pulled out a painted board with 'scarlet fever' written on it and hung it outside the door. "Nobody will bother us with this notice on the door," Boris said with a smile. And true enough any visitors departed very quickly after reading the sign.

We rested for a few days before setting off but I could not sleep or eat properly because my death cell memories came back to haunt me with a vengeance, and I suffered violent headaches and vicious stomach cramps. The old girl gave me a small amount of vodka with wormwood weed soaked in it, but this just got me drunk like a mad dog. On our first day there I apparently walked out of the house and the old girl brought me back from the other end of the village. After that Ted started keeping a special eye on me, in case I did it again. Ted and I were going for longish walks in the evenings across the snow covered fields to keep fit, and we came across a huge grain store. We could see hot shimmering air coming out of the top square vents and small open doors. Through pure curiosity we decided to have a quick look inside. There was some kind of very dim light in there. On the outside there were braziers at each corner of the building with guards standing next to them. I could not believe my eyes when I looked inside.

There was literally a mountain of grain just dumped on the earth floor. Despite the low temperature outside it was quite warm inside, as we could feel the heat coming from the heap of grain. I was amazed to see that all kinds of grain were mixed together, including corn and sunflower seeds. We stayed inside for some ten minutes until we heard squeaking snow under somebody's boots. On looking through one of the many gaps between the cladding boards, we saw a very fat man with his arms outstretched directing several geese along the side of the building. The man was swearing and talking to the geese. "You sons of bitches keep together or you will end up in somebody's pot," he said. The nearest guard shouted to the man, "Hey, comrade, give us a goose for our supper. We are fed up with venison". "Go to Siberia, and join the NKVD," came the answer. "I've got no geese for you." We heard some footsteps and jumped behind the huge stacks of empty Hessian sacks. I looked up and watched in amazement as five men climbed down from the top of the mountain of grain. The fat man walked in through the door and said to the men, "I bet you sons of bitches were asleep again on the job." Denying it they said it was time to go home and soon the next shift came into the store, picking up huge wooden shovels and climbing on top of the grain. Nobody took any notice when we departed soon afterwards. We told the old girl and she explained that grain was being brought from all over the place, sometimes on open railway platforms covered in snow. It was unloaded and then dumped on top of the already massive heap of grain inside. The men were shovelling the grain from place to place to prevent it from overheating. The authorities sometimes brought prisoners from the labour camp to shovel and turn the grain, but too many of them tried to escape, so mostly local villagers were employed.

The pay was good but the main attraction was you were given the right to shop at the Army store, mainly for tobacco.

The days were passing very quickly and the time was fast approaching for us to make our last dash to freedom. Olga was very busy making us vests out of the soft cured skins of Arctic animals, which were very light and warm. Ted and I made two trips to the railway line and back of some 30 kilometres to get used to skiing again. We both found the trips quite easy and we soon found our ski feet again. During our second trip we found the incredible value of white camouflage coats. We spotted an Army patrol going in the opposite direction and, despite the fact that we were only some 300 metres away, they didn't spot us at all. We just sat on our heels for some ten minutes and were completely indistinguishable from our surroundings.

Before we set off, I stupidly decided to steal one of the geese for the pot. On the railway line next to the building, there were a number of empty and partly unloaded covered railway trucks with sliding doors wide open. I jumped in and lying down on the floor of one of the trucks, I planned to grab one of the fat geese passing underneath it. Within minutes a bunch of geese went past the truck and I made grab for one, but over-balanced and nearly fell out of the truck. The geese made a hell of a racket and sped away.

My second attempt was much more successful and I managed to catch a bird by the neck. Its weight surprised me and I could hardly manage to pull the damn thing into the truck. Once inside I decided to break its neck. Holding its body between my knees and holding the beak tight so it could not make a noise, I twisted its head a good four or five times one way. Feeling the goose quite still I let the head go. To my complete surprise and horror its head spun round in the opposite direction, as if wound up like a spring, and it then made the loudest horrible noise. Its screeches in the empty wagon were like a prolonged thunderclap. I grabbed its head as quickly as I could and, after a struggle, finally broke its neck. With it stuffed in a Hessian sack I dashed back to the house. Olga thought I had taken leave of my senses and told me off. She said that the only way to get rid of the feathers and down was to burn them, but the wind had to be in the right direction, as otherwise the whole village would smell the burning feathers. Instead of pulling the feathers out, she very expertly skinned the goose with most of the feathers intact and stuffed the skin deep into the snow near the bathhouse to wait for a kinder wind. Ted, Boris and I had a fantastic sauna the day before our departure. We managed to get rid of all the ingrained dirt, mostly from our legs and arms and beat ourselves and each other with twigs all over the body to make them smart and red. On the very last night I didn't sleep a lot as we kept going over and over our route. Boris knew the way very well and was extremely helpful, telling us to follow the tracks of his tractor in the snow. He even gave us details of the landscape we would encounter so we could navigate.

Olga insisted that we spent the last hour in the bathhouse in front of the icon praying. I remember thinking, "Here we are, in the 20th century, in a medieval bathhouse, praying in our own ways to a 200-year-old icon and asking for a safe last passage from a living hell." Olga made a fantastic stew with the goose and by freezing some of it in her bread-making tins, we took some with us on the journey. After a few last adjustments to our skis and tender goodbyes, we set off. Olga, in a flood of tears, blessed us with the icon wrapped in a piece of cloth, so nobody could see it, as we set off with haversacks made out of Hessian sacks on our backs. The going was very good and brisk. The snow was well packed and even at night and you could clearly see the deep tracks of Boris' tractor in the snow. In an hour or so, when it became daylight, we increased our speed, as the grooves in the snow were more visible. He had made tracks in the snow all the way to the lake while delivering grain a fortnight ago. Our first planned stop was over 40 kilometres away in an isolated trappers' place.

We were warned against going to the house as sometimes an Army Patrol would stop for a rest and it might not be safe. To our astonishment we reached our goal well before dark and found a big stack of peat bricks and settled down for the night. After a fairly restless night, we were up and off well before daybreak. Our second leg was much longer, some 60 kilometres away, and it took us all day and into the night before we got there. It was a very isolated peat store where we spent quite a comfortable night by firing a couple of bricks of peat, which smouldered all night, giving off enough heat to keep the frost away. Another night we spent with two cows in a stable on the outskirts of a town called Konevo. The cows seemed to be pleased about our intrusion and we all kept ourselves warm together. In the morning they even provided us with warm fresh milk, which was very welcome. As far as I can make out from my practically unreadable diary, it took us eight days to cover some 400 kilometres. We eventually arrived very tired but in good spirits at Vytegra, which was located on the big lake. There was a safe house some six kilometres north, where there lived an ex-prisoner well known to Boris. We found the place quite easily and were greeted with open arms after showing the man a short note from Boris. Everyone called our new companion Kalmuk. I felt at ease with him straight away and he spoke White Russian, a language mainly spoken around our state before the War.

He pulled out a huge bottle of home-made vodka and insisted we had a drink, which gave us dreadful hangovers the next day. Our new host, like all Russians, had verbal diarrhoea and was forever describing the horrors of the labour camps, where he had spent a few years. His hatred towards the NKVD was as great as mine, if not greater. After all, he said, you have known them for a few months, but I have known them for years. He was passionately against the regime and the NKVD in particular, who he called 'devils of the earth'. From him, I learnt some of the real sinister aspects of Russian society, such as the Red Army's use of dumdum bullets, strictly forbidden by international agreements. When one of these bullets hits any part of the body it practically explodes. He said our friend Olekk had been hit by one of those bullets, which is why his head seemed to blow apart.

We told him about our plan but discovered that the lake could not be crossed by skis because of a slight thaw. It was a great blow to us, but he told us not to worry as there was a specially adapted light tractor unit going across the lake with a few sledges. Within a few hours he had found out all the details. The last sledge convoy would depart in a couple of days and private individuals could attach their own sledge to the tractor, and get it across by bribing the driver. Kalmuk was well connected locally. He had relatives in Leningrad and he was well informed as to what was going on. I asked him how so many people were held in terror by a comparatively small number of secret police, and he put it down to a system of terror. Masses of informers had been recruited by blackmail or intimidation. As nobody knew who the informers were, nobody was fully trusted, and a quarrelling society was easier to control. He also gave me an insight into the very sinister policy of kidnapping Polish children and bringing them up as Russian citizens.

The Russians and Germans were attempting to destroy the Polish tribe, which had been a thorn in their side for centuries. My mother, who re-settled in Russia, and others, confirmed the policy of the Communists to separate children from their mothers and place them in orphanages run by Russian staff. When in 1942 and 1943 the Polish Army, which included prisoners of war and labour camp inmates, was allowed to leave Russia under British command, thousands of young children were kept back by the Russians, and most of them never returned to Poland after the War. Even children who could prove that their fathers were in England were kept in Russia forcibly. As a result, there are many thousands of men and women in Russia and Germany who don't even suspect they were born to Polish parents and were kidnapped as young children.

Kalmuk and his friend stuffed bricks of peat on a very large sledge in such a way that a large cavity was left in the middle. There was just enough room for Ted and I to squeeze in and stay there for the 100-kilometre journey across the frozen waters of the lake. We were given one more contact on the other side, which was a district close to the Finnish border, but after that we would be completely on our own. I was warned that there were even more informers on the other side and no ex-prisoners were allowed to settle there. During our last night I went with Kalmuk to check on the fish traps he had set on the lake and, when we got back, we cooked fish from them and spent the rest of the night eating it and drinking home-made vodka. It was still dark when Ted and I were helped into our hide on the sledge, which was very cramped but cosy and warm. Our sledge was then attached to the end of the convoy of five or six sledges. At the beginning it took a long time to gather speed, but soon after we were going along at break neck pace. I was wondering what would happen when the driver decided to stop and the possibility of us jack-knifing was a reality I could not get out of my mind.

After only some three hours travelling we heard a signal from his horn and heard the brakes being applied by different brake-men. The whole stopping manoeuvre was done so expertly that our sledge finished no more than one metre from the bank. We pushed aside the sack with straw, which was blocking the way, and scrambled out, taking refuge in a low building on the bank, used for storing peat. Soon after, two Russians entered and started unloading the peat from our sledge. Somehow they did not see us. Either they were blind or were so used to seeing human cargo it didn't bother them, as their own countrymen often travelled without official permits from place to place. Maybe they thought we were heading to Leningrad as one of them said loudly, "Take left turn from Lenin to Leningrad", before leaving.

We walked into town but decided we must not speak to anyone as we would be immediately recognised and reported. The settlement was fairly large with some 400 houses of all shapes and sizes. We walked briskly on snow-packed roads and soon came to the square, where there were full-sized statues of Stalin and Lenin. We walked past a large number of people queuing outside a provisions store when a very thickly clad woman said to us, "There is another woman queuing after me." I answered in a garbled noise and just walked past. The woman seemed to be satisfied and spoke no more.

To our horror we saw two policemen ahead of us, checking documents in the queue. It was already getting dark and, thankfully, the police must have taken us for an Army patrol with skis on our shoulders and white coats on. At the last house of the settlement we put our skis on and checked our bearings. After establishing the line on the horizon was about 300 degrees we pressed on as quickly as safety would allow. Somebody must have been looking after us from above as within two hours we came across an isolated house. The occupant must have been a trapper as there were small dead animals hanging from a hook near the door. There was also an outbuilding where peat was stored, and we decided to spend the night there. The sound of a barking dog woke us up. It was an Army patrol and, from the conversation between them, I discovered there were a series of observation towers nearby, which were very difficult to spot as they were made of whitewashed wood. From then on we only travelled by night and by compass.

It was an exhausting fortnight and we lived on our nerves, especially when we rested in the open. The distance should have been 150km, but the amount of observation towers meant we had to make massive detours to avoid detection. The last few kilometres before the border were the worst and we had to crawl at times to get through the lines of towers. Frequent alarms by the dogs, who smelt us, were ignored by the guards, as there were many tracks made by wild Arctic animals.

We saw only two buildings on our way and were too afraid to approach them. We eventually came to within striking distance of the border and, after avoiding a lot of Army vehicles, saw a board saying, "Attention - Border Zone. Any unauthorised person will be shot on sight without warning." Soon afterwards, we saw smoke rising from the middle of nowhere and abandoned our skis, hiding them under the snow. We crawled a good mile and saw a building completely covered in snow. To our amazement a large Army patrol left there with two dogs and went towards the border. We rested on a one-metre square straw mat that must have been blown away by a strong wind, observing the movement of the troops. The pattern was always the same. Every two hours the soldiers would return to the hut, presumably to eat and rest, and be replaced by another lot. I crawled towards the hut after one lot of soldiers departed. There was a big partly-burnt log fire in the middle and a huge black steel cauldron with some stew hanging from above as well as sacks of dry bread, the staple diet of the Red Army. I quickly signalled Ted to join me, and he crawled inside.

We filled a couple of empty plates and ate like wild starving animals. Ted was on lookout when he shouted that some vehicles were approaching. We dashed into a wood store next to the hut and crouched down as far as we could get from the door. To our amazement, a number of men in prison garb got out of the truck's trailer and started unloading logs. Two guards were standing nearby with automatic pistols in their hands and rifles slung over their backs. Soon logs of all sizes started raining in on Ted and me. One hit me on the head so hard it knocked me out. I came to with Ted rubbing my face with snow.

We'd been completely covered by logs and Ted had dragged me out and brought me back to consciousness.

Soon afterwards the soldiers came back to the main building for a rest. They immediately started a party with cases of vodka left by the truck. Two of their dogs went completely berserk, as they could smell us in the wood store. After prolonged and vicious barking somebody came out of the main hut and took the dogs in saying, "There must be a son-of-a-bitch fox somewhere and the dogs can smell him." The troublesome wind was whistling through our hide and freezing the blood in our veins. Eventually an NCO got everybody out and they all went towards the border, which was only 500 metres away.

As soon as they left we started crawling on our bellies towards the woods some 200 metres away and saw soldiers patrolling a no-man's land, which was about 500 metres wide. We both realised that the moment of truth had arrived. After all the agonies of our escape we had to cross the last 500 metres. For a while, we contemplated just running as quickly as possible. Ted was all for rushing this last obstacle, but I was sure there would be machine guns hidden somewhere. We decided to wait for the guards to change, as we could have a better chance of slipping through the cordon. While we lay there, observing everything, a barking dog suddenly dashed through a barbed wire fence as if it wasn't there. A guard was swearing and pursuing it, but stopped at the wire and fell flat on the ground, keeping still between its coils.

We didn't have to wait long to find out why. There was a massive explosion and a loud scream from the dog. There was a fountain of dark soil cascading from the sky everywhere. We realised the dog had set off one of the mines in no-man's land. Within minutes two trucks arrived with strong spotlights and started combing the terrain, and we saw torch lights on the other side of the border. Soon the sky was filled with falling snow. This was a Godsend for us as it quickly obliterated the dark earth exposed by the explosion. The solitary guard left near the gap in the barbed wire went to relieve himself among the trees a few metres away. And I realised our time had arrived. It was now or never.

We crawled quickly towards the gap and in a few minutes we were crawling along, line abreast in no-man's land. We realised it was a minefield, but hoped that by distributing our weight over a larger area we might not set off a mine. The falling snow covered us completely and we literally disappeared into the surroundings. Ted was at practically an arms length away to my right and we were nearly there when my face touched something that felt like a taut wire. In a split second I realised it was a mine trip. I screamed at Ted, "Mines - stop". I tried to move sideways towards Ted and stretched out my arm towards him. My hand brushed the wire and there was a massive and sudden explosion. Ted just disappeared from my vision and I thought, "Ah, he must have dashed the last few metres to the Finnish side." In a panic, I kicked off my boots, jumped up, and started running like a man possessed. After several metres I realised I was sprinting the wrong way, towards a burst of machine gun fire. I realised my mistake, turned round and started running the other way. Within a few seconds I collided with a taut wire fence and fell heavily backwards. Before I could recover, I had been grabbed and was being dragged by my feet somewhere. I tried to get up but was jumped on by a big man in white overalls. I felt a burning sensation in my chest and neck and realised I was losing consciousness. When I came to, all I could hear was a high pitched whistling noise in my ears. I was lying on a bed, surrounded by strangers in funny uniforms. One of them was bending over me and I could see he was talking to me, but I could not hear him. He wrote something on a piece of paper and put it in front of my eyes. I could see it was written in Russian but, as it was not printed, I could not read it. I tried to speak but could not utter a word, as all I could hear was the terrible noise in my head.

When I woke up again, I could not believe my eyes. There was a Polish Army Captain standing above me. After unsuccessful attempts at conversation, he wrote on a piece of paper in Polish, "Where did you come from?" I groggily picked up the pen and wrote down how I had got there. The Captain told me he was a military attaché in Finland and that my dear friend Ted had died on the mine. There was only his blood stained Russian hat left, which had been blown across the fence into Finland. After identifying it as Ted's hat, I asked for my own, as it had my diary in it. They told me the hat had blown off my head in the explosion but they promised they would look for it. For some days I slipped in and out of consciousness. I just could not believe that after such a long journey with Ted he had died just a few metres from freedom. In the following days the noise in my head gradually decreased and I partially regained my hearing and speech. One of the Finns spoke Russian and told me what had happened. Apparently the exploding mine had killed Ted instantly and blown my body some five metres away. After getting up and running I had collided with their border fence and become entangled. They had grabbed me by my feet and dragged me onto the Finnish side of the border. The Captain asked me about Ted and I got very distressed, as I could not even recollect the shape of his face. A few days later another two Polish officers in uniform came to see me and filled in the details. They said that by rights the Finns should return me to Russia as an escapee. Apparently the Russians had forced the Finns into an agreement that all escapees must be returned, but as I was a Polish national they would try to obtain a Polish passport for me. After a short and very nervous period I was told that permission had been granted and my passport arrived, and I started travelling across Scandinavia. Looking back, that part of my journey went past like a dream. It seemed to me as if I was unconscious all of the time.

I eventually landed somewhere in England, I believe it was Hull, in May 1940 and then travelled by train to Blackpool. It was confusing at first and I had problems working out where I was, as whenever I looked out from a train to see the name of a station, all I could see were signs saying 'Gentlemen' and 'Ladies'. It took me a long time to gather myself together and start functioning in my usual way. The loud whistling noise caused by the explosion persisted for a long, long time. Eventually, my youth and strong constitution overcame all.

My notes miraculously survived and were sent to me in a big brown envelope while I was posted with the Polish Air force in Great Britain later in the War. I was debriefed many times about my experiences in Russia and was eventually told not to communicate any of it to anybody, in accordance with the Official Secrets Act. But that was a long time ago and it has taken me more than two years of unbelievably hard toil to tell this story. Finally, after my dramatic recollections, made with the help of the tattered pages of my diary, I will briefly take stock of my general impressions of Russia and the Russian people.

The regime is the most oppressive system in the galaxy. It is corrupt and rotten to the core. Its one aim is to spread its diseased beliefs throughout the globe and its disregard for human rights is an essential catalyst to keeping the masses subdued and subservient. I believe fear is like heroism, very difficult to define. A small percentage of individuals can control both and become heroes, others become cowards. The Communist Party knows it and takes full advantage of the fact. It condones, and indeed encourages, every human weakness to its own advantage but, like all deviant trains of thought and action, it will fall like the others did. But when it does, the resulting bloodbath will be too horrific to even imagine, making the 1917 Revolution seem like a Sunday School picnic in comparison. The members of this cancerous regime know this and are in constant fear of the future. They realise that as they showed no mercy to the millions who were murdered in the labour camps, there will be no mercy for them on the final judgement day.

Now let's turn to the masses in this living hell. All the peoples of Russia have this peculiar subservience in their blood. They were slaves in the Tzar's time and they are more than slaves now. And yet their unconquered will to survive helps them to overcome all the difficulties and tragedies of everyday life. They are born defiant fighters against oppression with no guns in their hands, but hatred in their hearts. My first eight months in this hell was not my last encounter with the Russians. After my physical and mental recovery I was destined to return to my personal purgatory under the orders of the Polish section of SOE (the Special Operations Executive). I was to go back with a Polish Army unit formed before Germany's attack on Russia. That gave me a chance to get to know the Russians quite well and I found they are a most remarkable people indeed. Their ability to adapt, survive and overcome the everyday hurdles of life is truly remarkable. Their hidden sadness and sentimentality is portrayed in their songs and art of all kinds. Their dumkas (folk songs), which have been passed on for centuries, from generation to generation, immortalising all the great events in their history, are very moving and sentimental. The Second

World War was no exception. They sang about their unsung heroes who defeated the German hoards with bayonets. Most of the blood of the twenty million Russians who died was spilt aimlessly and for no reason. They were thrown into massive battles, fought with practically their bare hands, by pigeon-minded Communist leaders, just to show the world the supposed strength and superiority of the Soviet system. All of this occurred while Stalin and his hatchet men enjoyed the good life in Kuybyshev and Saratov.

So, to the ordinary people of Russia, I give you my grateful thanks for the gift of life. Without your help, in defiance to all in authority, I could never have survived the first months of the War. As a parting shot to those in charge, there is no hiding place for you and your followers in the future. It is not enough to bury yourself in a casket in a wall in Red Square. If there is a God above us, you will have to stand before him and give an account of yourself. Well before then, descendants of your cancerous regime will have to face their fellow countrymen who will sit in judgement on them.

# Part 2

The following is the second part of Joe's remarkable story, written by him a couple of years after he finished the preceding chapters. It was dictated and transcribed in the same manner as the first part and details the second part of his War following his escape to England in 1940.

What follows are his words, with nothing added, and they continue his incredible untold story.

## Chapter 9 : Freedom in England

I arrived in Hull in May 1940 after my miraculous escape from Russia, through Finland and Scandinavia. I was physically and mentally exhausted after everything I had been through since the outbreak of war some eight months before. During that time I had experienced the invasion of my Country firstly by the Nazis and then by the Communists and had fought and killed invaders from each side. I had been captured, tortured, starved, thrown into a series of hell-holes, interrogated, sentenced to death and finally sent to an Arctic Gulag for a term of 25 years. I had endured a long journey in a truck on a cattle train to the foothills of the Ural Mountains and, following my escape, had endured another train journey back almost to the gates of Moscow. I had skied some 350 kilometres and crossed a lake to finally reach safety in Finland. That eight months had taken its toll on both my physical and mental well-being. I was the only survivor from the eleven who had made our escape from the train.

I was examined in great detail in a local hospital and was found to have some irregularities in my shoulder joints, as a result of the interrogation by the NKVD after the Russians arrested me in 1939. The doctors who examined me arranged for my arms to be strapped in a fixed position, making me feel like a trussed capon on a butcher's slab. I also started receiving physiotherapy treatment in the hospital, which was to continue for many months at different places. I was also interrogated by Polish Military Officers about my experiences since the start of the War. At that time there was a massive flood of Polish nationals into Britain, most of them fighting men, who had escaped through Rumania and Southern Europe into France, after the collapse of the Polish forces during the German blitzkrieg into Poland in September 1939. A Polish civilian I met, shortly after my arrival in Hull told me that a new Polish Government was being formed in London and that Polish pilots were already being formed into fighter squadrons to fight the Jerries. As I was not then an official member of the Polish forces, I asked immediately to join the Air Force. I had attended two gliding courses before the war and had successfully completed a flying scholarship so was keen to fly. I was told that, for the moment, I would be sent to a holding unit to wait for the selection board. To my amazement a parcel of my personal belongings was sent to me, containing three small books in which I had kept notes of my travels in Russia. By now, my Russian saga just seemed like a bad dream, but when I started reading my diaries, the past came flooding back with a vengeance.

I spent four weeks in Hull and it was a very sad and lonely time for me. My recent past, my horrific memories, and my lack of English did not help, and so I felt very isolated and unhappy during my early time there. However I felt that my luck had changed for the better when I struck up a close friendship with Mary, a physiotherapist from the local hospital, who was treating my shoulders. She was not in her first flush of youth, but was very kind and loving. We had great difficulty in communicating, although our mutual knowledge of a little German, learnt at school, helped a lot. She lived near the River Humber with her elderly mother and I spent many hours looking out of her bedroom window watching the boats go up and down it. I often scared her half-silly with my nightmares. She was a well-endowed lady and every time I woke up upset, she would hug me close to her and nearly smother me in the process.

In the backyard of their house was a small shed where four chickens were kept and so we had plenty of eggs – scrambled, poached, boiled, you name it. At the time Mary was good for me, giving me a thin thread of sanity and reality that kept me going, and I think I was good for her. At times she was rather overwhelming in bed, especially after massaging and manipulating my shoulders, which seemed to trigger off other activities on her part. One day, out of the blue, I was visited by a Polish Army Captain and ordered to sign the Official Secrets Act and told to say nothing to anybody about my Russian experiences. According to him, I was the first Pole to have escaped from Russia through Scandinavia and he wanted to know a lot more about every detail of that escape. For some reason, perhaps because my experiences of the last eight months had made me suspicious, I said nothing about my diaries. In our talks he mentioned my friendship with Mary and warned me not to get too involved with her. He told me that her family originally came from Ireland and that she wanted to marry me. This scared the living daylights out of me; I was only just 18 at that time and had no intention of getting married to anybody for a long while. I knew that there was a war with much fighting to be done and I was very anxious to get into the action.

So far I had been on the receiving end of the Russian invasion and I was anxious to get my own back on them. I was making good progress with my English, and with my German and the use of hand signals found that I could communicate with Mary quite well. Not that we did a lot of talking about our mutual interests. But, as everything in war has a beginning and an end, our idyllic existence came to a halt. The same Polish Captain who had lectured me previously arrived from London and told me I was to report to a holding unit in Blackpool, where my selection for the armed forces would be completed. He brought a railway warrant with him and agreed with Mary's pleas that she could accompany me on the journey.

The last night at Mary's house left me with a swollen and sore left shoulder, but it was well worth it. I packed my very few possessions into a small brown cardboard suitcase and we caught a very overcrowded train out of Hull. We arrived in Blackpool late the following day and found a small pick-up truck waiting to pick us up. The driver, a Sergeant, spoke to me in Polish, telling me I was to be billeted in one of the town's guesthouses, a pleasant semi just off the seafront. On arrival Mary had a long talk with the landlady who gave us a room practically overlooking the sea. We could also see the Tower ballroom, where I was to subsequently spend many days and nights dancing. Within a few days the Sergeant had arranged for transport to take me to a nearby RAF station for a selection board. To my dismay, he told me I would have to go on my own, saying, "Don't be daft man, you can't take your girlfriend with you." So I set off in an RAF car accompanied by two other Poles. Our driver was a girl in RAF uniform with beautiful, highly-scented chestnut hair. I manoeuvred my way so as to sit next to her, much to the dismay and annoyance of my companions on the back seat.

We spent our first night in a large dormitory with many other recruits. As the following day was a Sunday we were all gathered on the ground next to a huge black hanger for church parade. I had met quite a few other Poles at the station, so we all stood together. All Catholic and other non-Church of England personnel were told to fall out and stand facing a hanger, while the C of E's said their prayers. It was so humiliating and reminded me so much of my time in the Russian prisons, where one always had to stand facing the wall in the presence of guards. I was told that this was standard practice adopted in all military barracks and RAF stations on Church Parades.

The next two days were very memorable for me. I was asked to do a few simple sums, had an interview through an interpreter, and got my uniform, identity card and RAF cap with white flash. I then signed the Official Secrets Act again and was sworn in as a member of His Majesty's Forces. Separately I promised myself I would attempt to chat up the RAF driver on my way back to my billet so thumbed my way through an English-Polish dictionary for ages to find the right thing to say. However that all went to waste when, none the wiser as to the results of our final selection, some 20 of us were taken back to Blackpool by lorry, The truck dropped us at our headquarters in Blackpool, about a mile away from my billet, and there we were screamed at, in Polish, by a Sergeant who called us all kinds of peculiar names. I resented the fact that he dragged my father into his rant. I showed my disapproval in sign language that was unfortunately spotted by one of his Corporals so, instead of being released from the parade in peace, I found myself dragged in front of the Commanding Officer, who promptly confined me to barracks for seven days. I made a mental note of the eager Corporal who had got me into trouble. Before being dismissed by the CO he said, "Oh, by the way, you will find your girlfriend gone. I can't have a civilian living in an RAF billet." I felt very tempted to punch him on the nose at this news, but fortunately the calmer side of my nature prevailed and I refrained from this foolish act. I was told that I had been selected for pilot training and would probably go either to the US or Canada for my flying course. This news cheered me up and temporarily made me forget about seeking revenge on the Corporal, but I promised myself I would still try to catch him on his own. I did not have long to wait as he was detailed to take me back to my billet on foot. On the way he told me he was actually in the army and he had come from France with a Polish cavalry unit. He was a cocky little bastard with a boil forming on his neck. I waited until we got into the small backyard of my billet before I had a serious talk with him at the same time grabbing hold of his ripening boil. After a short, sharp session on his neck he began to shout like a wounded animal but solemnly promised to leave me alone in the future.

Next day, Mary returned and told me she had been promised a physiotherapy job at the local hospital, but would have to go back to Hull for the time being. As I still had to attend hospital for my shoulders she took me there and introduced me to my second girlfriend in this country. She was a beautiful black-haired girl, who turned out to be even better than Mary at all kind of manipulations. It took us about three days to come to some sort of mutual understanding. She was young, very energetic and loved gymnastics and dancing. She was less experienced than Mary, but made up for this with enthusiasm. There was a problem with privacy, as she lived in hospital accommodation, so we used the sand dunes a lot for our liaisons. Later she became an expert in sneaking into my billet via the backyard and we somehow got by. My love life became extremely complicated due to a lack of steady accommodation.

At this time problems arose in my dealings with various authorities, especially Polish Military Intelligence people. Also, for some strange reason, even the French decided to muscle in on the act. A French officer turned up to interview me one day with the aid of an interpreter who did not actually speak Polish. I never managed to find out what he wanted, even after getting the help of a Polish official from London, who could speak a little French but was not very fluent. After great confusion and much waving of arms nobody was much wiser about what the others were trying to say. It reminded me of the blind trying to teach the deaf to play the piano. After a while, the Frenchman just gave up and retired from the scene.

The British I had been interviewed by up until then were very polite, correct and thoroughly scrupulous, and always brought not one, but two Poles, as interpreters. The only trouble was that the Poles were constantly arguing about who was the better translator and so eventually one was removed. I found that the British were not really very interested about what was going on in Russia or about my countrymen's plight there. The Polish authorities, on the other hand, reminded me very much of the Russian interrogators I had met as they wanted to know the smallest detail of every name, place, etc. that I could recall. Unwisely, at one point, I mentioned that I could not remember the names of some of the places I had been without referring to my notes. On hearing this they nearly went berserk and proceeded to frog-march me back to my billet, demanding to see my diaries. I had them hidden in three different places in my room. They consisted of three thin Russian-made books, which had miraculously survived my travels across Scandinavia. Very reluctantly, I had no option but to hand one of them over and I never saw it again.

My landlady's son was a schoolboy who was always leaving his exercise books around the place so when I returned there I stole one of them and wrote my fresh memories down in it. A few years later, my conscience got the better of me and, on a return visit to Blackpool, I pushed half a crown through her letterbox – my late payment for the book.

The British authorities made sure that the declarations of the Official Secrets Act were signed by me and removed all misunderstandings about its content as the form had been translated and double printed in both English and Polish. The Polish intelligence people were particularly interested to find whether any Poles had collaborated with the Russians. They took particular notice of one of my own special adversaries, a local NKVD man, but were somewhat disappointed when I told them that his body was floating around in a huge tank of alcohol, and most probably still travelling around the Russian rail system.

For better or for worse, I decided to keep the names of the Russian nationals who had been very helpful to me to myself and said nothing about them. I continued to be examined by a whole stream of medical specialists and their x-rays showed my shoulders were improving.

They even arranged for me to have a session with a British psychiatrist which proved to be especially amusing for me as the interpreters' translations of the questions were very often quite suspect. Whilst all that was going on, I was learning English from the girls of Blackpool amongst the sand dunes and the streets behind the tower, while my steady girlfriend, the physiotherapist, was on duty. I found my inability to speak English no handicap with the girls. Every spare moment I would listen to the BBC in order to learn the language and gradually started picking up a few odd words, especially from the news.

There were also some English classes held and run by Polish officers who at least pretended they could speak English. At that time, in 1940, Poles were very popular and fashionable among the natives and they were forever being asked to go to parties or even to big country houses for the weekend. On one occasion a number of us stayed in Preston, where the lady of the house actually explained to my friend and me what an electric light was, and how we could switch it on and off. Despite feeling rather hurt to be considered as some kind of wild peasant from the middle of the jungle, it eventually struck me as funny, and we all had a good laugh about it. That was the first time I went to stay in a grand British house and the last for a long, long time. To our great dismay, we found that somebody, most probably the local lads, were spreading rumours that the Poles were so vicious in their sex lives that they were a danger to be with. So there was a period when only the boldest of girls would be seen around with us. But, in fact, the Poles old custom of kissing a woman's hand frequently won the day and we were accepted as normal human beings.

Eventually, a signal came from the RAF that I was to be posted to a pilots' school in the very near future. However, one day a Sergeant told me to accompany him to the very end of Blackpool pier. On our arrival I saw two civilians sitting on a bench. The Sergeant saluted smartly and requested their identity papers, which they showed him. He then shouted at me to stand to attention. One of the civilians turned to him and said: "There must be a mistake. I don't want to see this boy." At that, I turned and walked off, before being hurriedly called back by one of them, who introduced himself as Colonel X of the Polish Military Intelligence. He said they had been expecting to see my father, who had been in Military Intelligence (MI) before the war. This was a surprise to me and the first time that I heard that my father had worked in MI.

The Colonel told me that he believed my father had some information that might be very valuable to the Polish national interest and war effort. We sat on the bench and talked until it was quite dark. Afterwards, to my surprise, we set off to Blackpool Tower for a slap-up dinner after which they took me back to the bewildered Sergeant behind the desk. Colonel X told the Sergeant to have me ready in his office at 8am the next day in my full kit. The Sergeant took the order very seriously and sent a Corporal with me to my boarding house. He was ordered to sit outside my door on a chair all night and even charged me half a crown to let my girlfriend in for a last night of goodbyes. It was 6am when the panicky Corporal dragged me out of bed and from the arms of my girlfriend. By quarter past seven we were in the Sergeant's office ready and waiting for the Colonel, who arrived punctually at eight. His staff car in drab camouflage colours drove up and the girl driver in an army uniform beckoned me into the front seat with her whilst the Colonel sat in the back with his Adjutant. The Sergeant smartly put my kit bag in the rear compartment and we set off.

After a rather sleepless and exhausting night, I was tired and the longer we travelled the more my answers to the Colonel's questions became vague, so he told the driver to stop, ordered me into the back with him while his adjutant took my place in the front seat. Then there were more questions with the Colonel taking notes on the top of his briefcase on his knees. Our first stop was at RAF Newton near Nottingham. We had a meal and I was told that this was where I would probably train as a pilot. I mentioned to the Colonel that I was supposed to go to America for training, but was told abruptly that that posting had been cancelled with no explanation given. Afterwards we continued our journey eventually getting to London in a blaze of 'ack ack' guns during an air raid. At the time I wondered what I had done for my sins that the other bastard involved in the war, namely Hitler, was now trying to kill me. Up until that point only the Russkies had had a go at me. The car turned away from London and eventually we arrived at a large country house beside a beautiful lake. At the back of the house there were some army lorries and cars parked. At the last gasp of the day, I saw fish playing and feeding profusely in the lake and it reminded me so much of our home before the war. Some bad feelings came over me and I had a desperately restless first night at the hall.

The next day I was invited to take a solemn oath in front of a Catholic Polish priest that I would keep all my conversations secret. I wondered what was going on; I realised I was with a Polish MI unit but, because of my experiences, I did not trust them fully, nor anybody else for that matter. I had my remaining original diaries tucked into the top of my air force socks, where I had hidden them before leaving my room in Blackpool. But they found the stolen exercise book in my kitbag and questioned me about the notes I had made in Blackpool. At times the questioning was rather intense and quite unpleasant.

They could not understand how I had managed to get into England through Finland. Eventually, I told them I would not say anything further unless a British officer was present. After that I had a visit from Colonel X, who came to my room to talk. What was actually scaring me in this place was the apparent mistrust of me by the staff that were carrying out my interrogation. The Colonel was reluctant to talk in my room and requested a walk through the grounds. As we walked an armed guard followed close behind. When I saw the butt of an automatic pistol sticking out of the Colonel's trouser pocket it proved to be too much for me and I lost my temper and ripped into him. My outburst took him by surprise and he told me his story. He had arrived in England on a Polish naval ship just after the beginning of the war together with a German decoding machine built in the form of a typewriter. He said my father was an important contact in military Intelligence in our part of Poland and that they had met on a number of occasions in Warsaw in the past. Only when the Colonel was able to give me my uncle's address in Warsaw did I start believing him fully. At that point I told him all the details regarding my escape and about my diaries. He told me I could keep the diaries but that he would like to copy pages to which I agreed. The very next day an RAF photographer arrived with his camera and a pile of photographic plates. I was present in the room when most of the pages were photographed.

I spent two months in that house under constant questioning. Practically every day I saw the trails of fighter planes going up after enemy aircraft and my heart bled while I sat there, doing nothing at all. My heart was there with the Polish pilots who were actively fighting the Germans. I was given Polish Air Force bulletins describing the successes and tragedies of our pilots. Large numbers of our Polish lads were being buried in the cool of English cemeteries and I told the Colonel I was getting more and more restless. He solemnly promised me that the moment they had finished with me, I would be allowed to go straight to flying school, and he arranged visits to me from a Polish flying instructor and a warrant officer.

The warrant officer started putting me through the syllabus of the ITW (initial training wing) but could not figure out why I had been singled out for such exclusive personal tuition. He assumed I must be the son of a Polish VIP, hence this preferential treatment. Obviously, I could not tell him anything and eventually he stopped trying to find out more. During that time I was even taken to visit an RAF station for the purpose of trying my hand in the Link Trainer (an early flight simulator). However I started to feel that the flying instructor was only a sweetener to keep me quiet and in the clutches of MI. Then one day the Colonel dropped a bombshell, telling me that Hitler was bound to attack Russia sooner or later. This was about six months before the attack actually took place. He said that all the reports indicated that an attack would come in 1941 and that it was imperative that Polish MI should have their own contacts in that part of the world. It took a few days to sink in that the Colonel might actually suggest to me that I should go back to that hell. The whole idea upset me greatly and I started having nightmares over it.

Mentally I relived every day that I had spent in that condemned cell in Russia over and over again. The memory of the time I spent in the hole in the wall as a punishment especially came back to haunt me in a very vivid way. I suddenly developed a bad rash on my legs and experienced other strange symptoms. As treatment, doctors prescribed me to be painted from head to foot with a purple disinfectant. One of the girl orderlies in the sick quarters painted me from just below my earlobes down to my toes. The purple dye could be seen above my collar and I got really upset about it. In my anxiety to learn English, I had been taking private lessons from various local lasses and it was not very convenient to look like some sort of wild mushroom that had gone bad on top. There were a lot of female personnel in the building in the form of typists, secretaries and telephone operators, fortunately I found I was rather popular with them for some reason. After being been painted with this horrible disinfectant, one of the girls asked me if all Poles were like this and were born blue. In desperation I offered to date the girl who had painted me in return for her taking the dye off again. She was not exactly my cup of tea, but in desperation I had to sacrifice my pride to try to get the damn stuff off. Unfortunately, due to my bad English, I must have misunderstood her as I found there was no way to get rid of the stuff and it had to wear off over time.

I did not suspect at that time that I would have any further encounter with this damn disinfectant later in life. Later on during the War while I was stationed with the RAF at Hucknall, the local Salvation Army was holding dances for servicemen at the church hall. I got friendly with a beautiful woman whose husband was the local bobby. Due to my basic English, I did not realise she was married at the time and I thought that her husband was her brother. She would often ask me in for a cup of tea or coffee on my way to camp and, with her husband often being away from home, one thing led to another. Her home was an old pre-war semi-detached house with a number of untrimmed climbing roses in the small front garden.

One night her husband unexpectedly returned and I had no option but to jump into those bloody rose bushes. Despite the guardroom being only 400 yards away, there was no way I could walk to the station unaided with thorns sticking into my flesh and trousers. So a passing mechanic called an ambulance, which took me to the station. The medical officer was not very pleased to be called out from a party in the mess but had such a fit of laughter when he discovered what had happened, I thought he was going to peg out. The MO called two nurses who painted me with the same damn stuff again, after pulling several rose thorns from my bottom. The pain and embarrassment was very acute and it took me months to get over.

Despite having a fair amount of encounters with the fair sex, I was extremely shy and self conscious and hesitated when I was at this point ordered to "drop my trousers" in front of a female. The officer screamed at me, rather heartlessly, "Drop everything you stupid bastard. You were keen enough to drop them a little while ago. There is nothing you have got that my nurses haven't seen." As there was no answer to this, and as I could not find a mouse hole to hide in, I stripped down to my birthday suit. Once again came the moment when all my skin was painted with that purple disinfectant. It smarted like hell on my private parts but this time I made sure that my neck survived the onslaught of the nurses with the paintbrushes. I eventually got my own back on them and managed to date all of the nurses from that encounter in the sick quarters.

Anyway, I digress, so let's go back to my open prison, at least that is what I called the MI house in the country. I had nothing to complain about – I had excellent accommodation, good food, plenty of girls, but rather doubtful company. I did not need to have my brain laundered to hate the Communists.

The Colonel kept his word and I was posted to a flying school where I began by flying Tiger Moths. I found I had a natural aptitude for flying and passed my course with distinction. After taking more advanced training and getting my flying wings, I had another meeting with the Colonel, who had requested my presence in London. I had had no further contact with the British authorities and it was now February or March, 1941, at this meeting with the Colonel when the crazy plans of the Polish MI were revealed to me. Together with a group of others I was "invited" to go back to Russia. My nightmares had come alive.

"Don't worry, we will get you there safely," they told me. "All you need to do is to keep your ear to the ground and make a few contacts with some of our men who are already over there."

When I asked why they had picked me, they said that I had been in Russia fairly recently and had knowledge of present life within the country, which would give me more than a fair chance of survival. I was instructed to keep my eyes and ears open for any possible collaboration between the contacts and the Communists. When I enquired how the hell I was going to get back, I was told, "Well you got out once didn't you? So you can do it again." A stupid question I suppose, which deserved and received a stupid answer. And so I was given very long briefings of possible ways to journey back, however they would not tell me how exactly I was going to get into Russia. Shortly afterwards I was sent on a parachute course and, after a few jumps from a large static balloon, I decided this game was not for me as I was absolutely petrified. But, with the passage of time and a few more jumps, I overcame my fear and actually enjoyed it in the end. To my very great surprise, I was re-united with the battered garments I had come out of Russia in. They turned up in a sort of wax bag smelling of mothballs, having been chewed by mice or moths. Some joker had even put the remains of my shirt and long johns into the bag. The clothes were all freshly laundered so that I could wear them again. Luckily, there was plenty of pre-war Polish-made clothing that had been brought into the country by our fighting men available to supplement my meagre items. It was essential to wear something that would not seem suspicious to the NKVD. Very soon I had a complete set of clothing that had all originally been made in Poland. But I still had no idea exactly where I was sent to or how and when I was going to get there.

Eventually I soon found out. It was decided to send me somewhere that Polish nationals could still be found. Many of our people were still running around Lithuania, after the massive evacuations of 1939, and that was to be my new destination. A decision to go there had been taken after learning that there was still radio contact with Lithuania and that it was also possible to make ground contact with agents there. The Colonel was very active in all my preparations and I had long confidential talks with him. From my past experiences of being searched by the NKVD, we decided that a written list of names I had to remember would be best hidden inside the lining of a badly worn shirt collar. They would be written in code using the Greek alphabet.

## Chapter 10 : Mission to Lithuania

The Colonel told me that according to his information, a German attack on Russia was imminent and would probably come in May 1941. The main push would go towards Baku in the south and so the northern area, near the Baltic Sea, would give me a chance to establish myself in one of the Baltic States already occupied by Russia. Just before my departure I was briefed about three individuals who had to be killed as soon as possible, at all costs. They were Germans who had lived for many years in Poland and were active members of Germany's MI department, concerned with espionage and diversion. I was given very detailed descriptions of them. I remembered especially that one of the men had lost a forefinger in an accident with a field gun while serving in the artillery years before. It was a very strange feeling to be asked in effect to become a hitman if the situation arose, but it did not bother me much as I had found it quite easy to kill already, without any psychological after effects. As another of my tasks, I was also given the names of senior officers of the Polish MI who were believed to be in Russia as prisoners, and I had to try to deliver call signs and Morse messages to them later on.

During our talks in London's Rubens Hotel, the HQ of the Polish Army in Exile, we tried to anticipate what would happen to the thousands of Polish nationals who were in Russian prisons and labour camps or had been resettled, were Russia to be attacked and became an ally. The Colonel was adamant that he expected there would be a general amnesty and units of the Polish Army would be formed very quickly and trained for action on the frontline against the Germans. So it would be very important to open a line of communication from London to those units.

There was a discussion regarding call signs I had to give when sending all communications back to them. The Colonel at first suggested I should be known as "Cuckoo", the bird that lays its eggs in another bird's nest, but I refused point blank to have that as my name. We eventually settled on "seventeen", the date in September that the Russians had invaded Poland in 1939, a call sign known to London only. With all these details seemingly settled. I was put onto Red Alert, which meant I could be moved at a moment's notice. Now that they had made the final decision for me to go, waiting became a bore and I was anxious to depart as soon as possible. Eventually I was summoned to London and was told that everything was ready. The Colonel told me there I was not going to be able to go by air as there was nothing that could fly that far and get back in reasonable safety. Although there was a possibility of going across the Baltic Sea from Sweden or somewhere else in Scandinavia, it would take too long to organise. So with everything carefully packed we boarded a car and drove out of London. It was still daylight when we got to Portsmouth; we waited in the outskirts until darkness fell before we proceeded to drive through the gates of the harbour. At that point, all I was told was that I was going by sea and would meet a ground contact on the west side of Lithuania north of Klajpeda, near the gulf of Riga. Accompanied by the Colonel, I climbed into a rather flimsy dinghy and we were rowed for half an hour or more by two hefty men wearing dark overalls. There followed a small climb up onto the hull of a submarine. The dammed hull was so slippery, I very nearly fell overboard, but huge hands grabbed me by the scruff of the neck and lifted me onto the deck. There then followed very brief goodbyes, good-lucks, a hard handshake from the Colonel, and I was left on my own.

I spoke to the man in the conning tower in Polish but got no reply. There was an uncomfortable climb into the bowels of the monster, with my head banging on the sides a few times. I was ushered to my bunk by a Polish-speaking sailor who gave me a blank stare when I asked him the name of the boat. He was huge and powerful and said that he was going to be my shadow and helper throughout my journey. His name was Stan and he was in his late twenties.

My accommodation reminded me of my punishment hole in my Russian prison, the main difference being the lack of bed bugs in this bunk. I was frequently chaperoned around the boat for exercise by Stan, which was very welcome to me. The humming noise of the diesel engines was rather troublesome and got on my nerves. It looked to me as if the crew was a mixed bunch, as only a minority could speak Polish. I asked an officer for a breath of fresh air whenever possible and was allowed above quite frequently. It seemed to me as if we were sailing most of the time on the surface and during these periods I was allowed up into the conning tower, crouching on the floor against the wall. Everything on board was always cold to the touch and the confined space, smell and the realisation that water was all around us, scared the living daylights out of me. I remember thinking how brave these men must be who were prepared to fight in such atrocious conditions, and I promised myself that I would never volunteer to be a submariner. But for the moment it was too late to back out of my temporary role, so I decided to make the best of this self-imposed predicament. It felt to me that I was being considered as some kind of freak. I was treated as a VIP and always pushed down the hole first from the conning tower in an emergency, but at the same time kept away from the rest of the crew, who looked at me as if I had a horn growing in the middle of my forehead. Apart from Stan, I was kept well away from the others on board. As time went by, Stan became more talkative and claimed to be an agnostic, but once I caught him crossing himself while we were in the conning tower during the latter part of the journey. When I told him that I thought that agnostics didn't do that sort of thing he blamed his religious grandma for having brainwashed him years before.

Days and nights passed in a sort-of limbo without any visible difference between light and dark. I did not like the feeling and felt I had been buried alive in a steel coffin. I lost all sense of time. The worst part of the journey was at the beginning when we had spent a large proportion of our time underwater. Finally one day Stan whispered to me, saying, "We are in the Baltic now and are nearly home." From then, on the journey was less troublesome, as we spent more and more time up top in the conning tower. On the way along the coast of my homeland we stopped twice at night and I noticed some shadows depart from the boat in a small dinghy. The sea was kind to us except for a few days when many of the crew were very sick. This was a great surprise as I felt fine and had always thought that sailors would be immune to seasickness. Then at long last, after some 19 days at sea, I was told we were close to our goal and that I was to prepare to depart.

I got changed, checking my hidden notes were still safe in my shirt, and shook hands with a vile- smelling, bearded Captain, who wished me all the best.

I was ushered out of the conning tower onto the steel deck of the submarine where there were many handshakes and pats on the back. Adrenalin was flowing so vigorously I felt my heart thumping like a drum against my ribcage, but for some peculiar reason I also enjoyed it; masochistic tendencies I presume.

There appeared a large boat a bit like a kayak to take me to the shore. My first few steps on its deck were very nearly my last, as I tripped over a big nut sticking out of it and nearly fell overboard. Luckily the strong hands of a minder grabbed me and pulled me back from the brink of disaster, but not before I'd hit my left elbow, which then became rather painful. Eventually, after a lot of difficulty, they got me into the kayak, which was propelled by two burly men in black overalls wearing balaclavas on their heads. One of them was Stan. I had the top of a black stocking, which previously belonged to one of my female acquaintances from the House near London, pulled over my head. The sea was very calm but with quite a heavy swell and we moved swiftly through the water. It was nearly lapping over the sides of the kayak and I was far from happy. The two minders were paddling quickly and very, very quietly. There was not a sound from the boat and I could not see anything at all as the coastline was obscured by the burly paddler in front of me. Only occasionally did I get glimpses of the dark coastline as the kayak swayed from side to side in the swell. After a good hour or so of vigorous paddling, I spotted a cluster of dim lights in front of us at a bearing of about 2 o'clock.

The coastline was still not clearly visible when we stopped for a breather. Stan put his hands to his mouth as he whispered into my ear that he could not locate the pre-arranged light signal on the coastline. There was the possibility of a shoot-out with a Russian patrol if we were unlucky. At this point he asked me if I could swim. After all the long, careful briefings in London I just could not remember anybody asking me this before. I replied that I was prepared to fight if necessary, but could not swim very far with my clothes on. I had been given a 9mm automatic pistol, a box of ammunition and four mills bombs, and began desperately thinking about the story I could tell if I was captured. Scores of ideas went through my brain, but each of them seemed to be more unbelievable and ridiculous than the previous one. I knew very well the stupidity of the average NKVD Officer and of his low IQ, but there might just be one clever bastard who might not believe me if I told him that I was out fishing in a kayak armed with a 9mm pistol and British made grenades. After a long rest we moved off again and I very nearly capsized the kayak whilst trying to see where we were going. There was a very swift reaction from the man on the other paddle who, in cultured Polish, made some unfavourable remarks regarding my family. For a moment, my hand squeezed hard on a grenade and I very nearly hit him on the head with it. Luckily, the bark of a dog somewhere in the distance quickly cooled our tempers. Stan stood up and excitedly exclaimed, "Its him, let's go." They immediately started paddling feverishly towards the dark coast. The dog's bark was getting louder as we neared the beach and, as the swell was getting bigger, I was preparing myself for a dunking. The passing clouds momentarily uncovered the quarter moon and I saw the outline of some buildings. Seconds later, we hit the gravel on the beach. The swell turned the kayak sideways and we were all thrown into the water. A dark shadowy figure suddenly appeared and started wading into the water towards us. He seemed to have something long in his hand and I immediately cocked my pistol.

"Don't shoot for Christ's sake," shouted somebody in Polish from the beach. Very quickly, we all jumped to our feet and rushed out onto a sandbank. The pebbles on the beach made a very loud rustling noise under three pairs of boots and the voice from the beach hissed, "Be quiet, there's a Red Army patrol no further than 200 metres away." As quietly as we could, we followed the figure into a building some 50 metres away from the beach. It was a long low Dutch-style barn with the seaward side open and several boats parked under its roof.

"Identify yourself please," said the stranger and Stan produced some papers. The second paddler was angry that the signal light on the beach had been encased in a paper tube and so was invisible to us from the sea. He started a loud argument that was too much for my nerves, so I put a gun to his head and announced, "If you won't shut up, I'll blow your head off here and now." He replied, "I am a Polish Major and I order you to put that gun away." My nerves must have snapped completely as I was still holding one of the grenades in my left hand. Instinctively I hit the Major with it so hard that he went down like a sack of potatoes without making a sound. The stranger beckoned to me and Stan to go to one end of the building. We followed and got down to the business of exchanging information and planning our next move.

The stranger from the beach told us it was the last day of the month of May and the beach was being heavily patrolled by a Red army unit, who were still looking for escaped prisoners from a nearby camp for Polish nationals. Momentarily my heart missed a beat, then started thumping harder that ever, as I knew that my own father had been evacuated to Lithuania and had been in one of those camps. On closer enquiry, the man on the beach told me that most of the evacuees had already been transported into Russia and only a hundred or so had escaped and were still roaming around the countryside. The Russians were rather keen to round them all up and were combing the forest just a few kilometres away. All large sea-going boats had been blown up and only small ones up to three metres in length had been left alone. Captured escapees had been handed over to the NKVD, as the soldiers had strict orders to that effect. I desperately tried to form a plan of action and asked the man on the beach if war with Germany had started yet. He looked very surprised and said he'd heard nothing about it. That's charming I thought, so much for the intelligence of Polish MI in London, but said nothing aloud. Stan found that we had damaged the kayak on the beach and so he could not return to the submarine. He would have to implement plan B of his task and try to get back to Poland on foot if necessary.

By now the Major that I had knocked out had started to stir and groan. He had a cut on his skull and blood on his face. It took some time before he came round completely and straight away tried to take charge of the whole situation, telling me he had a written order for me hidden on him, and I was to be his guide. I took an instant dislike to him and told him to go to hell. I felt betrayed by the Colonel who had said nothing about this man and I began to wonder what else the Major had in writing in his possession. It was clear that none of our lives would be worth a small grain of sand on the beach if the NKVD found it.

Much later, I was severely reprimanded for the abuse I had dished out to the Major, but at that moment my only regret was that I had ever volunteered for this mission at all, and was mad that the Colonel had dumped an idiot on me who could easily get us all killed. There was no time to waste, however, as our most urgent task was just plain survival, which could only be achieved by a successful breakout from the beach. It was still quite dark when we heard some horses' hooves beating on the ground. It was the local man's friend with a two-horse cart on which lay a dinghy resting on straw. We unloaded the boat into the building and the local agent revealed his plan. They had obtained a pass from the local NKVD chief to deliver the boat to the beach, saying it was a present for him.

The Major, Stan and myself laid down on the floor of the cart and some straw sacks were thrown over us. The caravan set off and went slowly inland, with the local agent and driver walking next to the cart. They were stopped twice at army checkpoints to check documents, but had no problems as the guards remembered the cart going to the beach a short time ago and the pass had been signed by the NKVD chief. It was mid-morning when we stopped outside a barn-cum pigsty in a small village about seven kilometres or so away from the beach. The day was beautiful as only a May day can be in that part of the world. The sun was bright and warm and our new hide was full of straw, albeit rather smelly. The two remaining pigs in the sty were in a corner, behind stout wooden stakes. We all had a breakfast of huge amounts of scrambled eggs, fat pork and very tasty fresh home-made bread, prepared by the local agent's wife. We washed it all down with still warm milk, straight from the cow. Now decisions had to be made as to what to do next. I was determined to go on my own, as frankly I did not trust the Major. I was very angry and bitter that during all my briefings in London, nobody had mentioned they were sending someone with me. The Major turned out to be better informed than anybody else about Hitler's possible attack on Russia. He said that it should have already taken place in the second half of May, but he could not explain why there had been a delay. I started to suspect it was some kind of tall story, but could not understand why else we had been sent to our almost certain deaths. I realised that if I were caught with my secret list in my shirt collar, there would be nothing anyone could do to save me from a firing squad.

We slept on the thick straw in the loft high above the floor which, in the circumstances, was very comfortable, but my thoughts were bothering me a lot. Why was I so stupid to volunteer for such a crazy exercise? There and then I promised myself that I would be more choosy in future regarding my habit of volunteering. The great dilemma of what to do next was getting us all down. As all Lithuania was now considered part of Russia, there was no border between it and Poland. The local agent said that it was possible to get a pass to travel to Wilno, an old Polish city in the north of pre-war Poland. Within a few days he brought two passes and railway tickets for Stan and the Major, as they had both decided to try to get to Warsaw by crossing the Curson line, which was then the border between Germany and Russia. It was not until 1945 that I found out what happened to my companions. They both managed to get to Warsaw where the Major was caught by the Gestapo and beaten to death during interrogation at the infamous Pawiak prison. Stan died in August 1944, whilst fighting in the Warsaw uprising.

I decided to stick to my original task and instructions and stay in Russia and carry out my orders to the best of my ability. There was an emergency a few days later when a Red Army patrol found the 9mm pistol I had stupidly hidden under one of the boats on the beach. Luckily, I had tossed the British-made grenades into the drain ditch on the way from the beach. As a reprisal the Russians blew up and burnt the boathouse with all the boats in it. They searched the whole district very thoroughly and even questioned our local agent in whose house I was hiding. They actually searched the barn where I was up aloft, afraid to breathe. A few days later a Red Army unit quietly crept up to the village to search. When they were spotted I was alerted and, not wanting to compromise my contact, I bolted across the gardens and fields towards the woods. I would have got away if it had not been for a guard dog that followed me across the fields and into reeds near the stream. I managed to beat it off by pelting it with smelly mud but then soon after guards arrived on the scene. Several of them stood nearby and started shooting blindly into the reeds. I was stuck firmly in the mud with bullets flying around me like a swarm of angry bees. As there was no way out, I decided to call it a day and surrender. I waited until there was a short lull in the firing and shouted to them not to shoot as I was coming out. With my hands raised high in the air I walked slowly towards the line of soldiers.

With my hands behind my head, I was marched some three kilometres to the local NKVD headquarters. On arrival, I was searched very thoroughly but to my great relief the hidden notes in my collar were not discovered. I found myself in a compound that had been a factory yard before the war, with a very high brick wall around it. All the machines from the factory buildings had been removed so the 40 or so prisoners slept on the concrete floor. All the inmates were Polish nationals who had been captured after escaping from refugee camps. The stories they had to tell were horrific beyond belief. Apparently many Army evacuees had committed suicide to avoid being taken into Russia on the long trains of cattle trucks.

Many of the trucks, packed to and beyond capacity, with refugees who were members of the Polish Forces and police were sent into Russia. Thousands were also civilians, including women and children. The Russians classified most of them as prisoners of war. Before the war, the sandy Baltic beaches in Lithuania were a popular resort for Polish nationals, who travelled from the north of Poland. It was a short hop by train with the minimum of red tape. I was told that all youngsters up to sixteen years of age were separated from their families and taken separately into Russia. The only difference for children was that they were taken in passenger trains with Russian nurses wearing red crosses on their tunics, as well as an armed guard. Luckily for me, at this point, the NKVD took it for granted that I was one of the escaped refugees and left me in the compound with the rest of the prisoners. The only suspicious and questionable thing was that I could not name the camp I was supposed to have been in, but this was soon put right after I found this out from the other prisoners in the compound. I said I was from

Warsaw and had been in Wilno when the war broke out and this was accepted by the NKVD without question, to my great relief.

While in the compound I tried to find out if anybody knew any of the men who were on the list hidden in my collar. By coincidence one of the men in the compound had been in the same camp with two of those fellows. One had been captured after trying to escape and been sent to Russia, and the other had committed suicide in the camp. So I was able to cross at least one name off my list.

The inmates in the compound were mostly fed on soup and 300 grams (12 ounces) of bread a day. New men were brought in every day and, as soon as 200 inmates had been collected, there was another transport taking prisoners to Russia. Twice every day, political commissars called Politruks gave lectures in the main hall. As bread was handed out at the entrance, the lectures were extremely popular and very well attended. The Politruks were mostly illiterate peasants who all used the same phrases and slogans parrot fashion. There was always a good giggle during question time, when we found out a number of amusing things about Russia, such as their elephants were bigger than ancient mammoths, every swimming pool had an octopus to keep it clean with their suckers, and that there were camel breeding farms in Siberia, amongst a whole load of wild claims of Communism. So these brain-laundering sessions became proper hysterical comedies enjoyed by everybody. Some questions to the Politruks were so cheeky and grotesque that most of the inmates were terrified they'd smell a rat, but they never did. During one of the sessions, one of the Poles said that he had put wheels on his brick house in Poland before the war, so that he could take it on holiday with him. To that, the Politruk said. "We, the Russians, with our technology and engineering have been doing it for years. Even big blocks of flats are regularly moved from place to place to give hard-working workers a change of scenery". It caused such an outburst of laughter that many of the men were crying like children. Russians are actually very similar to Americans in their way of thinking and behaviour. They both have, or imagine they have, the biggest and the best of everything, and they like to be conspicuous by their behaviour. One can hear a Russian or an American from at least ten times the distance of any other group of people. The tragic and, at times, hilarious part of the Russian Politruks was that many of them were so brainwashed by their predecessors they actually believed what they were saying. With their pigeon-sized brains they believed it was conceivable that the party would find a way to grow oranges the size of footballs.

Very occasionally one could come unstuck on this assumption of their stupidity as when a high-ranking Politruk turned up at one of the lectures. When inmates asked him to confirm some of the statements his juniors had made, he became agitated and explained, "Those sons of bitches couldn't have been very good at school and they plainly made a geographical mistake. It is in the south, in Kazakhstan, where they have breeding farms for camels and not in the Arctic Circle, where as everybody ought to know, the camels could not walk on ice."

He ignored the octopus cleaning swimming pools altogether and the oranges that grew to be the size of footballs turned out to be melons. He seemed to be of average IQ and felt very silly about the whole affair, giving his juniors a proper rollicking over their statements. His parting shot was, "Well what do those sons of bitches know. They are stupid peasants." I suppose he didn't realise that he was talking about his fellow officers. He might have known the difference between oranges and melons, but his only knowledge of history was the one trotted out by Stalin and his henchmen. He foolishly allowed himself to be persuaded to answer questions on the history of Europe. Then to everybody's amusement he informed us that so many well known Polish nationals were actually born and bred Russians, including Copernicus, Paderewski, Chopin and even the first Marshall of Poland, Pilsudski, the conqueror of the Bolsheviks in 1920. They all became Russian citizens in his version of history The audience falling about with laughter somewhat upset him and he put the whole compound on 100 grams of bread a day for five days as punishment. As hunger among the prisoners became more acute than ever I stupidly led a raid on the bread store adjoining our compound, during which two Army guards were slightly clubbed. Unfortunately a Russian girl working in the bread store recognised me, retribution was very swift and I was put into solitary confinement. This was actually an outside toilet, which was next to both the bread store and the girls' sleeping quarters. My hands and ankles were tied together with my legs bent at the knees. Furthermore, the strong thin string was attached to my ankles and looped tightly around my throat, so any movement or attempt to straighten my legs put pressure on my throat. Everything was reasonably OK while I kept myself awake, but eventually, after some 36 hours, I started dozing off. As soon as I relaxed, my legs unconsciously straightened and pulled the string round my throat even tighter, cutting into the flesh. I had no food or drink for two days.

On the third day, Natasha, a young Russian girl from the compound bread store came in with about 100 grams of bread and a mug of water. My throat and the sides of my neck were swollen and bleeding, cut by the string, and she was rather shocked to see me in that condition. "That's those sons of bitches Ukrainians who always tie the prisoners like that," she said. "We've got three of them here and they are all cruel perverts. You wait here for a minute and I'll go and fetch an officer. He is an NKVD officer, but a good man."

Within a few minutes she returned with an elderly man in an NKVD uniform. He ordered the girl to cut off the string attached to my neck immediately and called for a medic. A young medical student with two years study in medical school, came and washed my bleeding neck, applying undiluted iodine to the open flesh wound. The pain was so acute that I instinctively punched the man on the nose making it bleed.

"You crazy son of a bitch," he said, stuffing a piece of bandage up his nose to stop the bleeding. "What else could I have done for you? That's the only disinfectant I have got to treat everyone, including our soldiers."

The incident amused Natasha greatly who said to the young man, "You son of a bitch are always trying to take my pants off. Perhaps that will stop you and give me a rest."

Natasha caught sight of me enjoying her young body dressed in a bright flowery summer dress, through which there was no sign of any underwear. Guessing my thoughts she said, "That's right, I don't wear anything underneath, but I am not going to tell that son of a bitch. I'm the sort of girl who likes to chose her own partners and not be pushed.

How would you like to help me to cut up the bread for the daily rations?"

Needless to say, I jumped at the offer. The bread cutting room was next to the kitchen where soup was always cooking in two huge cauldrons. A third cauldron contained just hot water for making a sort of herbal tea. The bread room had one long table in the middle and sacks full of bread standing against its walls. The bread was still hot, delivered from the local bakery every day, and there was an overwhelming smell of the freshly baked bread.

"And who is going to have a bath first?", she said with a smile, pointing to a huge wooden round, shallow container, standing in the corner of the bread room. "You need a bath as you smell like a wild boar after spending two days in punishment," she said. I helped her to fill the bath out of the hot water cauldron from the kitchen and cold water from a hose attached to the water hydrant, which was turned on by a passing soldier. The bath was soon overflowing onto the concrete floor when she just slipped her dress off and climbed into it with a big piece of soap. I stood there flabbergasted staring at her beautiful youthful body. I didn't know what to do next. "Come on, what's the matter with you. Aren't you going to wash my back?" she asked.

As the bath was not big enough to get into properly she stood up in it. "God, you're a funny fellow, haven't you seen a girl with nothing on before?" She produced a real sea sponge from somewhere behind the bath and handed it to me together with the soap and a charming smile. My sore neck was immediately forgotten and I even forgot I was desperately hungry and took up her challenge with enthusiasm. She stretched her arms as if just awake and said gently, "I feel lazy today. Wash me all over, my love." The suggestion did not have to be repeated and I thoroughly enjoyed the task. After all, at the time I was only nineteen and male throughout. I forgot about my predicament and enjoyed the feel of her firm body under my soapy hands. Knowing the human body from my two-year stint in hospital before the war, before passing my exams for medical school, I gave Natasha a massage, which pleased her enormously. She was twisting her body as the different muscles were massaged. It started to drive me quite mad as she wanted more and more. Even when somebody tried the door, she did not move but shouted, "Go away, I'm busy."

As it was rather hot in the room from the bread, despite the wide open window, I was perspiring and started slowing down in my task of gentle massage. "Wherever did you learn to wash a back like that," she asked. "Undress and stand in the bath with me. I'll wash your back now.". Somewhat hesitantly I joined her in the bath and she started to wash my back. After it was washed, I felt her teeth sinking into my back next to my shoulder blade. She held me long and tight, at the same time scratching my waist and rib cage with her nails. I was trapped and did not know what to do. I was determined not to make a fuss and so let her get on with it. Luckily her nails were well trimmed back so there was not too much damage done.

We must have been in the bath for a good hour before she let me go. Eventually we stepped out but there was not a towel in sight. "Well." she said, " I've never had a wash like that before, and now I'll pay you," she said softly. So with the scratch weals bleeding all over my body, I soon got over the shock of the bath, and despite trying to hide my feelings became visibly aroused. She looked me over and said softly, "Oh, let's not waste it. Come here."
She laid two sacks full of still warm bread on the floor and pulled me quite roughly over her. The session that followed was at least as rough as the bath and I ended up with even more scratches then before. I forgot I was starving hungry after my spell in the punishment hole. Eventually, with my help, she tipped the bath water onto the floor, and it ran into the low drain somewhere under the table. She went to a small box at the end of the room and pulled out a beautiful pair of men's underpants and a shirt. "Here you are. You might as well have these," she said. They had obviously been stolen from some local people, but it was a pleasure to put them on and I appreciated it very much indeed. "And now you are dressed go and get me some more hot water. I need another wash." I obliged and dressed, putting my own shirt on top of the clean one. Natasha jokingly got hold of the old shirt with a hard tug. It split and my hidden list of names fell on the floor near to the bread sacks. She spotted that something had fallen onto the floor and looked down to find it. It was then, to my great relief, I

realised she had defective sight and could not see the long piece of paper lying on the floor.

Her poor eyesight was a very fortunate twist of fate because if the list of names had been found by the NKVD I would have faced a very long and, most probably, very painful inquisition as they tried to beat the truth out of me. Natasha seemed to have the run of the place, thanks to a combination of her father being both a high ranking Civil Servant and a Party member, and also her continual half-promises of personal favours to local army members. She continuously spouted Lenin's quotations to the Politruks and younger members of the Red Army practically dribbled at the mouth whenever she spoke to them. All kinds of favours were granted to her with the hopeful anticipation that she might return them with others. She got permission for me to sleep inside the bread cutting room, managed to get a two metre long sack full of straw for me to sleep on, and fed me from the Red Army kitchen, where soups were so thick that the spoon would stand up in them.

She took a liking to having steamy love sessions on the hot bread sacks and was still active with her nails and teeth, but not as much as during our first encounter. My new clean shirt got firmly stuck on the bleeding bite marks on my back and she had to soak it off with warm water. She was very sorry for her robustness and tried to make it up to me as much as possible. We had very long discussions in the bread room and she told me all about her family. Her father lived in Moscow in one of the state-provided flats, which was very spacious and comfortable. They also had a country house well outside Moscow situated next to a large lake and surrounded by forest. By now, she had become so besotted with me that she was planning my escape from the camp, as she had been told that I was due to be sent to a Prisoner of War camp at Kozielsk in Russia for an indefinite period.

Impatient to put her plans for us into reality, she began to get signatures for the necessary travel documents for us both, and was planning for us to go to her family's country house to stay. She said that the property was very isolated and the whole district was out of bounds to all, and food was regularly delivered by Red Army trucks or sledges in the winter. Within a week she had everything ready for us both to slip away to the nearest railway station. She insisted they would never miss me, as they did not have a list of all our names, just a rough number of us. As some of the guards could not even count properly it would be easy and her father would fix all the necessary documents for me in due course.

Meanwhile, the days were slipping by like a dream. She was forever telling me how much she loved me although I kept mute. I just could not force myself to tell her that I loved her, as I had no plans for Natasha in my life. Needless to say, I hadn't spoken a word to her about who I really was and from where I had recently come. I did not have to attend the brainwashing sessions given by the Politruks, but insisted on attending at least once a day much to Natasha's great annoyance. Once I mentioned that I felt that Hitler would invade Russia because I felt like playing Devil's Advocate, but then kept quiet when I was told this was a counter-revolutionary statement; I knew only too well what happened to counter-revolutionaries.

Natasha moved into the bread cutting room with me and we spent every second of our days together. One day, on the 22$^{nd}$ June 1941, there was a rather loud and very urgent rattling at the door. We were in our morning clinch, saying hello, and she was not prepared to break off, and shouted angrily through the door, "Go away, I am stock taking." There was more urgent knocking than ever and the voice of one of the Politruks screamed loudly, "Natasha, Natasha. We are at war with Germany. Our mother Russia has been attacked by Hitler's hordes." Natasha was very shocked and dressed quickly. Everywhere political commissars were running around in a great panic. By midday a bombshell burst - Evacuation! All the officials were panic- stricken. They started burning all documents they could lay their hands on. After a while, Natasha said to me, "Those idiots burnt all the lists of prisoners and other documents and now they don't know who is here or why." They were anxious in case they were cut off by a rapid German advance eastwards. They were so panic-stricken that the Red Army boys were told to have their bayonets fixed on their rifles all the time. At the same time they were determined to leave nothing for the

Germans. All kinds of goods were piled hip high everywhere and inmates were employed to pack them for transport.

Eventually all prisoners were formed into columns five abreast and marched to the railway station some 15 kilometres away. The day before, on Natasha's insistence, three huge loads of bread were delivered as though for a journey and most of it was distributed amongst the prisoners. As an aside, I was summoned in front of a few Politruks, because I had somehow predicted the war, but they could not work out how, so they let me go. Natasha, needless to say, was put in charge of provisions and arranged for me to come with her as a helper. So we both went on the provision lorry to the station and eventually squeezed into the passenger carriage next to the provision trucks.

Overcrowding on the train was so atrocious that Natasha decided to travel in the goods truck with the food. So finally we settled down in a truck filled to capacity with bread, fresh and smoked meats, including yards and yards of continental sausage. A second truck was full of tinned provisions, a sort of dry toast and hundreds of bottles of various local spirits. Overcrowding was such that scores of soldiers were travelling on the roofs of the trucks. Between the two provision trucks there was fixed a rough platform on which an armed guard kept watch. From the very first day of this new war, Polish nationals found themselves being treated more as friends than enemies by the Russians. They were openly saying that all Slavs should join together to fight the German assault. After some 24 hours of feverish loading and packing, the huge train with two locomotives left the station and headed eastwards. It took two days to reach the old Polish city of Wilno, where, after a brief stop, we set off towards Minsk. Memories flooded back to me with a vengeance as I had been at Minsk prison in 1940 and also at nearby Orsha, where I spent 23 days in a condemned cell. Natasha realised that there was something wrong as I became more and more moody and she tried to extract an explanation from me. I was very tempted to say something about my experiences at Minsk and Orsha, but that would have given the game away, so I kept quiet.

To deaden the painful memories, I drank large quantities of alcohol with Natasha's intake not far behind. We got through litres of cherry vodka from the next truck. Shortly after, the train stopped just a few kilometres short of Minsk, as all the lines were packed full of trains evacuating people from the front line, which was approaching very rapidly. A Russian radio was blaring out their national anthem continuously and reporting stories of German atrocities against everybody, including civilians.

At Minsk the train was pushed into a sideline and there appeared to be no chance of going any further on it. I was told by the chief Politruk that I was free to join the Red Army and Natasha obtained a very special pass from him, which would allow both of us to travel on any means of transport throughout Russia. She then departed to see whether any tickets were available on passenger trains. Within two hours she was back with two passes for the Trans-Siberian train, which was due to leave Minsk within a few hours. "This is our last chance to get away as orders have been received to burn Minsk to the ground when the Germans get within 25 kilometres of the city," she said. The general panic was such that thousands of peasants were travelling east on horse and cart. It was like a vast flood of humanity flowing east.

Natasha and I walked nearly the length of Minsk to the station from where the Trans-Siberian train was due to leave. As we walked past an office where her brother worked we called in to see him. He greeted me warmly and told me in confidence that he felt that it was only a matter of time before Polish nationals would be conscripted into the Red Army or into their own army, which would be formed in Russia, although, so far he had heard nothing definite about it. We managed to drink a whole litre of strong Russian brandy in the 15 minutes or so we were together. Natasha was given a very special party identity card by her brother, which was to give us invaluable service in the future.

We eventually boarded a train packed to capacity and set off on a journey into the unknown. Within an hour on the train we found how invaluable the special party card was, as when produced it we were immediately invited by the conductor to share his specially reserved compartment. It had unlimited supplies of tea, which he continuously brewed in a samovar placed in the compartment. He was forever disappearing and returning with bread and an endless supply of salted pork fat. Two or three times a day he would announce he was going out for a quarter of an hour, and advised us to lock the door in case anybody tried to get in. We had visits from an NKVD man travelling on the train, who also advised us to keep our door locked and left a six-shooter 38-calibre pistol with us for self-defence. He got into the habit of coming in for mugs of tea and pockets full of rock sugar, a commodity which was almost unobtainable on the open market at that time in Russia. Remembering my past magpie habits, I stuffed much of the sugar in my pockets for future needs and "just in case". After a while, the NKVD man started making passes at Natasha who bluntly said to him, "Why don't you push off you son of a bitch. Can't you see I'm travelling with my husband?" I was rather taken aback to be promoted so suddenly to the role of husband, but was pleased with the result as we were left in peace, at least for the moment. Natasha apologised for the liberty but that night, when we were left alone in the compartment, she began to put pressure on me to get married. She said that we could jump off the train at one of the stations, get married at a wedding palace, as they were called in Russia, and rejoin the next train. I persuaded her that we had more pressing issues.

The train seemed to trudge along without hardly stopping and the stations became further and further apart. We were well past the Ural Mountains when the supply of coal started to get scarce and a lot of logs were taken aboard for keeping the steam up. As it was well into July, the weather was good and the sun was high and strong. During our fairly long stops to take on wood between stations, we took long walks along high pine trees, before running back when the driver gave three blasts about 5 minutes before pulling away.

It was after one of those longer stops that Natasha went for a shower. I was left in the compartment when, suddenly, I heard a muffled gunshot. A moment later Natasha rushed in and shouted, "We've got to get off the bloody train at the next station, as I've just shot that son of a bitch." Apparently the friendly NKVD officer had got in the shower room with her and tried to take liberties. She had put a bullet in his chest with his own revolver. I rushed to the shower room and there was the dead NKVD man bleeding profusely from his chest. With Natasha's help I opened the window of the outside door and pushed him out of the train, after taking all the money I found stuffed in his breast pocket. The moment his body left the window there was a shout and a rifle shot. Apparently a guard saw him falling out of the window and not knowing what it was, had fired at the corpse, just in case. Before a hue and cry could start, the train stopped at a station for provisions and Natasha and I hurriedly left it. The station turned out to be at Novosibirsk; we walked away from the station as quickly as we could, without being challenged by anybody. By then I had learned that my mother was somewhere further south in Uzbekistan, so I tried to persuade Natasha to catch a train to there. The weather by now had become very hot and she suggested we use her party pass and simply thumb a lift with Red Army lorries going in that direction. However we found that general nervousness had spread this far and that it was dangerous for strangers as there was a lot of shooting; one's life could depend on the whim of a local NKVD man, and an accusation of spying.

## Chapter 11 : To join the Polish Army

As the weather was so good, we decided to take a hike alongside a narrow gauge rail track going south. Soon an overloaded miniature railway train laboriously caught up with us going little more than at walking pace. We managed to get on and took a short ride. It was indeed a very short ride as, within half a kilometre the hot steam engine simply refused to climb so with grunts of "oh not again", everyone got off and pushed it up the hill, before clambering back on again. The poor train made a lot better progress and laboured on for at least five kilometres further without stopping. On one side of the track appeared a massive field full of ripe melons whilst we saw a large cluster of bushes on the other side. Strange noises were coming from that direction and I went to investigate. To my astonishment, there was a large lake behind the bushes, full of people bathing. I shouted to Natasha and beckoned her to come and join me. On seeing the lake she was overjoyed and immediately tried to get some soap from our travelling companions, but not of them had any. Undeterred, she said to me, "Come on, let's have a bath." We went to the side of the lake where we were covered by nearby bushes and Natasha stripped and got in. The water was very clear and warm. Nearby were people sitting around a small fire singing. I could not hear the words but the melody seemed to be very familiar. I suddenly realised the song was a traditional Polish Scout song, which I had sung myself around campfires before the war. Hurriedly I got out of my bath and headed for the group. On reaching the fire, I found it was surrounded by Polish boys, the oldest being about thirteen. Their clothing was in tatters. A woman called Zosia was taking them to join the Polish Army, which was reported to be forming at Kuybyshev. I could not believe my luck. On hearing this news I told Zosia briefly that I had a Russian girl with me and we were travelling South but at that moment we were trying to have a bath in the lake but without soap. To my amazement she pulled out a small tin of foul smelling jelly from one of the small boy's knapsacks, a delousing jelly that she had been given by the Russians to treat the boys with. I made an instant decision to join her and the boys.

Natasha was standing on the very fine sandy side of the lake rubbing herself down with the fine sand, which acted like a face powder and formed into a sort of china clay. Once again I was full of admiration for the adaptability of the Russian people. There she was determined to have a bath and, in spite of the fact that she had no soap, she was managing quite well. I touched her arms and found them quite clean and crisp, so the sand had done its job. Nevertheless, she was delighted to have some delousing liquid soap and we washed each other thoroughly and went for a swim.

Natasha washed herself with such very graceful movements, moving like a ballerina. I stopped and looked at her closely for her first time. She was of small stature, about five feet five tall, and her body was beautifully in proportion. Her skin was the texture of damp silk with the feel of the finest chamois leather. Her hair was dark in colour and her misty blue eyes were the colour of beautiful wild cornflower. I laid back on the sand and tried to think why I had not noticed her in the same light before. Perhaps I was feeling like this because I felt guilty about what I wanted to tell her, but I had to. I thought of all the good times we had had together and how good she was to me and for me, she had been like oil on my troubled waters. I now realised how important she had been to me and dreaded the approaching moment of separation. We lay on the sand and I started telling her quietly the history of Poland; her tragedies, triumphs and my deep love for her. She lifted her head off the sand and with tears filling her eyes she said quietly, "Jozef Jozefovich" (this is my proper name in Russian – the first name and the first name of my father), "I do not believe I could love anybody or anything more than I love you." On that she started crying softly, but very bitterly. "Why couldn't I be a Polish girl so you could love me in return?"

I could not contain myself any longer. I gently put my arm around her and, despite hating it, our tears joined together and fell on the hot sand, so far from my beloved homeland. The tears were flowing freely but for slightly different reasons. We seemed to lose all sense of time. Diplomatically Zosia, left us alone for a long while. Eventually it became evening and the whole group started singing a song, which was traditionally sung by scouts in Poland at the end of the day. I realised that much more than the day was at an end. With a lump in my throat, I quickly told Natasha who was on the other side of the lake, where their destination was, and the fact that I intended to join them. With her face still wet with tears, she said with wide open eyes, "If you think you can just go away and leave me you're crazy. I'm coming with you. Remember I have got a very important piece of paper in the form of a Party Pass and that can be of great help to you all. So we all got together and started planning our next move. We decided to go back to town by the small gauge railway. To do that we had to jump on a train that was labouring uphill. Natasha and I went to the local party headquarters, where they were impressed by her very special pass and issued an almighty piece of paper stating that we were all volunteers for the army. On the strength of this, our group was allowed to draw rations and be fed at any Red Army or NKVD kitchens.

While in town we witnessed the very unpleasant sight of the execution of a man and a woman, who had been accused of spying and were shot on the spot. They were crudely tied to a gatepost each. The man seemed to be too shocked to speak or to resist, but the woman became very violent and was shouting terrible obscenities at the Politruk in charge. They were to be shot for having some notes on them written in Hebrew, which nobody could understand. It made my skin crawl as I still had hidden on me my list partially written in the Greek alphabet.

There were four soldiers in the firing squad who took aim from not further than two yards and fired together. The man was killed outright but the woman was still screaming abuse. "Keep still, you bitch", screamed the Politruk with a revolver in his hand. Natasha was as white as a ghost and I thought she was going to faint, but stopped me from leaving the scene. "It's too dangerous to leave now," she whispered in my ear. And she was quite right, as an elderly man was immediately arrested while leaving the scene early. Eventually, the frustrated Politruk grabbed the woman by her long hair and, keeping her still, fired twice to finally finish her off. During our journey to Kuybyshev, we witnessed a number of incidents like this. We also saw a number of bodies hanging from trees, lamp posts and railway signal posts. This had been Natasha's first execution and it shook her rigid. She was quiet for a number of days afterwards and eventually wanted to talk. "I wish I had been born in Poland, as I am ashamed of my countrymen. Have you killed anybody in your life, Joseph?" she asked. I said, "Of course, there is a war on," and she burst into tears, slapping my face and screaming very loudly. "But not like that, not like that surely?" "Of course not," I screamed back at her, and that triggered off my thoughts back to October and November 1939, when I managed to despatch quite a few Russian NKVD men. But at that point in time my conscience was clear and I had no regrets. Natasha pressed me for details, but I said nothing.

The journey back West turned out to be a very difficult. All trains were full beyond capacity and we often travelled on the buffers between the coaches for miles at a time. Despite the weather being kind, it was very cold hanging onto all kinds of protrusions sticking out from the coaches. However we found it was a lot better to travel this way using goods trucks than in passenger carriages. At one of our stops, Natasha got a very painful leg injury when the buffer slid into the holding sleeve and took a long piece of skin off the back of her leg. For many days after, I had no choice but to admire her backside while dressing the wound. When after a few days her leg got a bit better, the cheeky girl went to a railwayman's hut and asked his wife if she could lie down as she had a headache, and asked if I could come in and hold her hand. I don't think for one second the woman believed her as she had a grin on her face while she let us into a very tiny room with a large feather bed. After a very vigorous half hour or so Natasha fell asleep and I had to explain to the woman that she was very tired.

To my amazement the woman suggested that we spend the night there as her husband was on duty in his signal box. When I explained the situation to Natasha, she said, "Fine Joe, we'll stay, but you are going to sleep next to the wall so she can't pinch you during the night". When the husband came in for a meal he fetched a litre bottle of home made vodka and we had a party. We got quite merry and he pulled me hard by the sleeve and whispered, so anybody could hear, "Comrade, see if you can put my wife in the family way as she blames me for not getting pregnant. I'll bring another bottle for breakfast and we'll drink to that." His whisper was so loud that Natasha overheard him and was ready for me with her nails. I tried to dodge the issue and explained that he was just drunk. "Well," she said " his wife is not drunk and she asked if we could all share a bed for tonight."

Natasha said she agreed and we all lay on top of the feather bed. Natasha seemed to change her mind as she clung very close to me. While in an embrace with Natasha, the woman kept pinching my bottom and ribs quite painfully. Eventually Natasha released me from the clinch and seemed to fall asleep. The railwayman's wife came to life and turned out to be more passionate than Natasha, but we had hardly got in a clinch when Natasha started pulling on me trying to separate us. After quite a long tussle, the vodka took effect and she fell sleep. Needless to say I had no sleep that night. Her husband came in next morning with an even bigger bottle of home brew. I popped outside and when I got back he had stripped down and, still holding the bottle, was joining both the women in bed. It didn't take more than thirty seconds before he gave out a howl. The bottle of vodka flew through the air and smashed on the hard earth floor. Apparently, Natasha had woken up and kneed the poor fellow in the crotch. I screamed with laughter seeing him jump out of bed doubled up holding his crotch with both hands. His wife jumped out of bed naked and gave him an almighty kick from behind. In the commotion, he screamed at her, "You crazy bitch. If you want children, don't kick me in the crotch." It took him a long time to settle down and dress as the poor fellow was in great pain. Every time he stood on one leg to pull his trousers on his wife thumped him and he fell over again.

Zosia spent the night with the boys in a makeshift waiting room at the railway station. The railwayman's wife and Natasha went to the village for provisions and came back loaded with all kinds of fruit. On the way from the village Natasha spotted a communal Turkish bath in town and managed to get a job as an attendant there. She returned three hours later with a full NKVD uniform, including a pair of smart riding boots that she had stolen from the baths. The uniform seemed to be rather small and while she tried the jacket on I found an automatic pistol with two spare ammunition clips, which I decided to keep for a time. Her plan was very simple; when needed she would dress in the uniform and commandeer spaces on road transport going west. I declined the offer to spend another sleepless night in the railwayman's hut, as I had not fully recovered from the last encounter, and we set off west on foot along the railway line.

We had just cleared the town boundary when we saw two army lorries being repaired on the side of the road by Red Army drivers. Natasha grabbed the sack with the stolen uniform and dashed behind a toilet hut. Five minutes later she came out wearing the smart red-flashed uniform which fitted her like a glove. With energetic and self-assured steps, she walked up to the lorries and asked for the officer in charge. A young man climbed out of the cab and, seeing the red flashes, saluted very smartly and asked her business. She showed him her party card and special NKVD pass and asked him where they were going. It was a relief to hear they were going our way once their repairs had been completed. We all squeezed aboard and set off. We stopped in simple but comfortable places with plenty of privacy, and found the Russian people very friendly when I told them we were Poles on the way to join the army. Practically every village had a primitive but very efficient sauna bath. Stones were heated and once they became very hot were sprinkled with some cold water from a wooden barrel. Heat from the fire plus heat from the stones made the well insulated room very hot and steamy. Natasha loved the combination and we had many steamy encounters in more ways than one.

Having over 800 Roubles, which I had taken from the dead NKVD man on the train, helped us a lot with accommodation and food. The villagers were willing to give us their home-grown food but our army rations had to be paid for. Our officer in charge, Misha, had given our group 200 roubles as army pay for volunteers so we were O.K. Whenever we were going through a large village, the local Politruk checked our papers. It always made me very uneasy and at times I felt I had a stamp printed on my forehead, "Came from London". I repositioned my secret list many times and Natasha carried it sometimes, not knowing what she had in her pocket. Some Politruks we met were very uneasy and suspicious. We were all searched on a number of occasions, except Natasha, because of her party card and NKVD uniform.

These gave her a very high position in the pecking order and the local Politruks did not fancy tangling with her. One of them supplied a lorry to the nearest railway station, which was in Omsk. He even helped us to get on the very overcrowded train going west to Sverdlovsk. The Russians at that time were rushing all their resources towards the advancing German line. When we eventually left Omsk station it was the 16$^{th}$ August 1941. There was such a panic at Omsk we could not find out anything further about Polish army units we believed were being formed in Russia.

The accommodation on the train reminded me of the trucks I had been transported in to the labour camps in the north Vorkuta district. We just huddled together for warmth as the nights were getting very cold. We got to Sverdlovsk on the 25$^{th}$ August, exhausted but in one piece. The huge smoking chimneys of heavy industry were the first things we saw when we arrived at Sverdlovsk, along with over a thousand flat railway trucks, most of them loaded with tanks. There was continuous movement on the sidings, as trains were being put together and leaving for the West.

Natasha and I decided to leave Zosia with the boys in one of the empty and partially demolished cattle trucks, and the two of us set off into town. It was quite a hazardous journey as we had to cross many lines of trucks, sometimes scrambling under them, not knowing whether they were about to move or not. I tried to persuade Natasha to ditch her NKVD uniform but she was adamant that it might help. I still had the small calibre revolver on me and about 20 rounds of ammunition, which I hid inside an axle oil bath container just before we reached the main station buildings. All around the station many military men were rushing around. Natasha cheekily asked the first man she saw wearing an NKVD uniform where the military headquarters was and he pointed to the huge building looking like a big store. We marched in and Natasha approached a table with some high-ranking officers behind it. "I am taking a group of Poles as army volunteers," she said. "Do you know where their headquarters is?" The man behind the desk shouted, "Hey, comrade Captain. Come here and see these people." To my absolute astonishment a man in Polish officer's uniform, including peaked four-cornered hat, came out from behind some parcels stacked high.

I was so flabbergasted that for a brief moment I could not answer him in Polish. I was shaken rigid when the Captain turned to the Red Army Colonel behind the desk and said, "He's not Polish." The Colonel gesticulated with his hand and four red army soldiers lowered their rifles with bayonets into my and Natasha's chest. Natasha screamed at the Colonel, "What the hell do you think you are doing?" And that is when we first found out that the NKVD officers had personal identity cards, which Natasha did not have. The Colonel gave two blasts on the whistle hung around his neck and all hell broke loose. We were very roughly manhandled by several burly soldiers and marched off to separate rooms in the building. We were both stripped down to our skins and searched very thoroughly. Natasha was absolutely livid and started slapping and punching everybody in sight. For no reason at all, one of the bastards punched me very hard in the back just above the kidney. That nearly knocked me out.

The NKVD officer in charge hit Natasha hard on the side of the head, knocking her out, and said to his aide, "Obviously they are spies. We'll shoot them today." There were quite a lot of people in the room, including the Polish Captain. I shouted at him, "You stupid son of a prostitute (a Polish variation on son of a bitch). What the hell have you done?" On hearing my fairly cultured Polish he looked aghast at the whole scene. Poor Natasha lay on the concrete floor, blood pouring out of her nose, and was still unconscious when a Politruk in civvies came in.

"Comrade Commissar, we need your signature on the execution papers". I watched the Politruk take a thick fountain pen out of his pocket, unscrew the top slowly and place it on the other end of the pen. I watched him as if hypnotised when he took it in his right hand as if to write. I realised we had very little time to live and try to explain our position. The Polish officer came up to the table and picking up our bundle of papers, started looking through them. To my great horror I saw my piece of paper prepared in London unfolded amongst the other papers. He examined the regular fold marks and looked at the paper against the light. Meanwhile, the Politruk signed his paper and, turning to the Polish officer, said, "Are those the papers found on the spies?" The Captain put the bundle in his outstretched hand and walked towards me. "Who the hell are you?" he whispered to me. "You bloody fool," I answered. "It's too late to explain."

I watched the Politruk examine the papers. He picked one out, throwing the rest on the table. I was certain the paper he was examining closely was my coded one from London. Meanwhile, the Polish officer started leaning on me. I glanced at him and to my real surprise saw my paper crumpled in the palm of his half-opened hand. Meanwhile, the Politruk said to an NKVD officer, "So you are going to shoot them as spies." "Yes Comrade," he answered. "Well before you shoot them, you'd better ring her father up," pointing to Natasha. He is not far from here, at Kuybyshev, where all the Central Committee has been evacuated from Moscow, and he is one of them. I thought the NKVD man behind the desk was going to faint.

"What can I do now Comrade Commissar?" he asked. "Well, first of all tear this up," handing him the execution order paper. "And what about him?" he asked, pointing at me. "You can shoot him if you like but do further checks first." Hearing that suggestion, the Polish officer stepped forward and said to the Politruk, "A word with you Comrade, in private". On that, the Russian put his arm around the Captain's shoulder and they walked away out of earshot. My attention was diverted to a now-revived Natasha, who, while dressing, had gone completely berserk. I have never heard anybody swear like it, before or since. The NKVD officer tried to calm her down but she just spat at him with a mouth full of blood, which had collected from her bleeding nose. To my relief, she was given her NKVD officer's uniform back and an officer asked her why she hadn't told them who her father was and where her identity card was. "You mad son of a bitch," she said. "I've been robbed more times than I care to remember, so how do you expect me to have all my papers?"

I still felt very uneasy about the two officers having a secret talk about me. It took a good half an hour before the Polish officer beckoned me to one side. He informed me that all our party had been recognised as army volunteers and would be issued with food and fifty roubles each. Then he said he was a Polish army intelligence officer and had spotted a watermark on the edge of my note. I tried to think how this watermark got on my note without me noticing it. Then I remembered that when I was making the note in one of the offices at the Rubens Hotel in London, I asked for a piece of appropriate paper, and those incompetent bastards gave me one with a watermark on it. I felt it was partly my fault for not checking everything. I was thankful we did not face the firing squad, which could have happened quite easily, as at that time all the Russians had a mania about spies.

The train journey from Sverdlovsk to the Polish headquarters at Buzuluk, due west of Kuybyshev, was uneventful. We had VIP treatment with adequate food and a not too overcrowded room. At Kuybyshev we had to change trains and Natasha stayed behind, as her father was there, evacuated from his Moscow office. She tried to persuade me to stay on for a few days but I was anxious to get to the Polish army headquarters. Seeing the terrible chaos everywhere I was afraid they might shift it to some other part of Russia, but I agreed to postpone my departure by 24 hours, so that Natasha could make sure her father was there. We found him quite easily, occupying a whole huge block of flats reserved for members of the central committee and their servants. A good-looking man with a huge crop of dark hair, he had a broad grin and greeted Natasha very tenderly. He was in charge of the whole building of about 200 flats. It was the first time I had come across the massive bureaucracy of Russian officialdom and I found that, before anybody could see Natasha's father, there were three rooms to be negotiated. The first two were called the "secretariat" and the third was for his personal bodyguards.

To start with, they wouldn't let me even enter the building. Natasha had to bring out her special pass before they would let me in. His personal guards frisked me for weapons before they let me into his office. After a firm and friendly handshake, his first words were, "So you are Natasha's lover and co-habit with her." I felt extremely embarrassed and for a moment was struck speechless. Natasha helped me by saying, "Don't worry, Jozef Jozefovich. He doesn't believe in marriage himself," pointing at her father. "You two must be starving," he said, "but we are in luck as I have a large piece of venison being cooked for my supper." The meal was really magnificent. I was very surprised when one of his many servants turned up with an original bottle of French champagne. We had quite a lot to drink and Natasha started getting very frisky, which embarrassed me greatly.

During the meal her father was talking a lot. He was very well informed regarding what was going on in general, and told me that the Polish army would eventually be sent to Mongolia to be trained for frontline duties. After saying he was surprised that so many thousands of Poles were found to be prisoners in Labour camps, he asked me how I happened to be in Russia and accepted my original story without question. To my amazement, Natasha told him how she had got her NKVD uniform. He waved his finger at her and said, "You crazy little bitch. You could have been shot for that. But as long as you have that smart uniform, I'll arrange a proper ID card for you."

The whole meal lasted a good two hours and at the end he got his secretary to issue us with a general pass to all facilities in the block. Natasha got a key to a flat on the first floor and, when we arrived there, a batman greeted us and told us about the facilities in the building. He said he would arrange dry cleaning of her uniform and bring me a new Red Army issue uniform as mine was past its best. He also gave us a key to the sauna in the basement. We had a very long sauna and when we got back all my clothing was gone, and a new set of quilted trousers and jacket was lying on the bed. To my horror everything including the list hidden in my jacket had disappeared. Luckily, I asked the batman for my old things back, which he returned straight away and I gave him twenty roubles I had hidden in the jacket and, at the same time, retrieved my original list. For most of the night Natasha tried to persuade me not to join the army. "We can go to Irkutsk on Lake Baikal where my father has got part of a house and we can stay there until the end of the war," she said. "Even if the Germans capture Moscow, they'll never get to Baikal." The argument was very powerful and very tempting. Maybe in different circumstances, I would have considered it, as I had become very fond of her, but I had a job to do, so there was no way I could agree to sit the war out. The night was very long and very passionate. This was the very first night we had spent together in reasonable comfort. In the morning I had to practically fight my way out of bed and the flat. Eventually Natasha gave up the struggle and accompanied me to the railway station. She said she was sorry, but she must stop for a few days with her father, as she had something confidential to talk to him about. To my great surprised and relief I got a seat in a reserved VIP compartment on the train and to my astonishment, in the compartment sat the Polish officer I had met at Sverdlovsk, who was returning to Polish headquarters after a spell of duty as a liaison officer at that station.

"There is something fishy about you," he said very quietly "But I can't put my finger on it. I want you to report to Intelligence and security company at headquarters, and we will get to the bottom of it." "Oh, bloody hell," I thought. "I might have a bigger problem with this lot than the Russians, who were pretty gullible in swallowing many of my stories."

He told me that many thousands of Poles were flooding in to join the Polish army. As all were released under the main order of general amnesty for Polish nationals, about fifty percent of them came in a terrible state of malnutrition and, by rights, they should have all been hospitalised. One of the main problems was the difficulty of delousing about five hundred people a day. I nearly fainted when he told me the name of the General in charge of the Fifth Infantry Division stationed nearby. His name was Bohusz-Szyszko, a regular visitor to our pre-war estate for the duck-shooting season. He had stayed at our house for fourteen days in 1938 and I had personally taken him in a punt for quite successful expeditions, so I hoped that my first contact would be with him, as I did not trust Polish Military Intelligence people.

The camp was about one kilometre away from the station. I saw many hundreds of half-starved men digging massive ditches in the open fields. On enquiring, I was told that it would be a complex of army barracks. As it was the beginning of September, the winter would soon be upon us and it was essential that these dugout huts were constructed, as they could be quite warm with one or two tortoise stoves burning inside. They were constructed under the supervision of Red Army engineers who had experience in this type of building. For the moment, the men were billeted in very primitive tents. I was ordered to report to military intelligence headquarters in town for an interview, where I was duly accepted into the Polish army. I was then temporarily allocated a place in one of the tents and realised that all the men were crawling with lice and other bugs, which were no stranger to me from my past Russian prison experiences. The Polish MI asked me for details of the Polish boys who had arrived with Zosia, but I could tell them very little. They were particularly interested in one boy who hardly spoke Polish, only white Russian, and the MI were worried he might be a Russian boy plant. Apparently there were a number of so-called volunteers in the Polish army who had turned out to be Russian nationals.

It was dark when they eventually finished with me and told me to go to my allocated place in the tent. When I said I did not want to sleep in the tent because of the lice and dirt, a staff Sergeant at HQ was given the task of finding me a place to sleep for the night. He was an old army sweat who could manage to survive anywhere. I later found that he had a good supply of Russian vodka and very strong home-brew stuff.

The two of us had a sort of party in the dim light of a paraffin lamp and later three or four other men joined us with their meagre supplies of drink and food. The party lasted nearly all night and practically everybody ended up the worse for wear. I had noticed the staff Sergeant had in his breast pocket a miraculously preserved fountain pen and I borrowed it, to copy some vital points from my secret list into the margin of a Russian paper, Izvestia, and destroyed the original. I hid my new note in a small crevice near the door of the barn.

I was called to the interview room soon after daybreak and they started on me all over again. This time the Captain from Sverdlovsk was there and the first thing he said to me was, "Let's have it." I played stupid and shook his outstretched hand as if in a greeting. He was after my list but I said that I had never got it back with the rest of my documents and stuck to that story all day. It was at this point, at the end of the day, when I saw someone with a shaved head standing bent double at a makeshift table in one of the rooms. The shape of the hairless head seemed to be familiar to me. When the man straightened up and turned halfway I suddenly realised it was my father. For a moment, I felt as if I was going to pass out. With as normal a voice as I could muster, I said to him, "Hello Dad, how have you been?" My father turned to me and could not move. He just stood there as if he was made of stone. It was the first time I had ever seen tears running down the old boy's face. He didn't ever cry but there were tears, as if from a tap, running down his drawn and hollow cheeks.

My father had shaved his head ever since he had been gassed in the First World War and had lost some hair as a consequence. We stood there staring at each other for a number of minutes, unable to speak. Eventually he said, "Come with me, I've got a room for you." Apparently, he had already been in contact with my mother, who had been resettled to the far east of Russian Mongolia by the Russians in 1939, and now was on her way to join my father at the headquarters. At that time, all letters and postcards had to be sent to Moscow, from where they were sent on to an addressee. He showed me the letter in which my mother was informed by Moscow that I had been executed for banditry.

My father hired two rooms in the village and waited for my mother's arrival. Needless to say, we spent all the following night talking about our experiences. To start with I told him nothing about being sent from London, but eventually I told him my whole story. He didn't seem to be shocked or surprised at what I had to say but promised to help in any way he could. It was still dark when we both went to the HQ. From a distance, we saw an NKVD man standing at the door. My father exclaimed, "What the hell does that bastard want at this time of the day." As we got closer to the HQ, to my great surprise, I recognised Natasha. As I had already told my father about her, he forced himself to shake hands with her. When I introduced them, she quickly put her arms around his neck and greeted him very warmly. It embarrassed him greatly and he was completely lost for words. All of his life he had been so bitterly against Communism that even the sight of an NKVD uniform gave him the creeps.

I was very surprised to see Natasha so soon after I had left her at Kuybyshev, but she said she was now officially attached to our HQ and had arrived as soon as possible to take over her duties. She said she would look after things from now on. I didn't quite know at that time what she meant but I left her to it. While we were talking, my father stood nearby and pretended he was not there. So far, I had not elaborated to him how important Natasha was to me in more ways than one and I was determined to put it right. But for the moment, I was preoccupied with close debriefings by the Polish MI who was not very satisfied with my explanations. It might seem strange that so much mistrust existed in and amongst the members of the intelligence unit, but the general motto was, "Don't trust anybody and you will live longer."

My father and I had always been very close, but the first sight of Natasha in an NKVD uniform was too much for him and he refused to talk to me for three or four days. To start with, all he said to me was, "Do you realise what the NKVD and this uniform stand for? After seeing what they are capable of, how could you form a friendly association with one of them?" All my efforts to try to explain to him came to nothing, as he just disappeared. He even moved out of his private room and into one of the hundreds of tents occupied by the army volunteers

My debriefing by the Polish MI became more and more intensive, as they suspected that I was not what I claimed to be. Looking back, I don't blame them, as a number of Russian agents were being unearthed and the Polish MI had the fantastic task to sieve through thousands of volunteers. Every new arrival had to be verified and cross-checked many times before being given the all-clear. All people in charge of Intelligence were pre-war members of MI and rather wise old birds. The presence of Natasha did not help me with my debriefings as she got two nice rooms in the house of the local schoolmaster-cum-NKVD informer, which had previously been occupied by a Polish Major from the MI, who made my life rather difficult.

My father's position in MI didn't seem to make any difference and I began to despair. I put in an official request to see General Bohusz but it was refused. Even my efforts to find out where he lived came to nothing. Eventually Natasha, who was liaison officer, found out the whereabouts of the General's quarters. But there was a snag. Polish and NKVD guards were posted outside his door 24 hours a day, and all seemed to be carrying automatic weapons. Natasha soon found out that only the Russians had ammunition for their weapons. She had to go to the very senior liaison officer, a politruk, for permission to see the General. Late one night I was taken under heavy guard to the General's room which was located in one of the railwaymen's small cottages. It was a tiny room, the size of a small pantry. The small and very narrow bed on one side of the room had a straw mattress on it. On the far end wall, there was a narrow shelf used as a desk.

Above the bed on a wooden peg, was a small crucifix hanging by a faded piece of ribbon. There was no ceiling so one could see the straw thatched roof of the cottage. The only light was from a hurricane lamp standing on his desk. I saluted as smartly as I could and, in proper military manner, asked for permission to speak. His first words were, "Why did you ask to see me? Do I know you?"

"Oh hell," I thought, "here we go again". Despite the late hour of the night he was clean shaven and looking quite smart in his Polish uniform. He pulled his eyebrows tight in concentration while I reminded him about our pre-war duck shoots and didn't relax until I reminded him about his batman, Jan, to whom he would shout most mornings, "Jasiu, where are my boots?"

I was very relieved to find that he remembered me well and asked where my father was. He was extremely surprised to learn that he was here under his own command. I told him about Natasha and my father's disapproval and disappearance. He smiled and said he would fix it for me. When I told him I was having a difficult time with the MI he wrote, by hand, a pass to enable me to see him in his tent the following day, and then said goodnight, indicating that our meeting was at an end. The following morning I had another tiring session with the MI and in the afternoon set off to the General's tent across very muddy fields. I was let in immediately. I told him there were very confidential matters I wished to talk to him about. The General said he realised there was something afoot but it was not the time nor the place to discuss it. Even his tent was not the proper place, so he invited me to go for a walk with him. We set off across the muddy fields as if on a troop inspection and went towards the nearby woods. He did not seem surprised when I told him I had been in England and said there had already been a number of agents in his unit from England and France. But he was taken aback when I told him about some German fifth-columnists roaming around Russia as Poles. He said that if they were still alive they must already be under his command, as his was the first unit to be formed in Russia. The General beckoned his adjutant to come forward and told him to call Jan to him. For a crazy moment, I thought his old batman was going to turn up. Instead a fairly short fellow in a very dilapidated Russian quilted outfit arrived, smartly saluted and asked what the General's pleasure might be. At the time it struck me as being very funny that this tramp-like individual was trying to click his heels army style in front of the general. The clay covered remainder of his army boots made a sort of squelching noise as if he was standing on a frog. The General noticed this and said, "Oh, for heaven's sake Jan, don't make that noise. It sounds like two rabbits having sex." It struck me as very funny as I had never given it a thought what sort of noise rabbits could make and I started laughing. The General said to me, "I am glad to see you can still laugh as there might be even harder times coming, and we all will all need the ability to laugh in future. Meanwhile, I leave you in the hands of Mr Jan, you can have complete confidence in him."

Mr Jan, was a middle-aged gentleman, about five foot eight inches tall, with a completely bald head and a slightly withered left arm. He took me for a walk and startled me by saying that first of all we must confirm my bona-fides with London. When naively I asked how he intended to do it, he smiled and said I should not ask such stupid questions. I found out later he had radio contact across the Caspian Sea with Teheran, and eventually London. It took three days for him to get a satisfactory reply and then a proper meeting followed. Mr Jan was very anxious to find the men I came especially to meet and, if possible, eliminate, but I had to be very careful as the NKVD Politruks were always at his elbow and forever looking over his shoulder. As a full member of the Polish armed forces, I had done very little soldiering as I had spent most of the time with Natasha or at MI headquarters. No other member of MI knew anything about my identity and somehow, despite being very inquisitive about me, left me alone.

Two days after, Mr Jan told me that my father had been ordered to report to MI HQ. We eventually all met in Mr Jan's office and my father was pre-briefed. As soon as I entered the room he turned his back on me and pretended I was not there, so I started telling him my story to the back of his head. When I came to the point of how I met Natasha my Father's very broad shoulders started shaking as if he was cold. I didn't realise what was going on until I walked round and faced him.

Despite his face being very serious and foreboding, huge tears were running down both cheeks. Eventually we held each other in a tight embrace for a long, long time before starting to speak. And this was when I found his hatred towards the NKVD was as great as mine, if not greater. He told me how he had been saved from getting on the mysterious transport that had left from the POW camp at Kozielsk and how all those on it had disappeared without a trace. Every new arrival to the camp was questioned about the transport and nobody had any idea what had happened to those thousands of men. Some other transports from other camps could not be traced either. So the big mystery of how the fifteen thousand plus men vanished had deepened every day. Even the local Politruks had no explanation for the disappearance of so many officers. It was only later in the war when the Germans came across Katyn woods that the mystery was resolved. At MIHQ these thousands of men appeared on lists, shown as "Missing – Whereabouts Unknown".

Natasha regularly attended briefings of all the NKVD liaison officers and kept me informed of what was going on. One day she came from a meeting more than unusually agitated and said that VIP NKVD officers were due to come and take possession of all lists that had been so religiously kept by Polish staff. I immediately reported the matter to Mr Jan. In the next 24 hours there was great pandemonium at HQ, as all available space was occupied by clerks rewriting all the lists. So when four high-ranking officers came from Saratov to pick up the documents, all they got were the lists of men already in the camp or those known to be still in labour camps or on their way to the army.

Natasha lost very little time at Kuybyshev with her father before joining me at the Polish army HQ in Tatishthevo. She still wore the stolen NKVD uniform but due to her father's intervention, she had joined the NKVD properly and was appointed as a Liaison officer to the Polish army in general. She did not waste any time in getting very comfortable quarters for herself and me. At the very beginning she told me to be very discreet in front of the house owner as he was working with his ears, as she put it.

My father had great difficulty in finding a place in a private house, but Natasha again turned up trumps and got him a very nice room in one of the houses only a few doors away from our own quarters. My father became more and more agitated as there was no sign of my mother, who was supposed to be on her way. Natasha was very keen to help and was forever badgering her chief to do something about it. With the great help of Natasha's father, my mother was eventually traced to a huge transit camp at Sverdlovsk and arrived at our railway station on the 28th September 1941. As bad luck would have it, my father was away at Saratov to get provisions for the army division. Natasha got to know about her arrival before me and without saying anything, went to the station to meet her and bring her into the camp. As the day was cold, Natasha wore her Red Army coat that covered her NKVD uniform, so my mother had no idea who she was. She just picked my mother up by name and brought her directly to my father's quarters. I waited late into the night at the rail station in an attempt to meet my father and tell him that my mother was in his room.

Meanwhile, Natasha got very friendly with my mother and got hold of a bottle of vodka. By the time my father arrived, both of them were quite merry. Mostly due to alcohol, my parents' meeting after two years and eleven days separation went without any special dramatics. I met my mother two or three days later, after my father and Natasha had warned her about my being alive and well. Despite these precautions, my mother fainted on seeing me and a Russian army doctor had to bring her round. With my mother's arrival came the frosts and soon afterwards the snow. Due to Natasha's position, we had unlimited supplies of coal and coke so life in general was quite bearable. The only problem I had was the Polish MI, who were forever demanding statements about my travels in Russia. Advised, and indeed ordered, by Mr Jan, I claimed I was in Russia all the time since 1939. The difficulty was that MI officers could not find anyone who was in a prison or camp with me during the time I spent in England. To my great relief, they eventually found somebody who had heard of me while in prison in Orsha.

It was round about Christmas time in 1941 when eventually a Polish welder from the furniture factory up North turned up who confirmed meeting me in 1940. That seemed to satisfy the MI that I was the genuine article and they left me in peace. Until then I had been under a type of house arrest and had to report to HQ every day. Co-habiting with an NKVD officer did not help my case and even after my investigation ended, I was still viewed with suspicion. At the same time I kept Mr Jan informed on many things that only NKVD officers knew. I found out from Natasha that our division was being moved to Uzbekistan, east of the Caspian sea, four weeks before it happened.

In November 1941 our unit had a surprise visit from General Sikorski, our Commander-in-Chief in temporary exile in England, and a number of other officers and senior NCOs from England. Later that month, on the 11$^{th}$, we had a big parade in front of our C in C and were told that our wooden guns were to be be replaced by real ones, and we'd be sent for proper military training somewhere in the South. The parade was an incredible spectacle as one could see thousands of men looking like tramps, marching proudly in front of General Sikorski on the snow covered plains of Russia. Many men were openly crying as it was a very emotional moment. British uniforms arrived at our army HQ a month later and were quickly distributed amongst the soldiers. The most welcome part of the equipment were the thousands of socks, which were immediately used as mittens to prevent frostbite in very severe low temperatures. All the time, Mr Jan and I were searching for German infiltrators we both knew were somewhere amongst us, and there was a big hue and cry when a Russian infiltrator was found in our MI HQ. I personally was treated with great contempt by most of the HQ staff as they knew that Mr Jan and myself had free access to each other and during our meetings, nothing was ever written down.

Christmas in 1941 was the most memorable in my life. Traditionally, in Poland we celebrated Christmas Eve supper. Natasha, on my Mother's advice, got ingredients for most of the traditional food which my mother prepared. We even managed to get a sort of Christmas tree to gather around. As Natasha and I had two fairly large rooms, we all gathered in our place for a sit-down supper. Surprisingly, we had five pre-war friends with us and my mother did us proud by supplying a twelve-course dinner. Despite being very anti-religion, the Russian authorities gave extra rations for Christmas. Every soldier was allowed 20 roubles worth of foodstuffs, which consisted of 250 grams of butter, 500 grams of cheese and sugar, 500 grams of white bread, 200 grams of smoked sausage and 100 grams of vodka. While collecting it from Saratov, the temperature fell to −43c with strong winds. The wind intensified the cold to such an extent that over 200 soldiers froze to death.

The scenes of finding people frozen to death were rather bizarre. Our dugout barracks worked very well but leaving them was very dangerous. The cold air was so vicious that it was impossible to breathe without some cover over your mouth. Within minutes of being outside, your nostrils were completely blocked by white frost with grotesque stalactites forming. Once you breathed in the cold air, your lungs went into some kind of spasm and death was very sudden. An order came that men were only allowed to go outside in pairs; even then there were a number of cases when both men died. Of course, the malnourished bodies of the men did not help matters. One benefit, however, was the elimination of lice and fleas, which perished in such conditions. In some dugouts the end doors were left open for two or three hours while the tortoise stoves were put out in order to kill off bed bugs. Natasha managed to keep our room fairly clear of vermin except bed bugs, which occupied every small crack in the house, but by hanging our feather bed outside the bugs were nearly gotten rid of. As we personally had the use of a rather splendid and effective sauna, which was situated in the house we stayed in, and kept ourselves fairly free of bugs. Unfortunately, one only had to walk into a room full of people to become alive with fleas. My almost daily visits to MIHQ did not help and I brought hundreds of fleas into the house.

But very soon, due to special request, with the British uniforms we did receive DDT powder, which proved deadly to our unwanted companions. Some men's skins were affected by the powder, but it was better to have a rash than hundreds of bugs feeding on you. The effectiveness of the DDT immediately created a black market in the stuff. Natasha got a whole pig for a big box of DDT powder acquired from NKVD stores. But before she swapped the box she mixed in 90% of rye flour with it, so my parents' house and our house were completely debugged and life became more bearable. I took the rest of the box to MIHQ, which helped to clean it up.

## Chapter 12 : Scoring a Double

The first inkling that we might be released from Russia altogether as a unit came from Natasha, who heard some Politruks discussing it. By the end of 1941 it was an open secret that we would be evacuated to the Middle East. Mr Jan was a wise old bird and his craftiness helped to unearth the first German agent. He alerted all doctors to report to him if anybody from the new intake had a little finger missing. One MO immediately reported that one of the men already present had indeed one finger missing, but could not tell who or where he was. So we knew that the man was amongst us, but where? When I discussed it with my father, by an incredible fluke he remembered that one of the MI officers always appeared with at least one glove on. I mentioned this to Mr Jan who at first dismissed it, but started to investigate. The individual with the glove turned out to be a Polish Major who was taking statements from some of the new arrivals. His presence in MIHQ was not under suspicion as he had supposedly been cross checked and cleared. In the end, three other Germans were unearthed who had verified each other's stories. Mr Jan had to make sure that the suspect was our man so, on the pretext of an anti-typhoid check up, he called in two Polish Army doctors. They confirmed the missing finger and a lot more. They found a very small tattoo in the armpit of the man, which indicated a very high-ranking person in the Nazi party. Many members of the elite SS troops had the same identification numbers in their armpits. It was one thing to find him, but another to do something about it.

London confirmed the necessity to get rid of the infiltrators permanently, but it was easier said than done. I had several long talks with Mr Jan who was my immediate superior. He told me openly that I was sent for one purpose only – to eliminate the infiltrators. He could not openly hand them over to the Russians, as a lot of things would have to be explained, such as the unofficial contact with London. The whole affair would undermine the Polish MI in Russian eyes and Mr Jan was not prepared to do it. I told him I would do it, providing he supplied me with some kind of firearm, preferably a handgun. To my great surprise, he could not get hold of a handgun to do the job. I took my father into my confidence who, after enquiring, said he could get hold of a rifle from a pre-war friend who had been a gunsmith and a few rounds of ammunition, but not a handgun, but I felt it was too dangerous to involve him any deeper.

In desperation I took a risk and asked Natasha for help. I told her that I had been approached by a relative of one of the villagers for a handgun in exchange for a big tin of DDT. "Where in hell did they get hold of DDT," she said, but was less concerned about what he wanted the gun for. Nevertheless, she said she could get a gun, but would have to go to Kuybyshev for it. Mr Jan was horrified at my suggestion, but supplied me with a large tin of DDT from the stores. Natasha returned on the third day and brought an old browning automatic with ammunition. On very close examination, I found the gun had some signs of rust, which had been crudely removed. As I never trusted automatic weapons, I had great doubts about this one, and knew it was essential to try it out. On further examination, I found extensive rust pitting on the firing pin. My father came to my rescue by suggesting that I could try the gun out in an underground food store full of flour and wheat sacks. My fears were justified as the firing pin only managed to dent the shell detonator slightly and nothing more. In desperation, with the help of our friend the gunsmith, I doctored the rifle my father supplied. We cut the barrel to within five inches of the bridge and I decided to use it as a handgun, but when I tried it out it very nearly broke my fingers as its recoil was so great.

Mr Jan found out that the German had a heavy Russian sabre that he always kept within reach. He slept in an earth dugout that was split into individual rooms for officers by Hessian sacks or blankets. The very final details were left to me, as I was the only one doing the job. While we were having Christmas supper the gun was hidden in the ashes of our sauna. As the fireplace was still quite warm, I kept the ammunition clip in my pocket. The following day it was Christmas and we went to midnight mass in the camp's small chapel. To see how alert the German was, I went to his dugout with Natasha and, on the pretext of a quick cuddle, we quietly entered the corridor. Within seconds the tip of a heavy Cossack sabre was near our throats. Natasha's reaction was quick and full of horror. "And what the hell do you think you are doing, you son of a whore", she screamed at him. Seeing her NKVD uniform unbalanced the Jerry somewhat, who started apologising profusely. To start with, Natasha was adamant that she would make an official complaint, but I persuaded her not to.

As preparations to meet the New Year were progressing, the temperature dipped even further. It was not unusual for some MI officers to work late into the night and Mr Jan asked the Jerry to check some statements. I planned to wait for him at his billet on his return, but the temperature was so low I had second thoughts, as his dugout was some 200 metres away. Instead, I crept up to MI HQ and looked through a small gap in the Hessian curtains. To my surprise, I saw the German in the company of his pal, another confirmed Jerry infiltrator. I opened the outside door leading to the main corridor quite noisily, shouting, "Coal, where is the fire?" "Here", shouted the Jerry, opening the door to Mr Jan's office and leaving it ajar. I quickly got the gun from under my brand new British Army overcoat and walked towards the partly-opened office door. The German was standing next to it with his side to me. I raised the gun and aimed the barrel at his neck. Holding the sawn off rifle so high, plus the fact that my hands were so cold, did not help when I squeezed the trigger. The kick was so vicious that the gun jumped sharply up, hitting me on the forehead so hard with the sight that it nearly knocked me out. The bullet or blast from the gun shattered the hanging hurricane lamp, which set the room on fire. While rushing outside through the main outside door, I pushed a second round into the breach. The second Jerry followed me very closely screaming in Polish, " Help, help." I jumped off the two steps leading to the building, turned and fired from a distance of not more than two feet. The impact of the bullet threw the Jerry backwards into the building and me backwards into a snowdrift.

I jumped up as quickly as I could and ran towards the main camp, leaping head-first into the first dugout, sprawling on the earth floor. Some men were still sitting around the tortoise stove playing cards. They picked me up from the floor. "Jesus, whatever happened to you?" was their reaction, seeing my face covered in blood. I mumbled an incoherent reply while the hut medic was washing my face. They eventually settled me on a long bunk near the stove and carried on playing cards. I could not sleep that night, waiting for the first sign of movement in the hut.

It was still deep night when somebody had to go to the latrine and I slipped out with him. I had a loud ringing noise in my ears. To start with I could not get my bearings, but set off to get away from the hut. The cold was so intense it nearly paralysed my lungs. After no longer than three or four minutes I started getting desperately worried about freezing to death when I heard the faint bark of a dog. As there were no dogs in the camp I knew it was one in the village but, as soon as I realised this, the dog, as if in spite, stopped barking. White frost started forming on my eyelashes, impairing my vision, when suddenly to my left I saw the glow of a fire. It was the MI HQ, which I had not seen to start with as it was shaded by the woods. By now the main fire in the tent had burnt itself out, but a big red glow was still visible.

On getting my bearings I managed to find my quarters. Natasha was fully dressed and very worried as she thought I might be at the HQ, which was on fire. The adrenaline pumping through me prevented me from sleeping for the rest of the night and the following day, which was New Year's Eve. The final preparations were being made by my mother for seeing in the New Year and the vodka flowed freely. We had plenty to eat, mainly thanks to Natasha, and Mr. Jan came to the party, which gave us a chance to have a confidential talk in the sauna room. He congratulated me on scoring a double and said London would be very happy about it. The headquarters building and the two bodies were burnt beyond recognition and the Russians had not show any interest in the matter. Natasha told me later that the Russian NKVD viewed the matter as the settling of some old scores amongst the Poles, while the Poles put it down as the doings of the NKVD, so the matter was closed very quickly. It is nearly 50 years now since I sent those two bastards back to hell and I haven't lost one minute's sleep over it. I still remember the wickedness and the chaos that people like the German fifth column created amongst the army and the population in general.

From the very first day of the formation of the Polish Army in Russia, the Polish MI were given the task of identifying and verifying every volunteer that arrived at the Buzuluk headquarters. This meant debriefings were a mammoth task as everyone had to make a detailed statement regarding their movements since the 17th September 1939, the day the Red Army entered Polish territory. All statements were cross-checked and, if at all possible, verified by at least one other volunteer. Men were arriving from prisons, labour camps (concentration camps), so-called POW camps and from forced resettlement. At this point, let's get a few facts straight. The Red Army crossed the Polish border on 17th September while bitter and ferocious resistance was in progress against the Germans advancing eastwards. There had been no declaration of war by the Russians, the excuse they gave was that their army was liberating Russian minorities who lived in the east of Poland before the War.

On the 17th and the following days, leaflets were distributed and displayed by Communist cells in Poland, stating that if Polish Army units laid down their arms, all military personnel would be released to their homes. Instead, the army, police officers and many army reservists were packed into cattle rail trucks and taken into Russia and herded into three main camps near Smolensk. One of the camps was at Kozielsk where my Father was an inmate, and from where he eventually came to join the Polish Army at Buzuluk.

In the latter part of '41 and the beginning of '42, fairly frequent small transports of up to one hundred and twenty men were sent from those camps to unknown destinations. My Father had been included in one of those transports but, by bribing an NKVD man with a silver cigarette case, he had been withdrawn at the last moment. None of these men reported into the newly formed Polish Army, and, as most of them were professional officers, were badly needed in the freshly formed units. Their whereabouts was puzzling to the Polish MI and there were very strong representations made to the NKVD, the Russian Government and the Red Army. The answer was always the same – that they must have been held up, but would turn up in due course. No-one seemed to have any answer as to what had happened to nearly fifteen thousand men. I spoke to Natasha about the problem and she was sure they must have been taken somewhere deep into Siberia and, due to disruption of the railways, their arrival had been delayed.

Mr Jan had a long talk with me and suggested that I should volunteer to go and gather some information regarding the missing men. Knowing my circumstances, the old bastard knew that Natasha would not let me go on my own, and he was right. Natasha wouldn't hear of me going alone, saying: "Don't be stupid. Any army patrol, NKVD man or Politruk will shoot you on the spot as a spy if you ask anything about the movement of army personnel. I am coming with you", she declared. She obtained two open rail passes and we set off to Kuybyshev where her Father had last been seen. She became rather thoughtful and nervous. When I pressed her for the reason, she said that there was bad news from the front. The Germans were making very rapid progress and her boss expected that Moscow could be overrun very soon.

She was also very worried about her Brother who was a Politruk in Minsk. The reports were that the Germans killed all NKVD members and Politruks immediately on capture. Thousands of people were being arrested by the Soviets on suspicion of spying. Many villagers were murdered because it was suspected they had sympathy towards the Germans. All minorities in race or religion were treated with brutality. Very many old grudges were settled and resolved by murder. Any breakdown in machinery, whether military or on collective farm property, was immediately put down to sabotage. Children more than ever were encouraged to report any counter-revolutionary activities, and any adults who expressed dissatisfaction were immediately placed in the most dangerous category. While on the train to Kuybyshev, our papers were continuously checked and re-checked. At times armed patrols were following each other within visual contact. Everyone wanted the same information. Our aim to achieve our goal fell a few kilometres short of its target. Our train was stopped by a massive detachment of troops and we were all just kicked off the train and we were escorted to one facing in the opposite direction. As all the troops looked trigger happy, we argued no longer.

On arrival back at Headquarters, I was summoned to Mr Jan and we had a very long talk. Apparently a few men who had been released from a labour camp near Ukhta up North had arrived. They made a statement that during the movement of Polish POW's from the Kola Peninsula across the White Sea, a number of barges full of men were sunk with explosives by the NKVD. This had led to an horrific loss of life. To start with, this report was taken with a big pinch of salt and Mr. Jan said it was essential to confirm the reports. As I had been in that district once, he asked me if I would I be prepared to go north and try to get some more details. I thought he was mad to ask me and I told him so. To travel over a 1,000 miles with such a panic everywhere was not only suicidal, but completely impossible. But true to form, he had a secondary task for me.

He said that on a tip-off from London, they had found another German who must be got rid of. By now the Polish Army was partly armed, so there was no problem getting a revolver. I started feeling uneasy as it was plain to me that I was being treated as a very expendable hooligan who could do any dirty job. Mind you, in principle, I didn't mind doing another job of killing, but luckily their attention was soon focused on a different problem. Natasha heard that her Father was still at Kuybyshev and she was determined to see him. As there was a real possibility of getting some true facts from him, I was urged by Mr Jan to go. Travelling by train turned out to be impracticable and too dangerous, so we decided on road transport. By now I had received a full British uniform, but for the journey to Kuybyshev. I put on a standard Red Army uniform, with the British one in a haversack. After numerous stops and a few swearing sessions with army patrols we eventually got to Kuybyshev and her father's apartment. The whole building had been turned into a sort-of hospital for the seriously wounded from the front. It smelt of carbolic disinfectant but there was also an overwhelming stench of gangrene that was quite revolting.

"Come in and have a vodka", was her father's greeting. "Only vodka can kill the horrible smell in this place." His breath stank of the spirit, making me feel quite sick. We spent three nights with him and he was adamant that the Red Army would eventually stop the German advance with their overwhelming numbers. "You see we can afford to lose ten million men but the Germans cannot," he said. "We can overrun them with wooden clubs if need be."

It was clear he knew more about the missing Polish POW's than he was prepared to say. On the last night we were there he got so drunk he started hallucinating and started seeing people who were long dead. In his drunken mumblings, he had flashes of sanity. Putting one arm around Natasha and another around me, he said, "Jozef Jozefovitch, I cannot tell you the whole truth about your army comrades as I don't know the full story myself, but I can tell you those sons of bitches in command of us made a massive mistake regarding those men.

"I hope they will have regrets one day but I doubt it. They have practised murder for so many years that to them it means nothing." I tried to pump him for more information but he passed out and didn't come round until the next day, when he and Natasha had a terrible argument. She wanted his help to leave Russia with me. After a lot of shouting and swearing he calmed down and said quietly to her, "Natasha if you leave, I will be executed for sure, along with your family. I know you love this young man (pointing at me), but can you do this to your family?" Natasha started crying uncontrollably for a long time but eventually promised him she would stay.

We left Kuybyshev on 10th February 1942 and went back to the Polish headquarters at Tatishthevo. The train was overcrowded to the point of madness. Most occupants were military claiming to be going to Saratov, which was actually in the opposite direction. Some two hours after the train left, a large contingent of what looked like military policemen joined the train and started checking papers. They eyed me very suspiciously as I was by now, on the advice of Natasha's father, wearing a full British uniform, including an overcoat several sizes too big. Natasha managed to rid of them but a load of drunken Red Army boys were not so lucky. They were openly accused of deserting as they were on the wrong train, going in the opposite direction. The MPs and NKVD Officers drew their revolvers and told all the military men they were under arrest. There were some scuffles, a shot was fired, and one of the soldiers was killed and thrown out of the window by the MPs. Soon afterwards the train stopped near a huge expanse of water which looked like a river in flood, with thick ice on the water. As soon as we stopped there was much screaming and swearing. The MP's were getting about 300 people off the train. MP's and NKVD officers were rushing around with revolvers drawn and Natasha and I watched all this in amazement from not further than 40 metres away.

We were in one of only two passenger carriages on the train. The rest of the train was made up of cattle trucks and open platforms all filled to capacity with people. More and more soldiers were being thrown out of the train, accompanied by the sound of regular gunfire. Then there was a terrific howl and a crowd of soldiers grabbed their tormentors. I shall remember what followed for the rest of my life. The crowd dragged the MPs and NKVD officers towards the openings in the thick ice and pushed them head first underneath. The openings had been made by the locals to set net fish traps. Now a lynch mob were using them. Someone screamed in our carriage, "Look there is another of the bastards hiding in here", pointing at Natasha who was in NKVD uniform. Natasha immediately drew the revolver she had got from her father. I realised that if she fired into the crowd, we were both finished. I screamed in broken Russian that I was Polish and she was with me as my friend and we were going to the Polish HQ. That seemed to cool the crowd down a little. After the mob executions, I wrenched the revolver from Natasha's hand and told her to be quiet. Then a huge fellow in an army uniform pushed through the crowd. He must have been at least eighteen stone in weight and stood a full head above the others. He grabbed Natasha by the coat near to her throat and lifted her off her feet. I put the revolver muzzle into his huge and hairy ear and told him to let her go or I would shoot. He turned his head towards me and spat in my face. As I smelt his disgusting breath I instinctively pulled the trigger. There was no loud bang, but a muffled thump and some blood spurted from his ear into my face. He made a noise as if he was gargling and fell forward, presumably quite dead.

At that particular time I was so mad I screamed at the others, "And who is next, you sons of whores?" To my amazement, the rest of the men in uniforms and two civilians immediately backed off. They all stared at my British uniform as it was strange to them. They could not make out who the hell I was. Only one chap, evidently the big fellow's friend, tried to go for me. Immediately I stuck the muzzle of my gun hard under his chin. Luckily for us, he was restrained by the others who shouted, "Leave the mad bastard alone," pointing at me. "There might be some more of them on the train."

Once the friend of the shot man was thrown out of the carriage, questions poured in my direction. "And what will we do now comrade?" they asked me. Taking the initiative I told the crowd to keep quiet and everything would be alright. I asked Natasha to go to the window and keep the remaining NKVD officers and MPs away. Understanding the situation, Natasha did just that. I gave her gun back, which she waved through the window shouting, "OK Comrades, I am in charge here and everything is under control". It seemed to cool the situation. The dead man was thrown out of the window and everyone settled down.

Food was then pulled out of people's pockets and everyone started eating. Unfortunately for the rioters, there was an NKVD unit of about 100 men in a nearby barracks. The train driver was ordered to move the train a few hundred metres towards the barracks and all the men pointed out by the few surviving NKVD officers were to be shot on the spot. Natasha, to everybody's amazement, went out to speak to the local NKVD chief and managed to get two armed guards at each end of our carriage, so nobody would interfere with us. She also got two big Hessian sacks of dried bread and a few kilos of back-fat pork. We heard her arguing with the local NKVD Major, saying that all counter revolutionaries from our carriage had already been executed. When the Major wanted to see their bodies, Natasha said to him, "If you don't believe me, you go up the line and see for yourself. We didn't want their stinking carcases in our carriage." This seemed to satisfy him and he went away. The train was moved once again onto a sideline and stopped for two or three hours before being cleared to leave. It was quite a sickening sight when a long line of men were examined by the few surviving NKVD men. Everybody pointed out as a participant in the riot was told to kneel and was shot on the spot in the base of the skull. Those refusing to kneel were shot while standing, but always in the base of the skull. All these executions were carried out in front of everyone and none of the victims seemed to fight back or protest. It was a sickening exhibition of Stalin-Beria rules at that period of Russian history.

Meanwhile, Natasha stood firm and did not allow anybody from our coach to join the line. It paid handsomely as the men in our coach made a collection amongst themselves and handed a very embarrassed Natasha an army issue peaked hat full of all kinds of goods, including 52 gold Russian pre-revolution roubles. Natasha gave me 40 of them. I eventually lost 20 of them in a pontoon game near Baghdad and the other 20 are lying on the seabed somewhere off the coast of West Africa, near Freetown, where German U-boats torpedoed my ship the SS Laconia. but more of that later. The rest of the journey back to the Polish Army HQ went by without further excitement. Most of the passengers were military personnel. There was still some checking of documents by fully armed patrols in progress and a few arrests, but not on such a scale as before. The rumours and stories about great battles and massive losses on the Russian side were on everybody's lips, except the commissars, who were very keen not to reveal their names in case the rapidly advancing Germans heard about them, as they were said to be killing all the commissars they captured. When quite innocently I called one "Comrade Commissar" he snapped back, "I'm not a commissar you son of a bitch." How things changed so suddenly. He would have been very offended if I hadn't called him "Comrade Politruk" only a few weeks back.

When we eventually got to the Polish Army HQ at Saratov, we found to our dismay only a skeleton staff left behind. Most of our people had gone to a new HQ somewhere East of the Caspian Sea in the Uzbek Republic. The few people left did not seem to know anything about me. I couldn't even get accommodation in the place and Natasha had to organise a room from the NKVD allocation. It was in a beautiful villa situated in the woods just outside the city, and we spent 14 days there together. It was a very private country rest house (dacha) for NKVD personnel. There was no shortage of food, drink or pre-paid prostitutes for male NKVD officers. Those girls were hand picked and really very beautiful. Natasha became rather short-tempered and would not leave me for a second in case I went astray with one of them. I intended to stay there just a few days, but on the second day one of the NKVD officers casually mentioned that he had been involved with Polish POWs near Smolensk, south of Moscow. He was about 30, with ginger hair and carried a small pointed beard Lenin style. He was also rather fond of drink, but his eyes were bigger than his constitution and insisted on drinking vodka from a thin glass, which held about five doubles. He could take two glasses with no problems but the third would turn his legs to jelly.

I told Natasha that I needed some information from him and she agreed to help. After all, I had specific instructions from Mr Jan that I should get as much information as possible regarding missing Polish POWs. Luckily, I could take up to four glasses of vodka without becoming incoherent, so I could pump him for information.

He said that at times he had been in charge of the receiving party at a railway station in 1940, where Polish POWs arrived after being transferred to the camp, but said that he had never gone with the POWs when they marched off to Katyn, towards the NKVD's so-called dacha (or rest-house). At that point he began crying uncontrollably. When pushed hard for more information, he said there had been very many parties of Polish POWs, mainly officers, but would not say what became of them. However hard I tried, he would not say any more, except insisting that he never knew what had happened to them. It was not until the latter part of 1943, when the Germans announced their discoveries in the Katyn forest, the mass graves containing bodies of the missing Polish officers, that the penny dropped and I realised the man involved in this mass murder had been my drinking companion. Even after so many years, I can still see his face in my mind and I regret that I did not shoot the bastard. At the time it would have been a very easy task.

Natasha secured train passes to my original place at Tatishthevo and, with some difficulty, we eventually got there. There was no sign of Polish troops; the whole camp was empty. The Red Army had taken over the camp and filled it with their own conscripts. We had great difficulty in finding out where the Polish Army had moved to, as it was a military secret. Eventually she got railway passes from the NKVD HQ and we found the Polish Army was stationed near the Afghan border. I found Mr Jan was some 100 kilometres away at an Army HQ, and on learning of my return, he came by lorry to see me. It took a few days to write very detailed statements for him. Mr Jan told me they had found a leader of a Communist secret unit from the Polish Ukraine and needed to get rid of him somehow, but it had to be done officially. To execute him officially we would need the approval of the Russians and that was not a simple matter. After all, he was a Communist, so some devious means had to be employed to get the Russians to sign the execution order. Eventually, the Polish MI arranged a court martial and he was sentenced to be shot. Surprisingly, the Russians confirmed the sentence. Mr. Jan insisted I took charge of the firing squad. After talking to a Polish woman whose whole family had been murdered by this man and his friends, I agreed. He was shot on the 28th March 1942 at 8 am and we buried him in the desert.

By the time I had rejoined the main body of the Polish Army, nearly all of its members had full British uniforms and were virtually free of body vermin. There were a number of Polish Army Officers and NCOs who came from England by road with supply trucks full of war materials from Iran. Hundreds of lorries were arriving every week at this time with huge land conveys full of war materials for the Red Army. The Polish NCOs and a few British personnel were running courses in English and the main syllabus consisted of a number of popular songs at that time, such as "Its a Long Way to Tipperary". We all learned this tune and the words parrot-fashion without understanding what the hell we were singing about.

On the day of the execution of the sentenced man, my had mother left the camp for Iran with the 14th Infantry Division of the Polish Army. My father was very anxious for her to go as it was not clear if the Russians would allow civilians to be evacuated with the army. She joined the transport as a nurse with false documents. By this time Natasha had managed to get a very large room for us in a nearby village. We settled down to the boring Army routine and Natasha made sure we always had a fair supply of food from the NKVD stores but even then we were half starving. Around the camp there were masses of large land turtles to supplement our rations and I managed to shoot a couple of huge goshawks for the pot. Despite the food shortage we undertook full and very exhausting army training. New arrivals from all parts of Russia were checked and cross-checked hundreds of times. Mr. Jan roped me into this work, which I absolutely hated. How can you possibly tell a fully-grown man, who is bitterly crying, that you don't believe his story. It was very monotonous and boring work. We trusted no-one and all the statements had to be verified by another person as, after past experiences with German infiltrators, it was essential to double-check everybody.

I badgered Mr Jan to let me join an ordinary unit and eventually he relented and allowed me to join a unit of Polish commandos. I started training as a radio operator and began weeks of Morse code on top of the physically exhausting training in hostile terrain. There were continuous rumours that we were about to leave for Iran. The main stumbling block at the time was the Russians' insistence that hundreds of Polish boys without parents must stay behind. I witnessed heartbreaking scenes when the Russians forcibly took boys of eight or ten from their parents, mainly Fathers who were serving in the Polish Army. One very handsome 12-year-old blonde lad committed suicide by head-butting a huge cast iron stove in a holding unit room for under-age boys. There were plans to take them by force across the Afghan border but the Russians smelled a rat and sent in three divisions of their own troops and closed the border completely. At the time we were armed, but we did not have sufficient ammunition for a real scrap with them.

The Polish MI eventually got used to Natasha and left us alone. What began worrying me was that she got herself civilian clothes and was hanging about the Polish hospital. She would not discuss the matter with me but I felt she wanted to escape from Russia disguised as a nurse. We left the camp-site at long last at 10am on the 3rd August 1942 en route to Iran. Natasha insisted on coming on the train with us all the way to the Russian port of Krasnovodsk on the Caspian Sea. The train was stopped by a Red Army unit a few kilometres outside the port itself.

As Natasha was the only NKVD Officer and our Division's official Liaison Officer, it was up to her to sort out the problem with the Commander of the Red Army. There was a lot of swearing and arm waving for nearly half an hour, but we were eventually let in and embarked on one of the boats. As all firearms were being handed in at the dockside, many men were crying as they remembered it was nearly two years since they put down their arms and were herded to POW camps in the depths of Russia. And so the time arrived to say our goodbyes. Natasha and I went to the dock master's office and hugged, as, I thought, for the last time. I walked quickly to the planks perched on the side of a trawler, which was loaded to more than its capacity. The troops started singing the national anthem while the last ropes fell into the sea. Most faces were drawn and serious. The men had been through absolute hell in the past two years and quite a lot of them broke down and cried like children. Others were very distressed as they were leaving their families behind who could not join them. A while after leaving port, I was called by the scream of a Sergeant Major to report to the bridge. It made me jump as he was standing above me on the bridge whilst bellowing my name. Pointing at a door he said abruptly, "You are wanted there." I opened the door and was guided to a hole in the floor where some steps led down to the lower deck. I felt very uneasy as I thought the Russkies were up to something nasty, but eventually climbed down cautiously with one hand on an illegal revolver. When I eventually reached the bottom my heart nearly stopped. There stood Natasha with a Russian naval officer. He stepped aside and, pointing to a side door said, "You will not be disturbed." It was a small cabin with one single bunk, a small table and one chair, and there stood Natasha with her arms on her hips, saying, "What is the matter Jozef Jozefovitch? You look as if you've seen a ghost." I felt my blood turning to red hot oil as I thought, "God what the hell am I going to do now." I was certain she had decided to defect into Iran with me and that was the last thing I wanted.

She grabbed me rather enthusiastically and for the moment I felt I was going to faint as she pushed the barrel of my gun tucked into my trousers into my private parts. The sudden pain took my breath away for a moment. Natasha thought it was very funny as she said, "You crazy son of a bitch. You fooled me. I thought you left Mother Russia in such good condition and it was only your gun." The door suddenly opened and somebody said, "Your luggage Comrade", putting a box and an army kitbag on the floor. To my amazement, Natasha started pulling out bottles of vodka, ten litres of the stuff, a large tin of black caviar and a loaf of brown bread. Then she explained that she had no intention of absconding, but just came for the sea trip. So here I was with ten litres of vodka, five kilos of best caviar, a beautiful girl and a pain in the crotch.

Natasha invited the Captain and his mate to come down, The Captain was a huge man with a big red nose and stale vodka on his breath, whilst his deputy was so big he had to come through the door sideways. They both had a few days' growth of stubble on their faces and looked really well-oiled. The Captain immediately opened a small cabinet on the wall and pulled out four very dirty glasses. On seeing Natasha looking at the glass against the light, he gave a deep belly laugh and said, "Don't worry, Comrade, the vodka will kill all the germs."

Within ten minutes we had drunk two half litre bottles and eaten the caviar with soup spoons. The second litre of vodka went in an even quicker time. Soon after the third litre, the First Officer fell over and threw up near the open door to the cabin. In his stupor, the Captain gave me permission to ask a few of my pals to the party. I managed to find three to start with and brought them down below and soon realised our stock of vodka would not last the journey.

The cabin and a corridor leading into it became overcrowded and Natasha started getting anxious to get rid of our company; they were eventually dragged upstairs for fresh air. In the excitement the Captain was sick all over two boy helpers who were pushing him from behind. Eventually we were left alone in the Captain's cabin with the remains of the vodka. The caviar was taken upstairs for the lads. The crossing took all night. I recovered from the gun in the groin injury and we said several tender farewells before arriving at Pahlevi on Iran's soil.

## Chapter 13 : The Thought of Freedom

While disembarking Natasha stood waving and sobbing at the very highest point of the boat. We had been together for a long time and had been through bad and good times, but the thought of freedom overcame my pangs of regret. One last wave and I turned my back on Natasha for the last time as I walked onto the golden sands of the free country. The sight that greeted me was incredible. A canvas town consisting of army issue khaki tents – there must have been at least a hundred of them pitched in straight lines. Lorries and pick-ups were rushing around everywhere. After delousing and a shower, we were issued with army log books. The same day, we were herded into big queues for a general medical and injections. All around the perimeter there were Arabs with all kinds of goods for sale and, to my delight, I found they were accepting Russian money. Despite warnings by the authorities to be careful with overeating, I joined forces with two pals and bought 60 eggs and one kilo of butter. We scrubbed clean an empty caviar tin with sand in the desert, made a small fire and scrambled eggs. I will always remember us sitting around the tin taking turns in scooping some of the eggs from it. It was a habit acquired in Russia to divide the food in equal portions amongst everyone.

When we had nearly finished the NCO arrived and insisted on knowing what we had just eaten. He was especially concerned if we had mixed any local pork with it. On telling him to push off in plain language, he called in an officer and we were put on a charge. I bought a beautifully juicy large melon for afters and we ate it before swimming in the sea, but all three of us got terrible cramp. Two of us managed to crawl back onto the beach, but the third had to be rescued by the lifeguard and was taken to hospital. The two of us who were still mobile were frogmarched to HQ and spent the night under guard in the punishment compound. I did not sleep a wink as my left arm was throbbing all night as a result of injections, so I crawled under the net surrounding the compound and soaked my arm in the sea. Next morning I was taken by the Red Caps to HQ and charged with disobeying a lawful order and escape from detention. The Sergeant tried to say I was a deserter or at least absent without leave, and all because I wanted to ease the terrible pain in my left arm.

While waiting for the Captain to make a decision, I asked him if I could see somebody from MI and a Lieutenant who I knew very well in Russia was sent for. He vouched for me and rescued me from the Captain's clutches. He told me that MIHQ was in Teheran and we set off later that day by lorry. We arrived in the late evening and I met Mr Jan within half an hour of my arrival. During a long talk he asked me whether I would like to fight the Germans for a change. On enquiring how could I, as there were no Germans in the Middle East, he answered, "Well, you have to go to occupied Poland to do that". For a moment I thought he had taken leave of his senses as I was not going to go back to Russia to get into Poland, but he explained that I would go by air and from England. Polish HQ in London were looking for volunteers to fight with the Polish underground. He told me I would be a suitable candidate as a radio operator. After very little hesitation I agreed and was told I would be transferred to Iraq within a few days on a special course. The next day I went to look for my parents and found out my mother was a patient in a Polish hospital. Due to her ordeal in Russia, she had a problem with her kidneys and liver. She was eventually sent to South Africa and spent the War in Lusaka, before coming to England in 1945, where she died in 1951 of kidney failure. My Father was in Teheran as well and on the 27 December 1942, he and I spent a last day together at my Mother's bedside.

Within a few days I left by lorry to Teheran and arrived at Khanaqien, about fifty kilometres north-east of Baghdad. We were stationed in the desert within sight of a mountain range and the Iranian border. Our driver was an Arab whose driving scared the daylights out of me. He hurtled along the narrow mountain roads like a racing driver; how we didn't go down the rock face I shall never know. We eventually got to our destination exhausted physically and mentally and I spent a week trying to remember the Morse code I had learned so well in Russia.

We started training in earnest, blowing up things, shooting things, driving things, etc. etc., and felt less of a human being and more of a machine that was geared up to destroy everything in sight. Our instructors arrived from different parts of the world and we even had an SAS hooligan from Egypt who taught us how to successfully blow up a petrol tank without putting the fire out during the explosion. Most of our group consisted of Poles but we had some Frenchmen and a Jewish group. The instructors seemed to want to try and break us both physically and mentally. We ceased to be members of the armed forces – all our letters, photographs and documents were taken off us and destroyed. Only by a miracle and my precautions did I manage to save my small diary, which I hid in the sand in the desert anticipating some dirty tricks by HQ. I saw Mr. Jan only once more, who informed me that London wanted me back and I would shortly be sent there by land and sea. I was warned that this training was only the start and I would finish it in England. The course was very exhausting as we were the only group of human beings out in the sun between 12 and 2 pm, when the Arabs were sitting under cover.

My training as a wireless operator was very intense and tiring and often went on into the evenings and nights. Dots and dashes became second nature and I learned how to both make a radio set and destroy it. The British Eighth Army Sappers were busy laying rail tracks and we were busy destroying them. I learned how to destroy any piece of installation and machine. Steam engines, radio stations, all kinds of turbines, aircraft, were all on the menu and were promptly destroyed by us. We also learned many ways of killing human beings, pigs, horses, etc., I soon found that the Arabs were even better at thieving than the Russians. They stole Bren gun carriers and even anti-tank guns, and so we had to sleep with the straps of our guns wrapped round our bodies or they would be stolen during the night. We never stopped at one place more than 48 hours and were continuously harassed by regular soldiers whose ambition was to catch us.

I swam in the River Tigris and soaked my aching feet in some of the most beautiful lakes in that part of the world. Other members of the group soon found that I could stalk and shoot wild pigs in the mountains, gut them and make a decent meal of the meat, so I was appointed as an unofficial supply chap and emergency cook. As far as our supplies were concerned, they were rather sporadic and delivered to us at different places and in different amounts. For cooking we used tins, crude oil and water. Among other things I learn how to swim with a wireless strapped to my head to keep it dry.

The only females around were prostitutes in Baghdad or travelling with wandering Arabs. I began to think I had turned into a eunuch, as I had no need at all for female company. On my $20^{th}$ birthday I got permission to spend the day swimming in the Tigris. I remember sitting on the bank of the river and eating masses of walnuts purchased from a travelling Arab. I used a large water-polished stone to break the nuts. That was a very tranquil day for me with my thoughts many miles away in Warsaw, where I would hopefully end up fighting the Jerries. One day I was ordered to report to a certain base and join a group of Polish volunteers who were going to England for air crew training, as apparently the Polish Air force in England were having heavy losses. We eventually left by road to Basra where, to our astonishment and delight, we embarked on a Polish ship, Kosciuszko, and set sail into the unknown. It was under British command and had Polish Officers, but most of the crew were from India, and they invited us to a festival.
To hide from the very hot sun we sat on the deck under a stretched tarpaulin. On the menu was rice and some kind of brown liquid in small bowls. I followed the rest of the crew and made a small rice bowl, dipped it into the liquid, and popped it into my mouth. It happened to be their curry and my throat was burning for two days. The next stop was a transition camp at Bombay. Many parts of the town were strictly out of bounds, so I felt no need to wander around, which was lucky for me as a number of lads came back with a dose of VD. One good thing that happened there was to get rid of four corns on my feet, which were removed by a local man near the gate for a small payment.

Our next stop was South Africa and we were told not on any account to have sex or be seen with black girls, as this was an offence. Before joining SS Laconia on the last leg of my journey to England I had a premonition of impending disaster. I placed my personal papers and money into two condoms to keep them dry and once again my feelings did not let me down as we were torpedoed off the West African coast. After rescue and a short stay in a transit camp at Freetown, and making a pig of myself on not quite ripe bananas, we left for England, arriving in Liverpool in May 1943.

And so the second part of my war wanderings was over. Back in England I rejoined the stream of men training to be aircrew again, qualified once more as a pilot, and started the third and last part of my private war. I do not think that I will ever be ready to recollect the last part of the War, as I feel exhausted with digging up the rest of my old skeletons. I will close my Pandora's box again and perhaps old memories will get buried for good. These memoirs were written from my old notes which were in the form of diaries. Many entries consisted of just places and dates, but it is amazing how many faces and happenings were brought back into my head by reading them. I did not carry out any research in books or documents while writing this in case it affected my recall of events and, as a result, it might not have been a true story to tell.

\* \* \* \* \* \* \* \* \* \*

In this book I intended to describe what happened to me and which events left a very deep imprint on me. These memories will remain with me until the day when I'm my released, by going through a chimney of the crematorium.

If my dust cannot be taken back to Poland, I hope that even a very small particle of dust from the atmosphere will find its way to my beloved part of the world and eventually settle on the fields and surroundings I loved so much. And now at the age of 62 unfortunately, through not entirely my own fault, I am left alone. Loneliness can be a very cruel thing, but at least it can give you a chance to look back on your past life and see things in a different light. This is not my first writing of this book and by now I know what an impenetrable jungle I got myself into. But with God's help and my friends' willingness to help, I hope to eventually finish it. Publish it? Frankly I do not worry about it. My main task is to write it in my own style and the language of my adopted country, England. Before I started writing in longhand, there was one snag I did not expect to come across – the psychological adaptation that is needed to recollect some parts of my life. A few times I came to a point when I had to stop writing for a few days, as the memories were too scary and upsetting to continue. The breaks were necessary to stabilise myself and recharge my mental batteries.

# EPILOGUE
## Joe's life after the End of this Chapter
### Summary CV

Service in the PAF/RAF: Flew many different aircraft but especially fond of his P51 Mustang flown with various squadrons finishing the War with 309 Polish Squadron

Demobbed in 1948 and decided to settle in Norwich.

**Working Life:**

Churchill Constructors, Salhouse Road, Norwich - employed as a coach-builder

Contal Washing Machine Hire - Self-employed hiring out washing machines to housewives around Lakenham in Norwich

Cabinet Making - Would put his hand to anything. A number of items of furniture hand-made by him are still in the family.

Wooden Pallet Repairing - on contract to Colmans of Norwich

The Little Shop - Taught himself jewellery repair and set up a jeweller's shop at St Andrew's Hill in Norwich

Boat Building - traded under the sign of the "Yellow Wheel" at Harford Bridges in Norwich making high-quality fibreglass and mahogany fishing boats, which can still be seen today on Sheringham Beach.

Fencing Manufacture - Manufactured and erected garden fencing around all parts of Norfolk

Glider Repairing and Inspection - for the Norfolk Gliding Club and others

Glider Trailer Manufacturing - both wooden and fibreglass

Founder-member of Norwich Judo Club - together with Eric Pleasants (worth looking up on Google)

Occasional interpreter for Norwich Speedway Club for visiting Polish and Russian teams.

Chief Instructor at Norfolk Gliding Club for 25 years - teaching hundreds of pupils and other Instructors

Chief Instructor at Rattlesden Gliding Club - when they were in danger of closing for lack of an experienced Instructor

Aerobatic flyer with Norfolk and Norwich Aero Club - often appeared at local flying displays, even showing off his skills at the request of the RAF at their Open Days.

After retirement became a volunteer driver for the local Cheshire Home. He met and was friends with Lady Ryder of Warsaw, the widow of Gp. Capt. Leonard Cheshire VC.

Other Achievements:

Received Royal Humane Society Award in 1950's for rescuing and reviving a drowning boy at Lakenham Swimming Baths

Received Chief Constable of Norfolk's Award for going to the aid of a policeman being attacked by hooligans in Dereham Town Centre in 1970's

And that was only the things we can talk about.....He truly was a character!

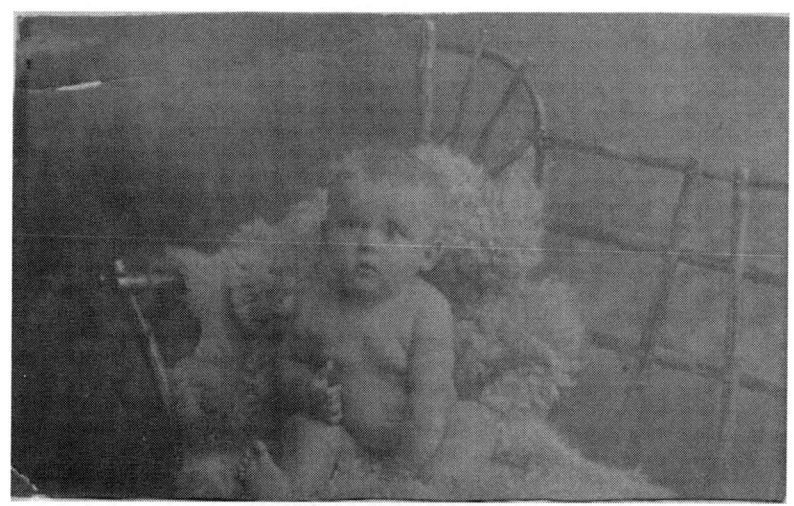

Baby Joe at 6 months of Age

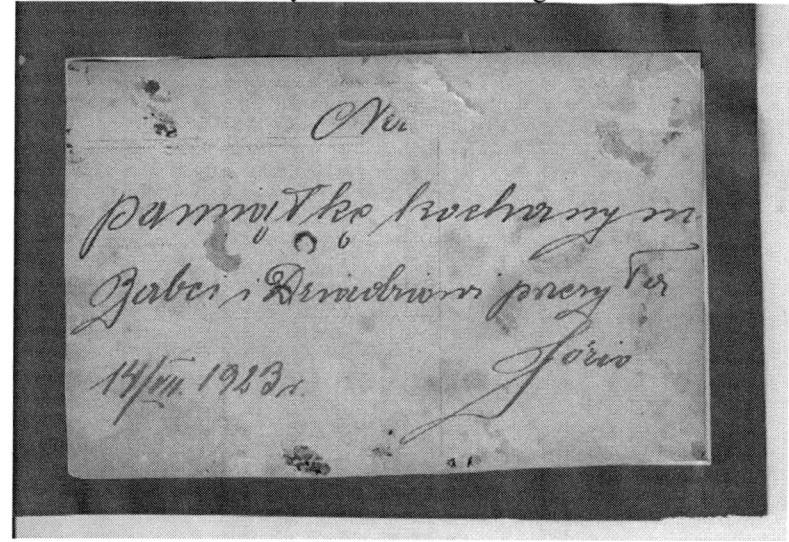

Inscription on reverse of photograph.
to my dearest Grandma and Grandpa, from loving Józio

253

My mother Maria 1931

My Dad Jozef 1945

At School 1935

Russian Justice 1939

Squadron Photo (2nd Left back Row)

309 Squadron 1945 (front row, last)

Family Group 1956
Joe with Dad Jozef, wife Mil, sons Andrew and Nigel